Virgil Thomson

HIS LIFE AND MUSIC

VIRGIL
THOMSON

His Life and Music

by Kathleen Hoover
and John Cage

BOOKS FOR LIBRARIES PRESS
FREEPORT, NEW YORK

STANDARD BOOK NUMBER:

8369-5376-2

LIBRARY OF CONGRESS CATALOG CARD NUMBER:

70-119933

PRINTED IN THE UNITED STATES OF AMERICA

Contents

Illustrations

7

Acknowledgments

IT WOULD BE IMPOSSIBLE TO LIST HERE THE MANY PEOPLE WHO HAVE graciously suffered my inquiries, but I would be remiss if I did not single out a few for special gratitude. My first expression of indebtedness goes to Virgil Thomson himself, who has placed at my disposal all his memorabilia and his voluminous store of letters. Other materials of invaluable assistance have been provided by Dr. Archibald T. Davison and Edward Burlingame Hill, former faculty members of the Harvard University music department; by the following associates of Thomson during his Paris period: the late Elizabeth de Gramont (Duchesse de Clermont-Tonnerre), Nadia Boulanger, Alice B. Toklas, Natalie Barney, Janet Flanner, Jean Cocteau, Henri Sauguet, Henry-Russell Hitchcock, and George Antheil; also by the following Kansas Citians: the late Geneve Lichtenwalter, Ruth Mary Weeks, Alice Smith Edwards, Gladys Blakely Bush, Donald Bush, and the late Henry Haskell, former editor of the Kansas City *Star*.

I am no less beholden to Donald Gallup, Curator of American Literature of Yale University, for giving me access to the Gertrude Stein collection; to the Robert Flaherty Foundation for providing data on Flaherty's film-making; and to Garrett Mattingly for his valued comments on the manuscript.

Alfred A. Knopf, Inc., and Henry Holt and Co. have generously permitted me to quote extracts from their published collections of Thomson's reviews.

KATHLEEN HOOVER

New York

Virgil Thomson

HIS LIFE

by

Kathleen Hoover

The Early Years

THE EIGHTEEN NINETIES HOLD A HIGH PLACE IN MISSOURI HISTORY. This was the decade during which William Rockhill Nelson, founder of the Kansas City *Star* and last great editor of the Horace Greeley type, helped to reform American journalism. His militant standards spurred middle-of-the-road editors to become progressive and outspoken. His racy writing style was adopted by the press of the nation, until then often magniloquent in prose. His readable daily, an influential medium in five states, gave color and purpose to the thoughts of millions of Midwesterners. The fortune reaped from it was to rear in Kansas City the art gallery that commemorates his name. Meanwhile William Allen White was serving his editorial apprenticeship as columnist for the *Star*, and Missouri was hatching genius of Nelsonian voltage in other fields. Thomas Hart Benton, a founding father of our American Scene school of painting, was learning to draw. Virgil Garnett Thomson, of tenderer years, was evincing zest for the art in which he was to become an equal force. Though only three when, at the close of the decade, Kansas City made world headlines by capturing a Democratic national convention, he had embarked informally upon composition. His first attempts, all improvised, were imitations of a grown-up female cousin playing the piano. His next essays were grandiosely announced as works of his own. The magnum opus of his infancy was a tonal portrait of the Chicago Fire, then still a topic of discourse in Midwestern households. Had the Deluge, the Siege of Troy, the Great Plague, or Waterloo entered his ken, he would surely have tried his hand at them, too, so boundless was his confidence in his powers. The élan with which he dashed off his extempore pieces, slapping the keys with his palms or bearing down on them with his elbows when his fingers failed to create the desired brio, is recalled with hilarity by former neighbors.

Virgil Thomson was a musical prodigy with a tone-deaf father.

Quincy Alfred Thomson never hummed, whistled, beat time, or took the least notice of musical sound. He could read or sleep during his son's piano practice as easily as the average person reads or sleeps on a train. Of Lowland Scottish descent, he was the first of a long line of agrarians to quit the soil. His forefathers appear in American records in 1717, when Samuel Thomson, son of a landed Ayrshireman, migrated to Virginia and became a planter. Four of Samuel Thomson's grandsons served in the Revolutionary army. Like many other young Virginians after the War for Independence, his great-grandsons trekked westward. One of them, Robert Yancey Thomson, settled in Saline County, Missouri, where he became a prosperous farmer. A Baptist, he married the daughter of the first ordained Baptist minister of the county and, as he tilled his acres, helped to plant the Baptist cause. As a lay preacher he was often drawn into public controversy, a fate Virgil Thomson was likewise to suffer—and enjoy. He was also a supporter of the Teetotal movement, a position his great-grandson was not destined to share.

On his mother's side, Thomson's roots in America go farther back. In 1607, when the recently founded London Company was encouraging colonization on the coast of Virginia, Thomas Graves, a Londoner of Middlesex gentry stock, embarked for Jamestown. He received from the Colonial government a grant of farmland, helped to develop Jamestown into an agricultural center, and in 1619 became a member of the Virginia House of Burgesses, America's first legislative body. But his descendants, like Samuel Thomson's, were caught up in the tide of westward migration that swept the Old South. John Graves, of the sixth generation of the family, was an early settler of Boone County, Kentucky. A great-granddaughter of John Graves married a Kentuckian of Welsh origin, Benjamin Watts Gaines, in whom we meet Virgil Thomson's maternal grandfather. Gaines's daughter Clara May became the bride of Quincy Alfred Thomson in 1883, and until 1888 they lived on a farm of their own in Saline County, Missouri. Here their first child, a daughter, was born. Because Clara May Thomson could not inure herself to the rigors of rustic solitude, her husband disposed of the farm and transplanted his family to a nearby village, where he opened a hardware store. On the failure of this venture, he sought the more promising opportunities offered by a brash metropolis that had sprung up earlier in the century at a confluence of wagon trails and waterways on the bend of the Missouri River. Here Virgil Thomson entered this world on November 25, 1896.

Named after Indians native to the district, Kansas City was then in the fifth decade of her corporate existence. She had expanded from her original site on a rockledge to encompass, in staggered levels, her background of bluffs. By exploiting her strategic location she had become a transportation center and a livestock market second in importance only to Chicago. From participating in historical experiences almost as intimately as New York and Philadelphia, she had also developed a flaming civic pride. The border skirmishes between pro- and anti-slavery civilians that turned John Brown into a legend began on her outskirts six years before the outbreak of the Civil War. (Some historians hold that war might not have come had it not been for these guerilla activities along the Kansas-Missouri frontier.) Geography gave Kansas City, in addition, an altogether central role in the winning of the West. The town's site provided an ideal Midwestern terminal for the river boats and the wagon caravans used in the transcontinental migration. At the suburban village of Westport the Oregon and Santa Fe trails began. From Independence, the neighboring county seat, Brigham Young had set out for Utah with his dissident Mormons. However, in acquiring metropolitan stature and historical prestige, Kansas City had remained a frontier settlement in spirit—all friendliness and "square shooting." Employment on any level could be found. Wages were high for the times.

After serving briefly as a gripman on the cable cars, Quincy Thomson secured an administrative job in the post office that enabled him to provide his family with a genteel living. An upright piano enhanced the parlor of their bay-windowed house on the rim of the town, and small Virgil could be heard thumping the instrument with gusto off and on through the day. May Thomson was warmly sympathetic to her son's delight in music, which asserted itself as soon as he could crawl, but like any middle-class housewife of the period she was largely engrossed in the practice of the household arts. Her skill in cookery was to enrich the local store of legends. She was no less expert at eliminating rough edges: the smooth domestic routine of her home was proverbial in Kansas City. Ruby, the Thomsons' first-born and Virgil's senior by eleven years, expressed herself, likewise unmusically, in china-painting. Both children were reared in the Southern tradition of *noblesse oblige,* without any strain of race prejudice. Culturally, Virgil brought up himself. He absorbed pioneer values and the Christian virtues in heaping measure from his family, but his artistic proclivities are not traceable to any forebears.

His pianist-cousin (on his mother's side) gave him his first piano lessons. From her amateur hands he progressed via a secondary professional to Kansas City's leading teacher, Geneve Lichtenwalter, pupil of the Berlin pedagogue Ernst Jedlicka. While Miss Lichtenwalter disciplined his fingers and musical tastes, other fields of music opened to him. Gustave Schoettle, a German theorist who had migrated to Kansas City, instructed him in the rudiments of musical syntax. Clarence Sears, organist of Grace Episcopal Church, gave him organ lessons. Robert Leigh Murray, tenor soloist of Calvary Baptist Church, gave him singing lessons, taught him to accompany, and schooled him in the techniques of first-class professional standards. Murray, in fact, shaped the course of his early artistic growth. A Briton, trained in oratorio-singing, he had come to Kansas City as director of a piano store. On discovering Virgil, he saw to it, by advising the elder Thomsons, that the boy studied with the right local masters and properly acquired the professional skills. Virgil came to his notice with nothing but talent. Murray provided the musical ambiance in which his talent matured. At twelve, he began giving, with all the *savoir-faire* of the trained performer, recitals in churches and schools. By then, he was substitute for the organist of Calvary Baptist Church, and Murray was using him as accompanying soloist in professional engagements.

In his book *The State of Music,* Thomson holds that of all
professional preparations serious musical training is the most
exigent: "Even medicine, law, and scholarship, though they often
delay a man's entry into married life, do not interfere with his
childhood and adolescence. Music does. No musician ever passes
an average or normal infancy, with all that that means of abundant physical exercise and a certain mental passivity. He must
work hard indeed to learn musical matters and to train his hand,
all in addition to his school work and his play-life." Virgil's record of virtually nothing but A's through primary, grammar, and
high school shows that he managed to combine with the grind of
four to five hours' daily practice an equal assiduity in general
studies. This enormous diligence, moreover, did not hinder a
rounded development of character. He was abundantly equipped
with common sense, intellectual curiosity, interest in the other
arts, and zest for living. He was further blessed with that demonic
energy that so often stamps the Kansas Citian. And he was not
without the aberrations of his age, being mildly anti-gregarious
and, despite his Baptist background, quite irreligious. As bud-
ding organist and son of a deacon, he had to go to church, but
the service appealed only to his musical ear. Sunday school was
bearable because his teacher, a grandniece of Jesse James,
charmed him with the glamor of her ancestry.

The rest of Miss Lichtenwalter's pupils stood in awe of Virgil,
but relished his playing and his talk. His skill with words and
his love for paradox had already manifested themselves. At discussions after studio recitals, he deflated platitudes, speared inac-
curacies, and leavened the atmosphere with quips. Once the topic
was Richard Strauss, whose businesslike attitude about royalties
and fees had disillusioned some of the class. Virgil saw no reason
why a musician of stature should not take a normal interest in
earning a living and reminded them, quoting Lamb, that "those
with laurels on their brows have a right to browse on their
laurels." *Also Sprach Zarathustra,* then regarded as Strauss's most
novel work, sounded to him "so much like Wagner that it might
have been composed by Humperdinck." A rising piano virtuoso
in whose pyrotechnics he found no lyric flight evoked the capsule

critique "technically a phoenix, for feet of clay a centipede." As a pianist, Virgil himself shone more by cleanliness of style than by bravura. His taste and good musicianship were needed to dispel the not-so-favorable impression often created by his professional preliminaries at the keyboard. He would survey the audience De Pachmann-fashion and improvise a little *à la Paderewski,* both gestures being tributes to his idols of the moment. In the same spirit he would imitate Nijinsky in the gymnasium. For all his preoccupation about the development of his gifts, he was not without boyish interests. As athlete he made up in agility and accuracy what he lacked in heft. But he could not pitch a ball or swing a bat without falling into a choreographic pose that evoked *Schéhérazade* or *Spectre de la rose.*

The rapid commercial expansion of Kansas City gave early impulse to projects for civic enhancement, which Nelson's editorials prodded into realization. The slogan "Make Kansas City a Good Place to Live In" was more than the cliché of a town-boosting chamber of commerce; it was a promissory note prodigally paid off. As soon as transportation facilities, public buildings, and other amenities had been provided, the schools and churches multiplied, while homes, hotels, and gambling establishments took on such cosmopolitan swank that by the seventies the town was reputed to be the most luxuriously appointed between St. Louis and San Francisco. At the same time the makeshift theaters of the frontier period were replaced by a grandiose Victorian-Gothic auditorium—the gift of Kersey Coates, a civic-minded settler representing an Eastern syndicate of real-estate developers. The spired and cupola-ed Coates Opera House gave Kansas City a claim to culture by providing programs comparable to the best in the East. Here Laurence Barrett played Shakespeare, Lily Langtry Sardou, Maurice Barrymore *The Bells,* Joseph Jefferson *Rip van Winkle,* James O'Neill *Monte Cristo,* and the Wallack and Madison Square stock companies their flamboyant repertories. By the turn of the century this stage had known virtually all the other actors of stature, including Salvini, Modjeska, Henry Irving, Ellen Terry, E. H. Sothern, Julia Marlowe, Richard Mansfield, William Gillette, and Mrs. Fiske. In 1901, a week

before Bernhardt and Coquelin were to appear, it burned to
the ground. Kansas City having by then acquired four more
first-class theaters, the French troupe was transferred to the stylish
new Auditorium, where visiting opera companies and symphony
orchestras played.

The experience year after year of seeing the best acting talent
in dramatic works of many periods would inspire in almost any
bright adolescent an enthusiasm for the stage. Virgil's reaction
went deep. The plays of Shakespeare, Sheridan, Shaw, Sardou,
Rostand, and other master dramatists enthralled him no less
than the operas, symphonies, and recitalists' repertory he heard.
Julia Marlowe's speaking voice shone as dazzlingly for him as
Gadski's high notes or Sembrich's coloratura. Paderewski's
pounding was matched in grandeur by Bernhardt's tirades. He
rejoiced in the nervous intensity of Mrs. Fiske's acting as he
rejoiced in John McCormack's *bel canto*. Only De Pachmann,
whose Chopin was "rain from heaven," and Busoni, whose Beethoven "married complete intellectuality to romanticism at its
most passionate," were for him without their equals in the spoken
theater. Mary Garden, by reason of the intelligence, originality,
and searching musical quality that made her projection of every
role so powerful, became his ideal of womanhood on the stage.

The Coates Opera House fire was taken in stride because one
briefly preceding it had put the Kansas City spirit to an acid test.
The civic heart of the town was a huge convention hall built
in the late eighties and opened with Sousa's recently formed
band. On the strength of this super-Crystal Palace the hustling
citizenry had made their bid for the Democratic national convention of 1900, which they captured from right under the nose
of Chicago. Three months before the convention was to open,
the hall went up in flames. Before its remains were cold, the pop-
ulation had organized a rebuilding job that still holds the world
record for speed in construction. By the eve of the convention a
new hall, electrically lighted and festooned with bunting, was
ready for the delegates. A boulevard system without peer and
the third largest municipal park in America, both representing
the best landscape design of their time, were subsequent tokens

of a civic pride that not even the great Missouri River flood of
1903 could daunt. Nor could exposure of underworld power in
the city administration, followed by a sweeping anti-corruption
campaign, quell aspirations for further enhancement. The artistic
ferment that was to bring into being the University of Kansas
City, the Kansas City Symphony Orchestra, and the Art Gallery
on the Nelson estate set in during these turbulent years. Each
of these institutions would later make the town an uncommonly
"Good Place to Live In," but none was realized in time for
Virgil Thomson to benefit from it. When he was graduated
from the Central High School in 1914, his formal education
seemed to have ended, for his father was not then in a position
to send him away for university training. Providentially, at this
point the High School was removed to more modern premises,
and in its antiquated quarters the Kansas City Polytechnic Institute and Junior College opened classes.

Junior College, as it was called, offered university-level work
in the liberal arts in addition to training in trades. The faculty
was a blend of experience and fresh blood. Foremost among the
veterans of the High School was its former principal, Edward
Bainter, who had conceived the plan of the new institution. The
newcomers, not long out of college themselves, included Ruth
Mary Weeks, first American to crusade for vocational high
schools, and mathematicians William Luby and Frank Touton,
co-authors with Herbert Hawkes of standard American textbooks
on algebra. Physically, Junior College was less auspicious. The
class rooms were cramped, and there was no campus. Even the
times were unfavorable, with the first World War in progress
and the United States expecting to be drawn in. When this
event occurred, the institution's existence was further endangered
by transportation problems, fuel shortages, and the grim first
epidemic of "Spanish influenza." But none of these obstacles
affected the exceptional quality of the first class that passed
through Junior College. The faculty members knew that they
must prove themselves. The two hundred students, coming
mostly from middle-class families of limited means, were more
earnest, on the whole, in their efforts at self-development than

the young Kansas Citians who could attend established universities. Though they would have preferred an older college, they
did their best to make a success of the new one. That they did
not do badly in the circumstances is borne out by the high per-
centage of prominent men and women among the first graduates.
These include the sociologist Rachel Stutsman, Hubert Kelley of
the editorial staff of Crowell-Collier, Richard Lockridge of the
old New York *Sun* drama department and long a contributor to
the *New Yorker* and to mystery fiction, and several outstanding
clergymen. The most eminent alumnus today is Virgil Thomson.

He entered college life with the advantage of professional experience. And it is certain that the student who has pursued
some vocation or avocation with a view to performance by professional standards knows the meaning of mastery better than
many others. He offers little if any resistance to drill in other
fields; he is disposed, as the student who has mastered nothing
for love or for necessity cannot be, to practice with new tools
and to persevere until he finishes any job. Ruth Mary Weeks,
who taught prose composition at Junior College, found Thomson docile in his willingness to practice literary finger-exercises.
But she disclaims credit for the crisp individuality, stripped to a
minimum of words yet not seeming quite to have been intended
for delivery by Western Union, that marks his early writing. She
ascribes it to the self-confident directness of one who knew what
he wanted to say and saw no reason to be ornate about it. Any-
way, Thomson had a native regard for simple people—for artisans
who know their tools and respect their craft, whether it be cob-
bling or book-binding—and liked to make himself understandable to them. He admired their relation to culture as much
as he scorned the half-learning of the dilettantes. These traits
do not seem to have precluded, however, a relish for startling
the crowd. Once after he had been at a students' tea given by
Ruth Mary Weeks, her invalid father, who overheard the talk
from his room, asked: "Who was the opinionated professor? I
thought only college boys were expected." Still, though assuming
himself to be nearly omniscient, Thomson lacked intellectual
snobbery. He was authoritative with his fellow students, but not

aloof. He behaved as naturally with faculty members as if he were one of them, but was never wanting in respect.

Bored by the usual kind of college societies, Thomson formed a group of his own for the purpose of bringing together boys of divergent interests. To arouse enough animosity to give them importance, he coined for them the impressive name "Pansophists." Their meetings consisted of readings and discussions. The female wing of the student body emulated them; and the Pansophists sometimes held joint sessions with their sister society, who less presumptuously chose to be called the Anons. For reading from *Spoon River Anthology* at one of these mixed gatherings, Thomson came close to being expelled from Junior College. The president of the Anons testified at a conclave of trustees and faculty members that he had not sprung the verse on the unsuspecting co-eds, as was supposed, but had warned them in advance so that they could stay away if they chose to. Her group corroborated the defense, and Thomson was allowed to remain.

The faculty and the trustees were further dismayed by his publication of a little magazine called *Pans,* in which his and other Pansophists' writings appeared, peppered with comments on the college and climaxed by his announcement of issues to follow. Here again is evidence of forward-looking influence. A decade later, in the twenties, the little-magazine idea was to sweep the country. Founded to circumvent a commercial culture hostile to experiment, *Blast, Broom, transition, The Little Review,* and other combative periodicals were to become recognized incubators of talent. However, at the time when *Pans* first saw the light of day, most other little magazines that existed were suspect publications filled with inept and doctrinaire "proletarian literature." To introduce into the student life of a junior college a similar platform for ideas—even without any of the "tainted" ideas associated with such a platform—called for courage in an undergraduate.

Thomson's editorials reveal the born journalist, already equipped with the intellectual audacity and crisp authority of the mature individual we know. In the first issue of *Pans* (May, 1916) he states the club's case:

The Pansophists herewith make their official bow. We are a group of young men organized ostensibly for mutual benefit. We are interested in anything that can be known. Like Bacon, we take all knowledge to be our province; and like a good governor, we hope to get acquainted with our province. Not that we expect to exhaust the world in our sessions. Our universality means rather this, that any sincere point of view is just as interesting as any other. We do not even require sincerity provided the performer does not bore us. . . . We bind ourselves to no principles or convictions, and we exclude nothing from our horizon. This, in brief, is the personality of the Pansophists. What our character is, is another question. If you wish a distinction between character and personality, let us say that personality is the mask one wears in public; character is the mask one wears to oneself. It is then a mark of higher culture to have no character at all. We are striving toward this condition. Our ideal of a club personality, though, is a unified development of an infinite variety of viewpoints.

He then urges changes in the college:

We are a new school with a small faculty and two hundred students, trying to do university-grade work and be a real college. As far as the scholastic work goes, it is better than that offered to freshmen at either Missouri or Kansas University in almost every department, and it is in no wise inferior to that of Michigan and Wisconsin. But being a real college is a job we have tackled with less brilliance. The school has been running for a whole year now, and we are still lifeless, dull, and indifferent. Our worst evil is in not being enough together. A campus would help greatly. We need a meeting place, a loafing ground where we can have class fights and hatch secret plots to get into devilment. . . . The trend of our life is so orthodox, so dignified, so unassailably correct, that it is in danger of dying of dry rot from lack of opposition. We want enemies. Give us something to take sides on and fight about!

To an unsigned letter addressed to the Pansophists he makes this open reply:

An anonymous enemy waxes wroth over our name. Granted we are not either "All of the Knowers" or "The Knowers of All," we still maintain that if we aim at such a distinction, we will probably become something better than those who do not. As for our sophistry . . . our enemy has here made a point for us by referring to the golden Sophists of Greece, who did not argue falsely or insincerely at all, but disputed for the sake of the dispute, and who discussed merely for the pleasure of talking well. If we were a debating club, the false argument accusation would apply, but we are not. And we believe that the emulation of the Sophists is no more presumptive than the imitation of Christ. The other charges against us are:

1. We are artificial.
   Any attempt to unite distinct classes of minds is necessarily artificial, since they do not gravitate naturally. The finest products of fertilization in horticulture are artificial, but that's no objection. Where's the argument?
2. We are narrow in our aim.
   Humanism itself is narrow. Certainly our field of interest is broad. But if our aim to add variety to the student life and provide a field for originality is narrow, we plead guilty on this count.
3. We are undemocratic.
   Of course we are! To pick the best and develop it is as ruthlessly aristocratic a course as the processes of nature. Democracy is a device to insure the survival of the unfittest, a plan to reduce the world to uniformity, a synonym for mediocrity. All men are not equal; they should merely be given an equal chance to prove their superiority. The equal chance we all have at the college, and it is only our effort to prove our superiority to the general average that makes the anonymous letter-writer call us snobbish. He is only proving our point when he tries to show that his ideals are higher than ours.

Youth, precocity, and the economic climate were all conducive to the unabashed smugness of this defense. Thomson was nineteen, acknowledged to be Kansas City's most brilliant student, and living in a world of what seemed to be endless security. Also, philosophic reading on which he had embarked had acquainted him with the doctrine of Nietzsche. However, the superiority he claimed to exemplify may have consisted of something besides intellectual prowess; it may have had a moral value potential, a strain of the "pluck that is not swankiness but the power to endure and to take a joke" that E. M. Forster holds to be the test of the true aristocrat. In upholding the equal chance and refuting the charge of snobbishness, the cocksure adolescent indicated that he was moving toward a view of aristocracy which, by the time Forster was seventy, had survived global wars, seen economic crises, and been confronted with the atomic menace, became the only conceivable one to a sensitive adult.

The first issue of *Pans* closes with the envoi:

> When a club is formed, the usual program is to lay down rules, specifications, and ideals for its perpetual continuance. The Pansophists have avoided everything of the sort. In our weekly sessions absolutely no dictation as to the nature of the program is given. Each member spends his hour in any way he likes, and the rest afford him an audience for the exploitation of his individual hobbies. Likewise our publication may be of any character the editorial board cares to make it. . . . We don't know what will become of us; we don't care. It is not our purpose simply to perpetuate the organization. It will perpetuate itself as long as it remains a vehicle for personal expression. It may fall into the usual hidebound club-for-club's-sake rut; it may be an ever-changing reflection of student ideas. If the boys of the college haven't the good sense to see that it provides a chance for them to do what they want in their own way, let them organize one of their own sort or else pervert the present club to their purposes. If they want the narrow-scope society, full of traditions and other limitations, they can have it. Conventionality is its own punishment.

The Pansophists who returned the following year spent their leisure in "doing what they wanted in their own way"; and during the year after that (1917), all of them enlisted in military service, while war work absorbed the younger students and the girls. The wave of frivolity that swept the nation in the wake of Prohibition engulfed the club in social pursuits. Though still extant, it has never regained the standards of its first years.

Thomson's circle accepted his leadership without question, though he vexed them as much as he impressed them. He scorned the jolly-good-fellow brand of popularity, and considered few boys outside his group worth notice. Nor did girls attract him much except as partners for mental sparring, though he seems to have had a way with them. At this time he became the organist of a Methodist church in the suburb of Westport. After his appointment, a marked increase took place in volunteers for the soprano and alto sections of the choir. Sunday after Sunday the musical forces discharged their duty and sat out the sermon in the organ loft, but he remained an "interesting stranger" to them. At rehearsals of chamber pieces that he introduced into the services, a courteous formality prevailed. Not even the minister's stalwart spouse, the director and first soprano of the choir, could break down his professionalism. She once sent him a sheaf of solos with the request that he transpose the accompaniments. They were returned untouched, with the message that it was "rather a good deal to expect of a five-dollar-a-week organist." The church went in for soirées designed to promote friendly relations. One "sociable" of this time presented a program of old-fashioned songs. Attics were searched for pre-Civil War costumes; libraries were combed for old parlor ballads. Thomson, who presided at the piano, found the poke bonnets, hoop skirts, and pantalettes so amusing that during an intermission he slipped backstage to compliment the singers. The prima donna, Gladys Blakely, prettiest co-ed of Junior College, was assured that she was the "cutest thing" he'd ever seen. The now musty adjective was at the peak of its vogue as a designation for all degrees of charm. No one could have read superlative connotations into Thomson's hasty utterance of it, but for the rest of the evening Gladys sang with a new sparkle and the performance took on a fresh bounce.

Thomson's one extra-Pansophist friendship was with another co-ed of Junior College, Alice Smith, daughter of the President of the Reorganized Church of Jesus Christ of Latter-Day Saints in Independence, Missouri, and great-granddaughter of the Mormon Prophet, Joseph Smith. She was the most intellectual girl student of the college, and for her years an uncommonly resolute character. She it was who, after founding the Anons, talked down the authorities bent on expelling Thomson for introducing them to *Spoon River Anthology*. Though she shared interests with him, her attraction lay primarily in her size and cheerful presence, which had something of the mother-mentor-monolith quality that the massive Egeria of Thomson's Paris period, Gertrude Stein, was to have. The rest of the students called the pair "Mind and Matter"—Thomson, who in those days was somewhat cherubic, representing the incorporeal element. But if Alice possessed anything of the Steinian faculty for imparting stimulus, she was given little chance to exercise it upon him. He, instead, spurred and quickened her. Without disturbing her Victorian ethical outlook except by sly digs, he acclimated her to twentieth-century values in letters and many other fields. He needed an audience, as he still does. Alice Smith was the most receptive he had found.

Even in the company of Alice's parents, Thomson maintained his preceptor role, bringing to it a nice edge of deference. He was often a guest of the Reverend and Mrs. Frederick Madison Smith, usually at his own suggestion. His aplomb at first put them off, but the skill, imparted by his mother, with which he helped to prepare meals on cook's day out soon endeared him to the household. His salads (nothing but greens, herbs, and French dressing), his rice (feathery, firm, bone-dry), his mushrooms (so broiled as to retain their own moisture), his soufflés (crusty without, creamy within), were gourmet's fare. His piano playing, especially his Grieg, his MacDowell, and improvisations of his own in a similar spirit of breezy freshness, gave added pleasure. Alice attempted a poem about his performance of the MacDowell *Sea Pieces,* which he had gone through for them by candle light during a blackout caused by an electrical storm. After many unsuccessful efforts, she perceived that the episode could not be caught in words, for, as so many were later to discover, the sum total of Thomson's nature eludes definition. It is a multiple nature, several selves under one skin and each complete in itself: egoist, altruist, realist, romantic, traditionalist, avantgardist, viveur, ascetic, and other contraries, all dovetailed into as integrated and fully expressed a personality as modern psychology could dream of. Within his more limited range he recalls the "harmonious human multitude" that Carl Van Doren found in Franklin, and a multitude does not fall into a pattern. The spell of his impromptu recitals for the Smiths was not infrequently broken by argument between the clergyman and the collegian. The elder did not always emerge from these dialectics with flying colors. Sometimes he took a trimming. On one such occasion, Thomson, after repeatedly seeing him repress Alice "for her own good" for venturing an opinion, questioned his right to ignore his daughter's mature status. He held that to refuse to recognize a girl of seventeen as an intelligent human being worthy of joining in family discourse was neither kind nor just. The quarantine of silence was lifted.

Outside his circle, Thomson was regarded as a young man with a destiny, but was thought to be conceited, eccentric, and even foppish: he managed to dress well on the simplest scale, but with the most dapper effect. He was also considered to be something of a poseur, and the romantic theory prevailed that his attitudes masked an inner loneliness. Needless to say, they did nothing of the sort. A life as studious as his was of necessity rather solitary, but to the creative nature solitude is not a vacuum. To Thoreau it was "the most companionable of companions," to Stevenson "the best society," to Wilde "the only tolerable company," to Emerson "the stern friend." To Thomson it was guide-philosopher-and-friend, so early did he master the art of living abundantly regardless of his surroundings. His apparent conceit likewise changes character on examination. His teachers had instilled in him an awareness that he had unusual ability both musical and mental. He had not yet decided whether to pursue music as a vocation and keep writing for a hobby or to reverse the two, but he was convinced that he could achieve success in either field, and in his intellectual honesty aired the belief. The fact that this confidence in his powers was the result of their sound training did not make it less irritating to his associates. It troubled even Alice Smith, who had boundless belief in him, but felt that he owed it to himself to assume a becoming modesty. His agnosticism was a phase through which the adolescent mentality is likely to pass. Such other phases as vegetarianism, sun-bathing, and outdoor sleeping were part of his self-preparation. In reading for a history course he had come across a theory from the Renaissance that there is such a thing as "physical morality." This, buttressed by Voltaire's dictum that the intelligent man should regard infirmity as debasement and by Samuel Butler's portrayal of it as a crime in Erewhon, made the preservation of good health as much a moral obligation as a common-sense measure. Thomson still views it as such, but unlike more doctrinaire health cultists, who wind up as invalids, he functions year after year in top form under pressures that would hospitalize the average adult after a season. Yet he is the least hurried of men.

When Thomson entered the army in February, 1917, his friends and foes alike speculated on the effect of an environment so fatal to eccentricity and conceit. Speculation gave way to astonishment as he rose to the highest rank attained by a Junior Collegian in the first World War: second lieutenant in the United States Military Aviation Corps. Foreseeing the entry of the United States into the war, he joined the Third Field Artillery Regiment of the Missouri National Guard, a mounted outfit with headquarters at Independence. After the declaration of war the state militias were not immediately mobilized. Summer came, and as he was still no nearer Europe, he went to Ann Arbor, where a friend at the University of Michigan had secured him a job as organist in a motion-picture theater. Knowing the advantages of possible aviation service or ambulance-driving (both highly romantic and reputed to get one rapidly across), he took a summer course in gasoline engines at the university. This kept him cramming automotive mechanism when he was not accompanying flickery Westerns, Sennetts, Keystones, and two-reelers featuring queens of the silent screen. (He prides himself on having introduced classical repertory into the cinema.) At this point the American Ambulance Service, previously a private society working under the French army, was taken over by the American army. At its chief camp near Allentown, Pennsylvania, volunteers who could drive a car were being accepted for immediate overseas duty. Thomson resigned his engine course and his motion-picture job, requested and received his discharge from the Missouri militia, took one lesson in driving a model-T Ford, and dashed off to Allentown, only to have the camp doctor misdiagnose his feet as flat.

He rejoined his old regiment in the Missouri militia, and on the advice of an ex-medical student in its ranks arranged to be assigned to the Medical Corps. Renumbered the 129th Field Artillery, and with Captain Harry Truman in command of one battery, the unit was ordered to "dig in" for the winter at Fort Sill, Oklahoma. Here Private Thomson inspected quarantine tents, vaccinated doughboys, and helped an army psychiatrist examine suspected mental deficients. Meanwhile, seeing Europe farther and farther away, he had applied for officer training in aviation. In January, 1918, he was appointed to the School of Military Aeronautics at the University of Texas, in Austin, where he would have a chance to qualify for a commission in the Signal Officers' Reserve Corps, Aviation Section. (American aviation was then attached to the Signal Corps.) The two-month course was an ordeal, but enormously gratifying. A letter to his parents describes the daily routine: from 5 A.M. until 10 P.M., except for three hours of drill "to keep us all from going stark mad," study of airplane construction, ballistics, bombing, meteorology, radio operation, military law, and the organization of foreign armies; most of the night spent digesting the day's rapid-fire lecture notes to make room for the next day's notes—"an effort that leaves you feeling like a stuffed boa constrictor"; every week a quiz in each subject with the alternatives of passing all or "busting out." Of the fifteen hundred cadets from many professions requiring special training, Thomson made the highest grades. But when he was ready for pilot training, a new complication arose: there were found to be more cadets than the airfields could handle. As radio-telephony needed men, Thomson secured an appointment to the air service school for radio officers at Columbia University in New York: it was promised that this would get him across sooner than piloting.

The course by which Thomson became a radio engineer was even stiffer than the Texas training, but on weekends he managed to avail himself of New York's hospitality to men in uniform.

He heard the Philharmonic under Josef Stransky and opera at the Metropolitan. He saw the cream of the plays and a filming at an Artcraft studio with Douglas Fairbanks, Sr. in action. He witnessed a Carnegie Hall rally at which the Bishop of Oxford electrified a capacity audience. He dined in Park Avenue palazzos that depressed him by their display of magnificence. A service at Saint Mary the Virgin, the Episcopal Church at Forty-sixth Street and Seventh Avenue in which the ritual is of medieval splendor, left a deep imprint. By now he had outgrown his agnosticism and had evolved for himself a creed that combined something of the liberal theology of Unitarianism with his frontier-nurtured faith in man's capacity to shape his own destiny. Yet esthetically he was and still is a High Churchman. He revels in the music of the Roman Catholic service, and no liturgical aspect of Catholicism or Anglicanism lacks visual charm for him. In Kansas City he had often dropped into the small Episcopal Church of Saint Mary to listen to the Gregorian singing. At Saint Mary the Virgin's in New York the "lovely fol-de-rol," as he described the procession of gorgeously robed priests, the chanting of the two choirs, and the rich music of a full orchestra and two organs, was followed by a sermon that awoke in him an awareness of his responsibility to others, hidden until then by an increasingly self-centered view of life. His years of absorption in musical training and academic study took on a new meaning. He resolved to go on after the war from where he had left off and, this time, to devote effort to helping others younger and less advanced in their careers. He had always been ready with the kind gesture, though he tended to camouflage it with a satirical quip. From now on he was to make a fine art of the practice. A full account of the scores performed, the paintings exhibited, the books and articles published through his exertions would require a special chapter. He has sponsored candidatures, bolstered morale, adjusted problems, lent money, and by this generalized bread-casting has become involved in endless, yet often amusing, complications.

After three months at Columbia, Thomson was commissioned, without wings, as radio engineer and ordered to Lake Charles, Louisiana, for flying practice. In September, 1918, he received his

overseas orders. But November 11 arrived before his troop ship
was to have sailed. The crowning irony of his war experience was
that his old regiment in the Missouri militia got to France in
time for some real fighting in the Meuse-Argonne offensive. His
flippant references to the blow, in letters of that winter, were
neither protective coloring nor observance of the wartime convention that demands indifference to moral, as well as physical,
suffering. It was a more basic restraint, motivated by a trait that
above all others in his nature is the least commonly shared or
understood. It passes with him for "social courage," and in casual
conversation can make him sound preposterous. In deeper experience it manifests itself as detachment. "If there is enough left of
me to perambulate after the war is over, I want to go East or
abroad," he had written his parents on notification of overseas
duty. Instead, when the army turned him loose, he returned to
Kansas City and re-entered Junior College. It was the only way
in which right then he could afford to continue his university
training, and he had a new incentive for completing it. His war
experience had clinched two decisions: he would make music his
career, and somehow he would get to Harvard. Lack of money
no longer seemed an insoluble problem, for he had become aware
of his competence in the practicalities of life. He was inordinately
endowed with this quality so rarely found in artistic natures. His
singleness of purpose, his ability to define the steps leading to it
and to persist until he accomplished it were, within the compass
he set himself, Churchillian.

The first step was taken that year—1919. One spring evening
Thomson sauntered over to the Frederick Madison Smiths', asked
for an interview with the clergyman in his study, and told him
he must secure a loan for him from a fund for young people
maintained by the Reorganized Church of Latter-Day Saints. Dr.
Smith, accustomed to having his young friend lay down the law,
advanced the sum. Having no illusions that life owed him a living, Thomson had already made plans for repaying the loan: he
would find an organist's post in Boston. Though his debt was not
to be liquidated until long afterward, not only an organ job but
also scholarship money and an assistant instructorship were all to

be made available to him during his first year at Harvard. Thanks to his sound musical preparation and natural self-confidence, he was to step without stumbling from the professional world of Kansas City into the metropolitan music life of the Eastern seaboard.

The Harvard Years

HAVING FULFILLED HIS SCIENCE AND HISTORY REQUIREMENTS AT
Junior College, Thomson could supplement his music courses at
Harvard with any others that especially attracted him. He chose
Italian, German, philosophy, and advanced English composition.
He wanted to acquire sufficient command of the two languages
to read their literatures and to make his way about Italy and Germany when a musical opportunity arose. As he meant to learn to
speak French impeccably, he tutored with a cultured Parisian
settled in Boston, giving piano lessons in exchange. A natural
taste for philosophic reading had already led him through the
writings of Schopenhauer, Nietzsche, and the English philoso-
phers; but except for Nietzschean reservations about the benefits
of democracy, he had remained unconverted by any doctrine.
Harvard's controversial approach to philosophic instruction was
therefore congenial to him. Since President Eliot's time, no one
professor in the philosophy department had wielded unique authority. All the professors honored diversity of mental attitudes
and opposed the development of a Harvard school of thought. To
help train students toward impartial thinking, opportunity was
provided to study every sort of philosophic system under a confirmed believer in it and to hear it refuted by expert opponents.
Thomson's philosophy teachers were Ralph Barton Perry, pupil
of William James, and Lucien Lévy-Bruhl, exchange professor
from the Sorbonne. Imbued with the Jamesian spirit of intellectual freedom, Perry encouraged clash of opinion, speculation
on one's own account, the achievement of an individual philosophic system. Lévy-Bruhl disputed the doctrine with urbanity
and formidable scholarship; but Thomson, though charmed by
Lévy-Bruhl, as well as by the British logician Alfred North White-
head, who was already expounding at Harvard the use of mathe-
matical symbols in reasoning, rejected all the European sys-

34

tematizations of thought in favor of Perry's homely and more specifically American do-it-yourself attitude.

Thomson's instructor in advanced English composition was Le Baron Russell Briggs, Dean of the College, who effected the shift of emphasis from rhetorical theory to actual writing practice that has raised his department to first rank in American universities. Discerning the students' need of a better working command of their language, President Eliot had appointed Adams Sherman Hill to reorganize the teaching of English. Hill, in time, required an assistant and chose Briggs, then an instructor in Greek. Harvard acquired with his appointment a singularly powerful teacher of English composition. He held that writing could not be taught, but that under the right conditions something about it could be learned. To provide such conditions, he supplemented his writing courses with discussions of contemporary life. His talks, which were less lectures than thinking out loud with wisdom and wit, awakened in his students an awareness that attitudes besides their own were quite legitimate. After an exchange of views on some aspect of the social machine or some puzzle of everyday affairs, he would ask them to put down their thoughts. His effort to train men toward perceiving their relation to the world around them and to write about it in a personal way gave a new direction to American letters. The movement to develop a literary art from the American soil, the American streets, and the American mores grew in part out of Dean Briggs's teaching. Bernard DeVoto, E. E. Cummings, Hermann Hagedorn, Conrad Aiken, John Dos Passos, and Frederick Lewis Allen were among the writers who came under his influence. Others perpetuated his tradition as teachers and editors. Virgil Thomson applied it to music.

An announcement in the Harvard catalogue of 1856–57 of "Instruction in Music with Special Reference to the Devotional Services" marked the pious beginning of the music department. This vague program constituted its whole activity until early in the sixties, when John Knowles Paine, first incumbent of a chair of music at any American university, introduced composition as an accredited academic subject. When Thomson presented himself in 1919 to the music department, Professor Walter Spalding found his knowledge of harmony out of date: he was required to take the elementary course. At the same time, wishing to improve his proficiency at the organ, Thomson signed up at the New England Conservatory for lessons with Wallace Goodrich, organist of the Boston Symphony Orchestra. For further musical experience, he joined the Harvard Glee Club and the Harvard Chapel Choir. Here began a long and fecund association with Dr. Archibald T. Davison, key figure in Harvard's rise to choral pre-eminence.

For the first century and a half of its existence the Chapel Choir had consisted of a handful of students who led the congregation at compulsory prayers. The service being Unitarian, their participation was minimal. With the change to voluntary worship in 1886, the Chapel service had been enriched to attract attendance. Noted preachers were called to the pulpit; and a full choir, picked and coached by Warren Locke, organist of Saint Paul's Church in Boston, was substituted for the untrained hymn-leaders. Davison, who succeeded Locke as choirmaster in 1910, adopted a wholly new repertory. Like Charles Bordes, whom he had known in Paris, he was a crusader for the liturgical music of the fifteenth and sixteenth centuries. He arranged its finest examples for male voices and so thoroughly drilled his men in diction and nuance of tone, that their performances matched those of Bordes's renowned Chanteurs de Saint-Gervais. The Glee Club was a descendant of a series of such short-lived societies as the Arionics and the Anacreontics that had cropped up at Harvard in the early nineteenth century. After years of performing the trivia that are the stock-in-trade of such groups, it attained its present scholarly status under Davison toward the end of World War I. He doubled the number of singers, arranged the best choral literature for them, drilled them in its presentation, and created opportunities for them to assist the Boston Symphony Orchestra in large-scale choral works.

Among Thomson's student associates in the music department were Walter Piston, Randall Thompson, Leopold Mannes, and several others now prominent in American music. They all remember him as a model of industry, a dynamo of enthusiasm, a dedicated "go-getter." Nevertheless, some of his letters of this year to a wartime friend show that his determination to reach the topmost level of his capacities was balanced by moments of misgiving. He wondered if absorption in classes, in organ practice, in Chapel Choir and Glee Club rehearsals was stifling inner growth: "In the immediacy of all this activity I cannot see what is really happening to me, but I suspect that rather than living and growing I am merely cerebrating. I dread becoming so incrusted behind my academic individuality that I shall be unable to reckon with the human things." That spring he was President Lowell's nominee for a Rhodes Scholarship, but the Missouri Committee's vote went to another candidate. The following year his activity doubled. He took Spalding's Advanced Harmony course, Davison's Counterpoint, and Edward Burlingame Hill's Orchestration. After the first semester he was appointed Assistant Instructor in the department and organist of North Easton's Unitarian Church. But the moments of misgiving ended when in the midst of this high-pressure cerebrating he was chosen one of the fifty members of the Glee Club to make a summer tour of Europe and also awarded a John Knowles Paine Traveling Fellowship for study in Paris. If Paris was all things to all men, she must be soil in which his emotional growth could catch up with his intellectual blossoming. There, he thought, his entire self could surely take shape.

The French historian Bernard Faÿ, a graduate of Harvard, had recommended to his country's Foreign Office that the Glee Club be invited to France. The Quai d'Orsay, eager to cultivate the friendship of the American student world, extended the invitation. A few persons active in fostering good Franco-American relations contributed the needed funds; and in June, 1921, the fifty members, Davison, and two managers—Avery Claflin and John Moore, old Glee Club men both—set sail aboard the antiquated steamer *La Touraine*. When she docked at Le Havre eleven days later, at midnight, the first to board her were the mayor, the municipal council, and a government representative from Paris. The significance of this reception becomes apparent if one tries to envisage the mayor of New York appearing at midnight with his councilmen and a representative from Washington to greet a French choir. The entire following day Le Havre fêted the Club. Charabancs festooned with French and American flags sped it from one end of the town to the other. Speeches of welcome hailed it at every stop. The mayor entertained it at a formal reception. The Association des Mutilés et Anciens Combattants bestowed honorary membership on it. Champagne flowed. The visitors boarded the Paris express unaware that they had only sampled the kind of hospitality that lay ahead.

They arrived at an ideal hour for first impressions, two o'clock in the morning, when Paris, deserted and wreathed in mist, is all ethereality. Mounted atop a four-horse omnibus, with luggage stacked inside, they rumbled through the moonlit streets to their quarters in a Left Bank students' club. The schedule planned for them was an endurance test. Every morning they rehearsed for their three Paris concerts, then for the rest of the twenty-four hours attended official parties, went to the Opéra or to the Comédie Française, did sight-seeing, and slept a little. They took part in the opening exercises of the newly founded Conservatory for American students at Fontainebleau. They spent another day at Versailles, and after strolling through miles of palace and park were presented to Marshal Joffre at a private château nearby. The Cercle Interallié received them with a luncheon at which Marshal Foch presided. Henri Bergson was host at a soirée given in their honor by the Institut de France. Their round of festivities was climaxed by President Millerand's first postwar reception at the Elysée Palace, where the spectacle of government dignitaries and prominent citizens pushing and elbowing for the free champagne was a gratifying revelation of European democracy. Though scowled upon by footmen for not wearing cutaways (none of them owned one), the boys joined in the scrimmage and downed their share of the refreshment.

Their rehearsal on the morning of the first concert could not have gone worse. All were tired; many were hoarse; none could keep on pitch. Their program (Allegri's *Miserere*, Lotti's *Crucifixus*, Handel's *Hallelujah! Amen,* an *Adoremus Te* at the time incorrectly ascribed to Palestrina, and a sheaf of equally exacting secular numbers) had been posted on the kiosks, making substitutions hazardous. It looked as though the Paris début was doomed. Davison, in despair, ordered the men to return to their rooms and sleep for the rest of the day. The cure succeeded beyond his hopes. The Parisians who filled the Salle Gaveau that evening heard the Harvard Glee Club give the best concert in its history. The press held the choral group to be unmatched by any other known to Paris; the organization of similar choirs in French universities was urged. Determined that they should keep up to the standard they had set, Davison had the men make up for further arrears of sleep on the days of their second and third concerts. On both occasions their performance was all he could have wished for. President Millerand summoned him to his box to congratulate him in person. Cardinal Dubois, who before the program had announced that he could remain for only one group, stayed till the end. Satie, Milhaud, Poulenc, Florent Schmitt, and other composers offered to write music especially for the Club. After its Paris triumph, it could embark with confidence on its Italian tour.

En route it visited Burgundy, Lorraine, and Alsace. In Dijon it performed in a public square; in Nancy, in the palatial opera house. At Verdun it was lodged in the citadel in underground officers' cubicles and driven in camions to the monumental ossuary of the bones of unknown soldiers, where it sang sacred repertory. In Strasbourg it took part in a service at the Cathedral, and from its place in the choir stalls witnessed a scene Thomson was not to forget. Sunlight streamed through the windows of luminous reds and blues. The vaulting rose in all the splendor of its sumptuous line and tracery. The altar blazed with tapers. The chancel glistened with vestments. The nave and transepts were a sea of Alsatians in native costume. After the service, Dr. Albert Schweitzer took the men to the Protestant Church of Saint Thomas, where he played Bach fugues for them on an organ that had been built under Bach's own directions. Later, the Governor of Alsace gave them a ball, after which the students of the University of Strasbourg fêted them at a cabaret. At nearby Mainz they boarded the private steamer of the Chief of the High Commission for the American Army of Occupation and rode the

Rhine to Coblenz. Their concert took place in the town's former Festhalle, where the Y.M.C.A. had set up its "Hut." It was the custom of men in uniform to come and go as they liked, as many a dwindling audience had previously shown. The Club did not vary from its usual scholarly program, and at the end there was no gap in the khaki surface presented by the three thousand seats. After a jaunt by truck to Ehrenbreitstein to view the Rhine and its castled banks again, the men entrained for Italy.

In a temperature of 120 degrees they gave three concerts in Venice—one at the Lido for the American Colony, one at the Casino for the Venetians, one at the Liceo Benedetto Marcello for students—and visited the Accademia and the cream of the churches. At Pesaro, where they sang in the conservatory founded by Rossini, they proved their musical independence. Davison having left Venice with a touch of malaria, Thomson directed for him without notice and learned, from leading an entire concert with confidence and competence, that he was a born conductor. The Bishop of Ravenna had offered the use of a church, but when the Club arrived, the Pope had withdrawn the privilege. The concert took place in a theater, where secular Ravenna made up for the Vatican's coolness, climaxing her ovation by escorting the men to their quarters with a torchlight procession led by the municipal band. Before leaving, they devoted a day to studying the sixth-century mosaics of the town's early Christian churches and basilicas. The splendor and searching realism of these scenes from the New Testament and from Gothic history made Dante's exile appear less grim; the heap of wreaths at his tomb was enhanced with a fresh one and a Harvard banner. The response to the concert in Milan was less boisterous but no less warm than the responses of Pesaro and Ravenna. Though puzzled by the Club's stately pacing of sacred works, as Anglo-Saxons ever are by the brisk Italian tempos, the Milanese marveled at its mastery of Renaissance polyphony. Harvard, in the opinion of one critic, had "opened the eyes of Italy, acknowledged land of song, to the possibilities of choral singing in academic life."

The Geneva concert marked the end of the tour. This occurred in the Calvinist Cathedral of Saint-Pierre and consisted of Roman

Catholic Church music. While revisiting Paris on its return journey, the Club was presented by Aristide Briand with a Sèvres statuette of the boy Mozart, a reminder of his visit to Paris a century and a half earlier. The Club, in turn, left with Paris its own musical ambassador, no statue yet; and the parting was painful to all. To Davison, Thomson had been a dependable assistant as well as the mainstay of the second tenor section. To Claflin and Moore, he had been useful in practical ways. To the men, he had been a bracing comrade. If their quarters contained a piano, he had entertained them with musical jokes, also with Debussy, Satie, Ravel, and Bach. In the tedium of train journeys and official receptions, his pointed wit and the vitality of his presence had kept everyone in high spirits with a healthy dash of exasperation. No one could fill his tonic role in the Harvard Glee Club.

In 1921, Paris was just beginning to fill with Americans. Some were there for study, some for the fun of it, others for getting away from home at any price. Many ex-servicemen were impelled to do so by the unfriendly social and political climate they found in America after demobilization. There was no provision for easing their adjustment to civilian life, no concern over the economic irregularities that eventually brought about the bonus march of 1932. The postwar boom was in progress. America, preoccupied with getting and spending and with circumventing Prohibition, seemed, in Samuel Putnam's phrase, to have "turned into a trollop." Thomson shared the expatriates' discontent, but not their disaffection. The human and the esthetic potentialities of America remained as real to him as to Stephen Vincent Benét, Van Wyck Brooks, and the others whose loyalties stayed with their roots. If anything, distance strengthened America's hold on him. His year in Paris was to bring about growth, but not deracination. France was to give him perspective, teach him to view his American heritage in the light of international values, equip him to move freely in the main stream of world art. But homespun Americana was to remain the chief substance of his expression, and in his hands to prove gratifyingly compatible with world standards of craftsmanship.

One of his first Paris friendships was with Alice Woodfin, a music-loving New Englander who had gone to France with a war unit and settled there. When she met him in the fall of 1921, he was already making strides. An introduction by Bernard Faÿ to the Ministry of Foreign Affairs gave him entry to cultural events. By reporting on special musical occurrences for the Boston *Transcript,* at the request of its music critic, Henry Taylor Parker, he received passes to the lyric theaters and the concert halls. (His articles about a particularly brilliant concert series fired Boston with such interest in the Russian leader that when Pierre Monteux's conductorship of the Boston Symphony ended, the trustees sent a committee to Paris to offer the post to Serge Koussevitzky.) With the *Transcript's* fees to supplement his Harvard fellowship, Thomson was managing to live in Paris in a manner satisfactory to a student of sense and taste. His furnished room on the rue de Berne, near the Place Clichy, was just wide enough to contain a grand piano with organ pedal attachment, just adequate for the requirements of sitting and sleeping. But it was central, high, and quiet; and a roofscape topped by the dome of Sacré Coeur compensated for want of elbow room. He had mastered the bus and Métro systems, and had drawn up a list of bistros chosen for the excellence of their food, the discreetness of their charges, and the friendliness of the *patron.* He had even acquired the Parisians' knack of sauntering through traffic. Alice Woodfin recalls with a shudder his sprightly chatter as he crossed crowded thoroughfares, looking neither right nor left, confident that the vehicles would miss him if only by millimeters. *Le vieux Paris* was the quarter he liked best. Walks through the Marais and the Cité had made him at home among the tortuous streets whose names spell history and among the *hôtels particuliers* that are seventeenth-century urban architecture at its loveliest. He had reacted to the Latin Quarter with some reserve—not to the Sorbonne, the Institut, the antique shops, and the book stalls, but to the international Bohemia of Montparnasse. Added to his distaste for the garish, he had geographical reasons for not frequenting much the Left Bank bars in which Hemingway was to set *The Sun Also Rises.* Nadia Boulanger, with whom he was studying, lived just off the Place Clichy, and he practiced the organ daily at a church near the Parc Monceau.

Like all men of all classes in Paris, Thomson had a favorite meeting place. His particular night-spot grew out of a wartime habit of *les six* of dining at a Montmartre restaurant before going up to Darius Milhaud's bachelor quarters to try out their latest compositions. After the Armistice, a former classmate of Milhaud's at the Conservatoire, Jean Wiéner, proposed that they transfer their meetings to a bar where he was playing the piano with a Negro saxophonist and banjo-player. Milhaud, accompanied by Jean Cocteau, visited the bar; and both were charmed by its jazz. The counterpoint of regular against off-meter accents that provokes a muscular response, the wailing melody that quotes from all sources without losing its African tribal rhythms or its gospel character, caught their imagination. Their patronage of the bar attracted so many new clients that the proprietor moved to larger quarters, which he named after the Milhaud-Cocteau ballet on Brazilian dance rhythms, *Le Boeuf sur le toit*. Diaghilev, Stravinsky, Raymond Radiguet, Louis Aragon, and many other artists, musicians, and writers of the "advance" frequented Le Boeuf. Through an American painter-pianist who replaced Wiéner, Thomson had known the boîte since its opening. He listened to much of its excellent talk and responded with his share of brilliance.

But such pleasure had to be restricted to the few hours remaining to one engaged in study with Nadia Boulanger. The third generation of her family to join the Conservatoire faculty, Mademoiselle Boulanger is at heart a classicist. At the same time, she abhors dogmatic systems and imparts creative stimulus as much by intuitive as by scientific means. A pupil of Gabriel Fauré, she has let her sympathies, spurred by an acute spirit of inquiry, carry her as far in the knowledge of contemporary music as in that of the past. Her interpretation of anything embodies both allegiances. With this range of outlook she combines a psychologist's understanding of the musician's nature and a saint's willingness to key her approach to a pupil's individual needs. At Harvard, Thomson's teachers had made him feel that to write music was to compete with Bach or Brahms. Seeing every effort unfavorably compared with one or the other had turned composition into a constricting enterprise. Nadia Boulanger's instruction had a very different effect. It was marked by the utmost strictness in the disciplines of harmony, counterpoint, and fugue, and yet by a great freedom in the approach to composition. Without imposing models on him, she made him understand that the inspiration of any trained composer is as authentic as anyone else's is or ever was, and that if he expressed clearly and sincerely what he had to say, his music would be worthwhile.

This concept of the art of composition as a function of the musical mind rather than as an attempt to emulate the classics restored Thomson's ease in front of music paper. His pieces of this year—a *Fanfare,* a *Pastorale,* a *Prelude,* and a *Passacaglia,* all for organ, and a *Tribulationes Civitatum* and a *Sanctus* for mixed voices—are the peak and the end of his student period. The musical atmosphere of Paris was charged with acid post-Impressionist sonorities, with Stravinskyan intensities, and with the deliberate levity of *les six,* but he kept to church forms and brought to his modal-sounding idiom a high degree of expressiveness and no small technical aplomb. If any kinship could be read into it, it would be with the early music of Erik Satie. Thomson was not yet sure what attracted him in the art of that independent spirit, whose war against pomposity and everything else official had anticipated the esthetic of Dada. He knew only that its simplicity was far from naïve, that it was a congenial climate, that it might be among the lasting values of the twentieth century for him. He was presented several times to Satie, but attempted no talk with him. Acquaintance with *Socrate,* Satie's muted, strangely expressive setting of passages from the Platonic dialogues, had so sharpened his admiration for the composer that he became skeptical of knowing the man too well.

In the hope of spending another year under Nadia Boulanger, Thomson applied for a renewal of his fellowship. The Harvard music department refused to consider his request until he had taken his degree. They offered a scholarship, an assistant instructorship, and the post of organist in Boston's historic King's Chapel if he would return. He was adequate to the post, having mastered under Mademoiselle Boulanger such formidables in organ literature as the Bach D Major, D Minor, and "Wedge" fugues. Having also gained confidence in his creative powers from her, he was eager to apply them to the expressive problems of his own country. But the temper of the homeland did not encourage such expression. H. L. Mencken, in New York, was flailing America for its reverence for wealth and its indifference to art. T. S. Eliot, from London, was advancing his doctrine of disillusionment and despair. Hemingway, in Paris, had privately convinced many of the younger intellectuals that they were indeed lost. Even such Middle-West-rooted Americans as Carl Sandburg and Sherwood Anderson were full of misgiving. And isolationism was the Senate's foreign policy. In a letter written after his return in the fall of 1922, Thomson avowed that despite his country's fabulous prosperity he "can only say of her 'A poor thing but mine own.'" He kept reminding himself this year that when civilizations have turned worldly and crumbled, others have sprung from the ruins; that it was out of the Dark Ages that Gregorian chant, Gothic cathedrals, and the poetry of Dante arose; that Grotius evolved his philosophy of law during the direst phase of the Thirty Years' War; that Beethoven matured in the tumult of the Napoleonic struggle. Living in France had taught him that the world is large and that one's country, a part of that world, is bound to forces in remote places that eventually shape its destiny. He did not doubt that America would perceive her global position, but he suspected that the discovery would be slow.

Slipping back into academic life, Thomson sct up a typical schedule for himself in the Harvard music department. He took Advanced Orchestration under Hill and assisted him in his History of Music, Modern French Music, and Modern Russian Music courses. He shared Davison's History of Choral Music course with him, and became assistant conductor of the Harvard Glee Club. At the same time he discharged his duties as King's Chapel organist and, with an assisting soloist, performed programs of new French music at the Harvard Musical Club. His scholastic hours were relieved by "gabfests" at the Liberal Club, where he

formed hardy friendships—with Garrett Mattingly, now Professor of History at Columbia University; Henry-Russell Hitchcock,
now Professor of Art at Smith College; Henry Sales Francis, now
Curator of Painting at the Cleveland Museum; Carleton Sprague
Smith, now Music Librarian of the New York Public Library;
and several others of future achievement. On being graduated in
1923 as of the class of 1922, he received a Juilliard Fellowship
with which he went to live in New York and to study with Rosario
Scalero at the David Mannes School of Music.

In his teaching Scalero used exercises learned at the Vienna
Conservatory from Eusebius Mandyczewski, a pupil of Nottebohm and devotee of Brahms, but he combined with the rigor
of this Germanic schooling a purely Italian francophobia. Dis-
approving of French instruction in counterpoint on the ground
that it was too rigid, he made Thomson return to the study of
counterpoint once again and encouraged him to give the maximum expressiveness to part-writing. After going through the
counterpoint mill three times, Thomson felt that he could write
eight-part double choruses in his sleep. Actually, he often wrote
them during orchestral rehearsals, for he had meanwhile enrolled
for a practical course in conducting under Chalmers Clifton, director of New York's short-lived American Orchestral Society.
He practiced free composition without benefit of Scalero, however. At his first lesson he had submitted a few pieces and found
the response so hostile to their French influences and to modernism in general that he never showed Scalero anything again.

The experience of conducting Clifton's student orchestra
taught him that for a trained musician who knows composition
and the periods of orchestral style and who is accustomed to performing in public, leading an orchestra through a score is no
more recondite a matter than playing the piano or training a
choir. But the New York symphony concerts made him fear that
in America the profession of orchestral conducting, under the
influence of Leopold Stokowski, was dangerously approaching a
state of mountebankery. He saw that the successful conductor
must key his art to the American tendency to react to music emo-

tionally rather than cerebrally, that his programs must present famous masterpieces rather than unfamiliar works, that his readings must be personalized rather than abstract, and that he must always play the lion. During that one season Brahms's First was programmed eleven times and the sure-fire romantic scores almost as often. Had distorted display performances of the "fifty pieces" not gone out of fashion before Thomson became a critic on the daily press, they would surely have summoned many a slashing philippic from him.

His immersion in counterpoint and conducting was relieved on Sunday evenings by ensemble playing. On arriving in New York he had engaged a room on East Thirty-fourth Street in the apartment of a professional accompanist. Felix Salmond, William Kroll, Joseph Fuchs, and other young instrumentalists of quality regularly made music in her parlor. Thomson frequently joined in the sessions as pianist; and through them he became so interested in the cello that he took lessons with Luigi Silva, who was also studying at the Mannes School. Learning how many are the pitfalls in the technical handling of the cello challenged him to compose for it. Such was the origin of his Cello Concerto (promised to Silva at the time, but not written until many years later), in which virtually all the potentialities of that eloquent and difficult instrument are brilliantly exploited. And such was the source of the acute critical judgments that cello playing has summoned from Thomson.

After the year in New York, Thomson was again offered an assistant instructorship at Harvard, which he accepted for bread-and-butter reasons. The King's Chapel organ loft had a new incumbent, but he secured that of the Congregational Church at Whitinsville, near Worcester, and made up for the lower salary by writing for *Vanity Fair*. Then in its sixth decade, this monthly magazine, after a period of volatile editorship under Frank Harris, had been transformed by Frank Crowninshield into an organ for expounding in light vein modern art, music, and letters. Though its accent was on fashion advertising, the nubbin of editorial content in its glossy pages was worth hunting down.

Aldous Huxley, Erik Satie, Wyndham Lewis, Jean Cocteau, Colette, Gertrude Stein, and E. E. Cummings were among those who had availed themselves of its liberal fees when Thomson became its music correspondent. His essays on the contemporary music scene were so sound in judgment that many of his colleagues advised him to adopt criticism as his life work. Then, as now, however, composing was for him the paramount concern. As he expressed it, "My business is making music, not talking about it." If he could not devote himself wholly to composing, he would pursue it concurrently with writing. Letters of Berlioz, Debussy, and other composers who have also worked as journalists bitterly set forth the disadvantages of such a course, but for Thomson their admonitions were defeated by their own wit. He wondered why no anthologist of humor had ever compiled the cries of despair to which composer-critics had given vent. In addition to teaching, filling his organ post, and doing his critic's job he continued, therefore, to compose. A second version of his *Missa Brevis* No. 1 (written in New York the year before), his *Three Antiphonal Psalms,* his *Agnus Dei,* and his *Three Sentences from the Song of Solomon* (for tenor and piano) date from this time. However, Thomson the critic and Thomson the composer represented no duality of purpose. His aim in each role was to help establish and to advance a native musical culture.

At the end of the academic year he was invited to direct the music department of the University of South Carolina for a salary no one else in his circumstances would conceivably have turned down. While visiting his parents in Kansas City that summer, he was offered the organ at the Protestant Episcopal Cathedral of Grace and Holy Trinity, also a major post. He refused it, too, and in September, 1925, left for France. No Eliot-inspired thoughts of foreswearing his country motivated the step. He was merely seeking the musical and esthetic climate that he felt to be the best for him at this stage of his development. He had five hundred dollars and a third-class ticket; and *Vanity Fair,* he had been assured, would keep him afloat until he could establish himself as a composer. But he had no illusions that establishing oneself as a composer is a shortcut to economic independence.

Twenty-eight years old and leaving his country forever, for all he knew, he addressed to its receding shore no Byronic-ironic "My native land, good night!" He merely remarked with his characteristic flippancy that if he was going to starve, he "preferred to starve where the food is good."

The Paris Years

IT HAS BECOME COMMON TO LAUGH OFF DADA AS THE SUPREME HOAX of a period when hoax was in high fashion in Paris. In origin, however, it was anything but a joke. As a product of World War I political disillusionment, Dada represents an attempt on the part of some of the finest minds of its generation to jettison established values in society, literature, and art. Positivism, humanitarianism, and patriotism having betrayed their highest aspirations, they chose as a substitute goal the attainment through art of the infinitely irrational. The upsurge of creativity that ensued was the latest link in a long chain-reaction of creative impulses in France. The romantics, seeing their political ideals frustrated by the defeat of the 1848 Revolution, had turned for inspiration to opium and exotic climes. The cubists, in protest against a commercialized academic tradition, had hermeticized their content and broken form into its geometric components. Finally the Dadaists, unhinged by the collapse of their once-secure world, used Freud's ideas to explore the possibilities of psychic escape. Like Gauguin, they felt an irresistible urge to go back beyond the horses of the Parthenon to the rocking horses of their childhood. For their very name they chose the French infant prattle term for that toy. To the earnest-minded the exploration was a technique of liberation from bourgeois values. Cocteau, Eluard, Aragon, and others among them stand today in the front rank of French writing. To the exhibitionists it provided a retreat into the defeatism that is associated with the movement.

Dada was born in the darkest year of World War I, when gifted refugees from all over Europe had taken their pacifist convictions to neutral Zurich. Improvised entertainment in a cabaret founded by local sympathizers climaxed in a pledge to reject a civilization that seemed to have degenerated into a tragic farce. If the world wanted to destroy itself with bombs and poison gas, they would speed its extinction with ridicule. A gaily blasphe-

50

mous manifesto proclaimed their intention to live by non-reason: sources of inspiration hitherto inhibited must be opened; primary mental processes—that part of the self in which the individual remains a child or a savage—must be utilized; the creative process must become pure psychic automatism, art a compilation of the accidental. By 1921 Dada had swept Central Europe and Germany, burst briefly over America, and settled on the banks of the Seine. Thomson, then studying with Nadia Boulanger, was charmed by its iconoclasm. Much as the use by free impulse of incongruous material clashed with his whole academic training, it suggested a new and vital mode of extending music's vocabulary, a way of saying fresh things by fresh means. He did not relax his application to counterpoint, but something of Dada seeped into the music he wrote. The year 1921 saw the apogee of the movement, but the interminable disputations (as stormy as any in the annals of French polemics about art) that made it the focal center of artistic life that year also ended it prematurely. Dada was talked to death.

By the middle twenties, dissidents within its ranks had launched a movement of their own: surrealism. In coining this term ten years earlier, Apollinaire had intended to convey that the three-dimensional world of conscious reality is but a pseudo-reality, a pattern of habits and codes; that absolute reality resides in the secret instincts and atavistic memories of the individual psyche, which he held to be the *fons et origo* of creative power. The surrealist writers confined their revolution to their subject matter, using conventional literary techniques to portray astral fantasies. Their painters, in turn, adopted a super-academic treatment to depict visions never seen on land or sea. However, before the movement became dominant in France, its founders began to perceive that there are limits to the exploitation of dream-imagery, which is essentially monotonous. Their inspiration was waning for want of steady relation to the hurly-burly of life: they were diving for pearls in a dead sea. To balance their introversions with an objective interest, they decided to adopt a social goal, to represent Marxism in art. Their attempt to fuse the Freudian and Marxian postulates resulted in a naïve dualism:

accepting the doctrine of dialectical materialism, they nonetheless claimed exemption, as artists, from the necessity of participating in the class struggle. They proposed instead to introduce the proletariat to a new culture compounded out of the preoccupations of both Freud and Marx: primitive instincts, socialist doctrine, political facts, artifacts, dreams. Their efforts to synthesize these elements were cut short by Moscow's demand that they join the Communist Party. Not all complied, most of them preferring to uphold Trotskyan Marxism. The few who engaged to follow Stalin's straight party line were forced to resign from the group. With the outbreak of the second World War the leading surrealists became bards of the Resistance or exiles committed to patriotism. Existentialism elbowed their doctrine into desuetude, and a new youth arose to stop belief in the absurdity of the universe. As an enthusiast of Dada, Thomson sympathized with its offspring as long as it represented a purely intellectual anarchism. When surrealism turned into a propaganda organ for psychiatry and socialism, he lost interest in it.

Meanwhile his articles for *Vanity Fair* had opened a broader field of writing to him. After resettling in Paris, in his old quarters on the rue de Berne, he received offers from the *New Republic*, the *American Mercury*, and *La Revue européenne*, all promising a steady market. But he refused to contribute to any of them more than once or twice a year, for he sensed that at this stage of his musical development over-verbalization would be harmful. A nostalgia for the climate of pure inventiveness possessed him; he longed to devote his whole time to composing. Though this necessitated subsisting precariously by giving piano lessons, he did not repress the urge; and his rejection of criticism in favor of music itself released a burst of creative activity. He tried his hand with a set of *Inventions* for piano and with four sets of *Fugues and Variations* for organ on American Sunday School tunes, in each paying his compliments in parodistic vein to baroque structure. He even experimented in the dissonant neoclassicism current at the time in France. This venture took the form of a *Sonata da chiesa* for five strikingly disparate instruments: clarinet, trumpet, viola, horn, and trombone. He then

revised and added to his earlier setting of quotations from the
Song of Solomon. Each essay, particularly the *Sonata da chiesa,*
in which twentieth-century dissonance is married to the fugal
style, was pruned and polished until it was exactly what he had
sought after. Had he known how soon some of them were to have
public performance, he could not have taken more pains. "Quality
is largely a matter of revision, improving in proportion to the
degree of rigor with which one re-writes," he informs Ruth Mary
Weeks in a letter of this year (1926), adding that the year has
been as rewarding in personal contacts as in creative work. Among
old friends mentioned are two Harvard associates: Arthur Train,
"learning the arts of being a novelist and spending an income,"
and Maurice Grosser, "studying painting and *savoir-vivre* on a
traveling fellowship." A few people he had known in his first
year in Paris had disappointed him: "gone Right-Bankish or
otherwise died." But there were exciting replacements: "James
Joyce is interested in my music. . . . Sylvia Beach is being angelic
to me. . . . And there is George Antheil, a thorough leftist." (In
his vocabulary of the twenties the word "left" meant simply
avant-garde.) This contact with Antheil triggered Thomson's professional début as a composer.

Ever since the end of World War I, "Shakespeare & Co.," a
bookshop founded by Sylvia Beach, bibliophile ex-ambulance
driver from New Jersey, had been a Paris rendezvous for American readers and writers. With her publication of Joyce's *Ulysses*
in book form in 1922, her establishment at 12 rue de l'Odéon
became the center of English language belles-lettres on the Continent. Whenever the Sitwells, Virginia Woolf, Eliot, Yeats,
Aldous Huxley, and other London authors of stature visited
Paris, the shop was their literary point of repair. Ford Maddox
Ford, E. E. Cummings, Ezra Pound, and other resident literati,
including Joyce himself, were often to be found at the end of the
day browsing at its tables. The areas of its walls that were not
filled with books were an unofficial Hall of Fame, lined with
photographic studies by Man Ray of current literary lights. In
the middle twenties a composer briefly dominated the gallery.
One shot out of the many exhibited showed, against a back-

ground of black and white squares, a wistful-eyed youth with a prize-fighter nose and his hair cut in bangs. Others displayed the same young man in acrobatic poses (scaling a wall, dangling from a balcony) and similar manifestations of the *enfant terrible* ebullience with which George Antheil, gifted son of a Polish shoe-storekeeper from Trenton, New Jersey, titillated the intellectuals of the Quarter. He was passing through his period of swagger. His compositions, modeled after Stravinsky and stridently scored, excited the literary mind somewhat more than the musical. Writers fancied that they discerned in them the symbols of a mechanized civilization. Joyce expounded in an article for the *transatlantic review* the "machinery-in-art" idea he read into Antheil's clangorous *Ballet mécanique*. Pound wrote an esoteric monograph, *Antheil and the Treatise on Harmony* (Three Mountains Press, 1924). Thomson, who met Antheil through Joyce, was not taken in by his shock tactics or by his pose as Stravinsky's heir; but he knew that beneath the rowdy texture of his scores there was responsible content, the deliberate parody of an over-mechanized world. He admired Antheil for his skill and bravado as a satirist. A common interest in being contemporary (and in getting their music performed) drew them together.

Parisian music criticism has not always been incorruptible. Lesser critics and even a few top men have at times operated on a price-list basis. After the first World War the practice prevailed on all levels. None but inexperienced foreigners paid the sums demanded for favorable reviews, and no notice was taken of the reviews. Nor did audience reaction count high in postwar France, where the claque was ubiquitous and applause depended more on an artist's or composer's largesse than on quality in performance and compositions. Judgments were formulated rather in the salons of Paris, where a recital was a recherché occasion. It occurred in the historic *hôtel* of some millionaire or member of the French aristocracy, among choice works of visual art. It was attended by bearers of historic names and by key figures on the cultural scene. There was no more influential audience in the world, nor any more exclusive one. Neither fortune nor

position alone could open these doors. The only passports were
artistic or cultural distinction. Thomson's acquisition of this
carte d'entrée for a friend is an episode that could have happened
only in the Paris of the twenties.

Alice Woodfin had introduced him to a member of the Crocker
family of San Francisco, Mrs. Christian Gross, whose husband
was then First Secretary of the American Embassy. Convent-
reared and still in her thirties, Mrs. Gross had breeding, charm,
and intelligence in addition to fortune. Her one foible was a
social ambition that her husband's merely diplomatic status
could not satisfy: she craved admission to the intellectual salons.
But she had neither the calculating faculty essential to social
ambition nor the patience for rising through the rung-by-rung
technique, with its detailed maneuvering to meet persons who know
the upper hostesses and can be cultivated into wangling invita-
tions. Thomson suggested, through Alice Woodfin, a more rapid
course. He recommended that she present concerts of avant-garde
music in her *hôtel particulier* on the Avenue Charles Floquet,
to which he would bring some of the intelligentsia; in other
words, that she set up an intellectual salon of her own. Mrs.
Gross was willing to experiment, and gave him a free hand with
the arrangements. He entrusted most of these to Antheil, who
had boundless aplomb and plenty of scores awaiting performance.
Antheil chose the three Friday afternoons following the Grand
Prix week, engaged the rising Vladimir Golschmann as conductor, and mustered assisting artists of rank. He and Thomson
then invited every presentable author, composer, and painter of
their acquaintance, exacting from each the promise to bring his
aristocratic patron if he had one. With coaching from William
Bullitt, formerly United States Ambassador to the U.S.S.R., but
then free-lancing in Paris as an author, they interested various
ambassadors in their enterprise. They also made it clear to Mrs.
Gross's chef and major-domo that they must surpass themselves.

Each afternoon began with champagne and a fabulous buffet.
The programs were exclusively Thomson and Antheil. At one
concert of the series, Golschmann conducted Antheil's *Ballet
mécanique,* for which seven player-pianos, a pair of airplane

motors, a battery of buzzers, and other sonorous hardware had been installed in the Gross drawing room. At another, a soprano and a percussionist, the latter playing in turn on cymbals, a tom-tom, a gong, and a wood block, performed Thomson's *Five Phrases from the Song of Solomon*. The fullness with which the rhapsodic melodies, accentuated by contrasting percussive accompaniment, convey the spirit of Hebrew chant charmed the poets as well as the musicians among the guests. At still another afternoon, a trombonist, a horn-player, a violist, a trumpeter, and a clarinetist under Golschmann's direction played Thomson's *Sonata da chiesa*. What with its disparate instrumentation and deliberately out-of-focus harmonies, it is a bewildering piece to the ear. Nevertheless, its structure is pure baroque. Like true Parisians, who admire originality but prefer it achieved within a traditional framework, the aristocratic patrons present were pleased to hear dissonant harmonic coloration applied with skill and taste to classic form. After the modernism-gone-berserk of Antheil, so proper a marriage of fancy to rigor was doubly admired by many. By the next morning a vogue for contemporary American music was on in Millionaire Bohemia, and Mrs. Gross was launched.

She expressed her gratitude with a small commission, and Thomson invested her advance payment in a visit to Thonon-les-Bains, near Evian, for a summer's work on a well-pondered experiment. He wanted to apply the Dada outlook to composition, to achieve within a disciplined musical structure a collage of incompatibles. For this trial mixed-marriage he dispensed with the usual procedure of inventing by formula and drew on melodic memories of the Midwest and the Old South, a working method he was increasingly to employ. Earlier in the century, Charles Ives had tapped indigenous wellsprings for thematic material in his use of native hymns and folk tunes. But he had handled them as a primitive, whereas Thomson exploited them in his *Symphony on a Hymn Tune* with the best Parisian rhetoric and syntax. Such treatment was all they needed to pass, in time, into common currency. Square, inflexible revivalist tunes were slyly woven with buoyancy and wit into a symphony of impec-

cable structure. The result was a classic in musical satire, the
first to convey through scholarly form the feel of rural America,
evoking all the color and bustle of a Currier and Ives print.

In the fall of the year 1926 the most decisive artistic association
in Thomson's whole career set in. Gertrude Stein had first entered his ken at Harvard, when the poet S. Foster Damon—then
a lecturer in the Harvard English department—introduced him to
Tender Buttons. The crackling word sequences appealed so
forcibly to Thomson's flair for the rhythms of English that he
experimented in transcribing them into music. Their sound,
their images, their flashes of humor replaced for him any need
of clear meaning. He read Gertrude Stein's writing as one watches
a delightful circus, expecting it to make no sense but its own.
And he saw it for what it was: a true literary cubism. When
Gertrude Stein wrote *Tender Buttons,* in 1911, she had already
settled in Paris for a residence that was to span two world wars.
Until then she had lived detached from local contexts, having
been born in Pennsylvania and having grown up in Vienna,
Paris, San Francisco, and Baltimore. On emerging from adolescence and from the inwardness that had resulted from her lack
of geographical roots, she had entered Radcliffe College, where
she found a congenial intellectual climate amid the psychological
investigations of William James and Hugo Münsterberg. From
there she had gone on, at James's advice, to Johns Hopkins for
medical studies and then had returned to Europe for more travel.
Soon after she had embarked on her Paris period, her eyes had
been opened by Leo, her art-critic brother, to the painting of
Pablo Picasso. Inspired partly by Cézanne's late works, partly by
African Negro sculpture, Picasso and his friend Georges Braque,
both then unknown, were reducing natural forms to their abstract components, investing these components with a dynamic
reality, and reassembling them into designs that were anything
but a sum of their parts. Gertrude Stein could scarcely have
helped being receptive to this new painting. William James had
implanted in her the idea that consciousness is an activity rather
than a receptacle for impressions; that it acts outside of events
and values; that the current of present "disengaged" thinking is

the final reality. Her writing from the first was oriented by this hypothesis. Though the whole literary movement of our century has been centered around the stream of consciousness, her use of it as a form of expression differed from that of Proust, Joyce, Virginia Woolf, and all the others. Experiments in language interested her more than communication, and from her study of automatic writing under Münsterberg she had learned that there is more in language than the dictionary discloses. She viewed words as entities rather than as utensils, though she felt no Mallarméan urge to give them non-utilitarian meanings derived from their sound or association. Their sound in itself—the shock and humor of unexpected word combinations—and their pure immediate meaning, stripped of associational emotion, defined at this time the scope of her literary endeavors. Perceiving that an exciting affinity existed between her aims and those of the cubist movement, she set herself to achieve with written words what Picasso was achieving with visual symbols. Her break with naturalism was precipitated at this point by a trip to Granada.

Donald Sutherland, in his revealing guide to her writings, *Gertrude Stein: A Biography of Her Work* (Yale University Press, 1951), offers a reason for the decisiveness of this trip. She had been to Granada before, but this time she went with new ideas to which Spain gave concrete meaning. These ideas dealt with her view of existence as immediate and final—a view probably best embodied in the landscape of Spain. "It does not change and melt and grow like an English landscape," Sutherland says, "nor can it be reduced to distances like an American landscape. After all, Spain is a peninsula, and one soon runs out of all except perhaps vertical distances. The landscape and the things in it or on it are absolutely and fully there. They make a challenge to man to be as absolutely, as unchangeably as they are. Man has to counter the landscape with an equivalent reality." Which might explain why the religion, the literature, and the painting of Spain are dense with images, why the architecture looks over-ornate, why the cathedrals loom over-large, why hill towns give the impression of being the highest in the world. Confrontation with such excessive primacy of physical presence in both landscape and artifacts strengthened Gertrude Stein's sense of words as existences in themselves and challenged her to affirm it. *Tender Buttons* (Marie Claire, 1914) was her answer. Choosing familiar household objects that correspond to the classical subjects of cubist or other still-life, she abstracted them from their practical context, splintered them, and clothed the shards in clusters of unrelated words. Picasso defined his paintings as "a sum of destructions." Gertrude Stein attempted a similar demolition of traditional literary form. Though the effect of her verbal jugglery on literature was slight compared to the effect of cubism on art, it at least jolted English writing out of its Edwardian rhetoric.

After early years rich in musical experience as a listener, she had finally put music behind her. She held that what appeals to the ear is of lesser intellectual value that what is directed to the eye or to the mind. Writing represented to her the highest achievement of man's imagination; music was an art for adolescents. Her own writing abounds in references to creativity without any mention of music. She associated little with musicians, and to ward off the subject claimed to be ignorant of its ABC. Until she was seventy, she refused to listen to a radio. After finally acquiring one for the purpose of receiving communiqués during the second World War, she deplored in letters to friends the vast amount of music that was broadcast. In her opinion, literary programs would make for better understanding between the nations. However, Joyce's enthusiasm for the *Ballet mécanique* was so infectious, and Pound's so importunate, that she invited Antheil to call. Dreading to present himself in a salon so demandingly intellectual, Antheil asked Thomson to accompany him.

Even Thomson was nervous as they neared the pavillon-atelier at 27 rue de Fleurus. It occurred to him that its location—in the heart of Montparnasse, yet for all but a few as inaccessible as Tibet—was eminently symbolic of its mistress's discontextuated writing. They crossed a stone courtyard and entered a windowed door through which an elderly female had eyed them skeptically. (Gertrude Stein's *bonne à tout faire* was so used to admitting Picasso, Braque, Matisse, and other callers of that famous gen-

eration that she could not take young newcomers seriously.)
Through the half-open inner door were visible two middle-aged
women seated by the fireplace. One was mannish with features
that reminded Thomson more of a medieval abbot's than of
a Roman emperor's or of an Indian chieftain's, to which they
had often been compared, though he subscribed to the dictum
of sculptors that they might have been hewn out of a mountain-
side by Gutzon Borglum. The monastic robe she wore made him
envisage her as an altarpiece. Her massiveness blew up the impression to that of a cathedral in human form. The other woman was
delicately built and gypsy-featured. Distance in the large room
lent each a slightly sinister look. He found himself thinking,
" 'Will you come into my parlor?' said the spider to the fly." But
instead of the snug parlor of the jingle, he entered a gallery hung
from ceiling to baseboard with canvases that summed up most
of the significant idioms of twentieth-century painting: a portrait by Cézanne; *fauve*-period creations by Matisse; Picassos of
the blue, the rose, the cubist, the African primitive, the neo-
classic, and the surrealist periods; portraits by Tchelitchew and
Kristians Tonny; landscapes by Masson; abstractions by Gris,
Braque, and others less recognizable to Thomson. The hundred-
odd paintings, placed tier over tier and exploding with color, all
but covered the whitewashed walls. Yet none impinged on another. Each seemed to belong where it was. Nor was there the
flavor of a museum. Renaissance furniture, old porcelains, and
liturgical objects relieved the modernity. Chintz armchairs and
a huge sofa covered with horsehair gave a tone of "homeyness."

Gertrude Stein's usual procedure with a young newcomer was
to greet him with cordial brevity and then turn him over to her
companion, Alice B. Toklas, known as her "sieve and buckler."
Miss Toklas engaged him in discourse long enough to size up
his background and achievement potential, discharging the function with grace, dispatch, and uncanny precision. If rated worthy
of more prolonged contact with his hostess, he was invited again.
Thomson made the most of his preliminary contact while
Antheil was being sieved. He avowed his attempts to set passages in *Tender Buttons,* and Gertrude Stein recognized the type

of reader for whom she wrote. His comments on her paintings showed him to be conversant with art. The verve with which he mentioned Satie's *Socrate* roused her curiosity. He offered to go through the score for her—in his room on the rue de Berne, as she had no piano—and she accepted. Before Alice B. Toklas had a chance to pass on him, he had been admitted to the Stein circle.

Gertrude Stein enjoyed discovering likenesses to historical figures in her friends. She had spotted a "Lincoln look" in Picasso, "something of the Norman crusader" in Marcel Duchamp, a "domesticated Viking" in Bravig Imbs. Edith Sitwell was "Queen Elizabeth painted by Modigliani," someone else a "caricature of Uncle Sam made French," still someone else "Heine in petticoats," another a "feminine Talleyrand." It was soon borne in upon her that Thomson resembles in more than name the author of the *Aeneid;* that he shares his homonym's attachment to his country, affection for indigenous things, fastidious tastes, and faculty for knowing the great of his day. He became the "Lutetian Maro" of her côterie. Being no Latinist, she drew on the phrase "Maro Lutetiensis" coined by Sherry Mangan, a Harvard associate of Thomson's, poet, and, later, *Time* correspondent in Paris.

Members of this côterie passed through carefully graded degrees of intimacy, the highest being the right to quarrel. Gertrude Stein could inspire friendship in all and sundry types, but friendship meant less to her than contact with genius. She infinitely preferred brilliant insincerity to sterling dull worth. Moreover, a belligerent strain in her nature had been sharpened through coaching in the art of *brouille* by Apollinaire, a past master. Her autobiographical writings abound in allusions to ruptures, but mention no causes. That vanity was among them is indicated by the historic brush with the surrealist poet Georges Hugnet. She had translated his poem *Enfances,* and expected to have her name appear first on the cover, in the same size type as his. He adduced the universal custom of placing the original author's name first, in larger type, and was dismissed. Another reason was the dislike of the vanguardist for the inertia of habit, even in friendship; another, the propensity to conceive of opinion as her special province. Like Verhaeren, she admitted that the only writing that interested her was her own, and this reserve tended to apply also to talking. Yet when she did listen to others, her concentrated attention and searching gaze made them know they really kindled her curiosity. Quick to recognize talent, generous in fostering it, she expected of its possessor submission not only to her guidance but also to her whims. Magnificently eccentric herself, she disliked eccentricity in others; in her presence an Edwardian decorum was *de rigueur*. All of which bears out Thomson's theory that there were several Gertrude Steins: "the Doctor Johnson Gertrude Stein, laying down the law; the salonnière, equally avant-garde and of the grand tradition; the *homme de lettres—homme,* not *femme;* the hermetic poet, humble before a piece of paper if not before the views of others on her work; and the generous, gallant, and charming woman that was Gertrude Stein at her best." His friendship with her was not to deviate from the established pattern. It was to head more than once for the rocks, though he was always to manage to salvage it. But few others in her wide circle set in so effortlessly or sprang so full-fledged into being.

Soon after their first meeting, he introduced her to Satie's *Socrate.* She was struck by the score's refreshing asceticism, but Thomson's lack of the pianist's usual emotionality as he sat at his Pleyel, being all at once conductor, orchestra, and vocal soloist, left the deeper imprint. Piloting her Ford homeward, she commented to Alice B. Toklas that he was "singularly pure *vis-à-vis* his art"; that it seemed to mean to him "discipline, humility, and loyalties rather than egocentric experience." He became a frequent guest at 27 rue de Fleurus, and in its atmosphere of passionate experimentation formed associations with leaders of contemporary movements in all the arts. One of the first thus engendered was with the Duchess of Clermont-Tonnerre, Gertrude Stein's favorite salonnière. Happening at the time to be looking for an intellectual novelty for her Grande Semaine costume fête, she engaged Thomson to produce there his *Capital, Capitals,* an onomatopoetic setting of Gertrude Stein's dialogue among a quartet of Provençal towns. The piece was such a resounding success that Thomson suggested to Miss Stein that they collaborate on an opera. Because it meant wider scope for his prosodic gift, which she believed to be unmatched by that of any other living composer, she accepted and, after hearing his requirement for a serious mythological subject with a tragic ending, suggested as protagonists Saints Ignatius of Loyola and Teresa of Avila.

Loyola was a natural choice. Gertrude Stein had grown up in San Francisco, where there is an impressive church dedicated to him, and had from early youth been familiar with the Ignatian literature. Later she had visited Avila, of all Spanish hill towns the most dramatically placed, built as it is on the flat summit of a mountain that springs abruptly from a treeless plain girded by higher mountains. Only Assisi in all Europe conveys so completely the flavor of its saint. Thomson had never set foot in San Francisco or in Spain, nor was he especially versed in hagiology, but the experience of spending much of his youth as a church organist had placed religious music at the core of his nostalgia, made it part of his melodic self. Any saint would have been congenial subject matter, and Ignatius Loyola and Teresa of Avila were uncommonly dynamic ones, both born leaders and disconcertingly modern in their passion for purposeful activity.

Gertrude Stein set these persons, with thirty others, against a picture of Spain and surrounded them with a sound-pattern of words suggesting the atmosphere of the country. Though she had no "ear" for music as she had an "eye" for painting, she composed poetry in the way a composer works, choosing a theme and developing it, or rather letting it develop itself, through free extension of sound and sense. Creativity, with her, consisted of minimal, though daily, writing, and a vast amount of germinating. It was a matter of simmering in her own juice, so to speak. However engrossed she became in a literary project, the tenor of her existence never varied. Except in time of war, when she was a tireless relief-worker, her days were a round of strolls, drives, calls, visits to exhibitions, and having company. All these pastimes served her literary purposes. The parks of Paris filled

Four Saints in Three Acts with their pigeons; a Left Bank
antiquarian's shop suggested an image in terms of porcelain; the
orchards of Bilignin, her summer retreat in the Rhône Valley,
contributed "pear trees cherry blossoms pink blossoms and late
apples"; the remembered skies of Provence gave their magpies.
Yet the play marks the culmination of the Spanish spirit in
Gertrude Stein's writing. From France she recalled Spain in the
clearer focus a painter achieves by turning from a contemplated
scene and looking back. *Four Saints* is dominated by the landscape of Avila as *Tender Buttons* is dominated by that of Granada, and like Avila it abounds in contrasts. Not involved with
making literal sense, it induces a mood. Static in form, it lends
itself to all manner of stage treatment. (Maurice Grosser, who
invented the scenario for it, holds that other interpretations than
his would be equally valid.) Neither saint, nor any of their ap-
prentices, has dimension, yet all have immediacy. They are talk-
ative abstractions rather than characters, but their patter gen-
erates an intellectual excitement as continuous as crisis in
melodrama. In this sense *Four Saints* touches the dynamics of
the Spanish theater, based on sustained verbal excitement rather
than progress of action. Its failure to emulate the brevity of
native Spanish opera could be considered its only shortcoming:
ambiguous art is a potent drug best assimilated in discreet doses.
In handing Thomson the completed libretto, Gertrude Stein expected to have it cut to pattern, but he found the words so
singable that he condensed it little. He even added characters,
though no words. Saint Teresa Number 2, who enables Number 1
to commune with herself, and the explicatory Commère and
Compère of the French reviews were his brain children.

Like many another of Nadia Boulanger's pupils, Thomson
went his independent way after receiving his first impetus from
her. This led to his ultra-dissonant phase, exemplified by his
Sonata da chiesa. With mastery of the use of discord and of the
Dada outlook, his interest in discord and in Dada as esthetics
exhausted itself. He continued to compose with all the syntactical
devices, old and new, and he did not abandon the whimsey
methods of Dada; but he employed them all for direct com-

Quincy Alfred Thomson—May Gaines Thomson: wedding photograph, 1883.

Virgil Thomson at ten.

Thomson, 1916: the editor of *Pans. (Photo by Moore, Kansas City)*

Thomson, 1918. *(Photo by White, Kansas City)*

Paris poster, 1921.

The Harvard Glee Club in Milan.

Sanctus for male choir, 1921: composer's manuscript.

Page from *Susie Asado,* 1926: composer's manuscript.

Thomson, 1927. *(Photo by Man Ray, Paris)*

Erik Satie, circa 1921: drawing by Pablo Picasso. (*Ex Paul Rosenberg collection*)

Thomson composing, 1930: water color by Maurice Grosser.

GertrudeStein, 1934. (*Photo by Carl Van Vechten*)

Alice B. Toklas, 1934. (*Photo by Carl Van Vechten*)

Mary Butts, circa 1926: drawing
by Jean Cocteau.

Thomson, 1929: water color by
Christian Bérard.

Page from *La Valse grégorienne*, 1927: composer's manuscript.

Cover design by Picasso for Thomson's *La Valse grégorienne*, published with *L'Usage de la parole*, Paris, 1940.

Gertrude Stein on the terrace at Bilignin, 1934. *(Photo by George Platt Lynes)*

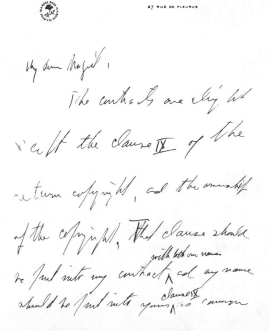

Gertrude Stein's stationery.

Florine Stettheimer, circa 1925.

Forty-fourth Street Theater, New
York, February 20, 1934. (*Photo
by Carl Van Vechten*)

Four Saints in Three Acts, Act I, opening curtain, original production. *(Photo by White, New York)*

Four Saints in Three Acts, Act I, angels and chorus. *(Photo by White, New York)*

Four Saints in Three Acts, Act II, the heavenly mansions. *(Photo by White, New York)*

Four Saints in Three Acts, Act III, Saints' procession. *(Photo by White, New York)*

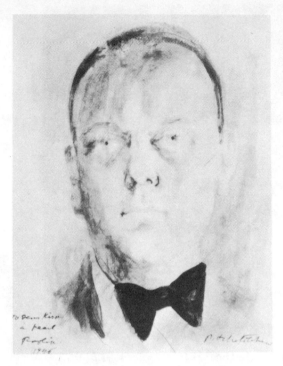

Thomson, 1935: ink-and-wash drawing by Pavel Tchelitchew.

Robert Flaherty filming *Louisiana Story. (Robert Flaherty Foundation)*

Thomson receiving the Legion of Honor to music by the band of the First Moroccan Regiment, Nice, 1947. *(Photo by Paul-Louis, Nice)*

Thomson, 1948. *(Photo by John Long, New York)*

Thomson rehearsing the Pittsburgh Symphony Orchestra, 1956. *(Photo by Benjamin Spiegel)*

munication, thereby unmasking himself as a neo-romantic and helping to found the movement so named. It was this new use of his tools that sparked his friendship with Christian Bérard, begetter of neo-romanticism, and with the composer Henri Sauguet, Bérard's frequent theatrical collaborator. Personal feeling colors the songs he wrote on poems by Gertrude Stein, Georges Hugnet, Max Jacob, and the naïvely Parnassian Duchess of Rohan while the libretto of *Four Saints in Three Acts* was brewing. In the setting he worked out for it, expression has primacy. His Americanism, too, asserted itself, with the special eloquence that nostalgia summons from the exile. For the libretto's devout episodes his music has the grave beauty of Anglican chant, but the brass choir of American revivalist meetings and echoes of the harmonium of rural American chapels pervade his instrumentation. Where there are secular implications, the parlor piece, the Stephen Foster ballads, and the dance tunes of nineteenth-century America are evoked. Gertrude Stein's esoteric fantasy emerged from Thomson's hands clad in homespun. Yet his setting is anything but monotonously local. It has Spanish overtones, madrigalian echoes of Elizabethan England, and a Satiean humor resulting from the deliberate discrepancy between text and score.

To most composers the lack of sense-meaning in Gertrude Stein's words would have posed a problem. Thomson gave them their natural speech inflection with the same meticulousness he would have applied if their meaning had been accessible, at the same time taking pains to make clear the emotional intention of his music. The inverted shock produced by this anti-modern treatment of an ultra-modern libretto precipitated a reaction against the turgidity of much American music of the time. If for no other reason than its tonic influence, *Four Saints* has a title to immortality. But it is more than a refreshing mélange of the homespun and the abstract; it touches within its compass a grandeur known only to conventional opera, based on winged arias, pliant recitative, oratorio-like choruses, and lilting ballet music. And its parody of stereotyped features of these elements brought to the lyric stage a new brand of wit, demure, yet devastating. Many were to challenge Thomson's choice of material. His treatment of it was to be admired by all.

Before beginning work on *Four Saints,* Thomson had moved from the rue de Berne to the Left Bank. Lodgings in that quarter of Paris during the twenties were all but impossible to find, but Gertrude Stein learned that one might become available and advised that he investigate. He took it on first sight on a long-term arrangement with the privilege of subletting. It is located on the Quai Voltaire, a short street that runs between the Pont Royal and the Pont des Saints Pères and where every house has literary or artistic associations. Voltaire occupied number 27 during his last visit to Paris. Number 11 was one of Ingres's residences. The young Delacroix had his studio at number 13. Wagner completed his *Meistersinger* libretto at number 19. Number 25 served Musset for *pied-à-terre,* and number 29 was the setting of Countess Marie d'Agoult's début as salonnière. Thomson's domicile in this genius-haunted neighborhood was the converted attic of number 17, where he lived on a variety of levels. The actual habitation was Directoire. One climbed flight after flight of wide stairs and at the end found a modern elegance. There was no concession to the "picturesque," no attempt at "atmosphere," only the simplicity that bespeaks a feeling for the quality of things, an imagination that does not override a sense of fitness. Two of its high walls were bare except for a wide expanse of window through which the Louvre and the Sacré Coeur could be glimpsed. On another hung a portrait now regarded as one of Christian Bérard's best. On the others, for the studio was octagonal, appeared still-lifes by Maurice Grosser, drawings by Kristians Tonny, and a polychrome wood bas-relief by Hans Arp exuberantly bearing out his dictum that "sculpture need mean nothing other than itself." These decorations were mostly gifts of the artists. The furniture, except for a piano, was the landlord's and consisted of Louis-Philippe pieces.

The concierge of number 17 was skilled in cookery, and out of respect for Thomson's admiration for the art prepared his meals with a motherly moderation of fees. She was also challenged by his shipshape arrangement of his belongings to sweep and dust with a very un-Left Bank thoroughness. The rent was not low, even by present standards, but it was reduced by being shared from time to time with Maurice Grosser, who, having no fixed abode in Paris, could always avail himself of a cot on the balcony. Grosser's lively mind made him a congenial housemate. The turpentine fumes he brought with him were an added pleasure, evoking the resinous odor of sister Ruby's china-painting in the Thomsons' Kansas City home. But the arrangement had its lumps, for Grosser, like most painters, felt little need of order. Still today, wherever he is, he manages to create a turmoil in his surroundings. The co-tenancy was to father these comments on the profession in Thomson's *The State of Music:* "Disorder is of the essence in a painter's life. . . . Their houses are as messy as their palettes. They view life as a multiplicity of visible objects, all completely different. A dirty towel in the middle of the floor, wine spots on the piano keys, a hairbrush on the butter plate are for them just so many light-reflecting surfaces. Their function is to look at life, not to re-arrange it."

When Thomson first settled on the Quai Voltaire in November, 1927, he was happily alone with the libretto of *Four Saints,* overjoyed to be living for the first time in his life in a flat of his own, and quite without economic worries; for he had acquired a patroness, Mrs. Chester Whitin Lasell, a San Franciscan long resident in Massachusetts. (Gertrude Stein later persuaded a friend from Chicago, Emily Crane Chadbourne, to contribute also to his living expenses while he worked on his opera.) During his tenure of the organ post at the Whitinsville Congregational Church, Mrs. Lasell had been in the background of friendships formed with her daughter Hildegarde and with her nephew Philip Lasell. Philip had re-entered Thomson's life by migrating to Paris. Hildegarde had remained in it by corresponding with him. Married to J. Sibley Watson, editor of *The Dial,* and a musician herself, she was genuinely sympathetic to Thomson's association with advanced literature and music. In the spring of 1927 she had written him that her mother planned to summer in France. He had met Mrs. Lasell at Cherbourg, having been invited to motor with her to Paris via the cathedral towns. A head cold had necessitated her breaking journey at Rouen, where a local physician found symptoms of mastoiditis. Thomson had motored to Paris and returned to Rouen with a French ear specialist under whose care Mrs. Lasell recovered without having to undergo operation. As soon as she could be moved, Thomson had taken her to Paris and settled her in suitable quarters. She had expressed her accumulated gratitude by offering to help him with funds and by putting her daughter's New York house at his disposition during a "repatriation visit" planned for 1928, when a concert series organized by Aaron Copland and Roger Sessions was to introduce his music to New York.

Ironically, the benefits of this temporary security were offset by a problem of more baffling nature: at this point Thomson fell in love. Through Philip Lasell he had met a woman of Circean attractiveness, the British author Mary Butts. She was seven years his senior and had weathered assorted vicissitudes: a ruptured marriage, a disappointing liaison, an addiction to drugs, a cold shoulder from the Bloomsbury set. As the London critics had found high distinction in her work, this powerful set may be assumed to have ignored her for reasons of incompatibility. The fact that the Dorsetshire gentry of which she came was a singularly difficult breed, to judge by the portrait of it in her story of her youth, *The Crystal Cabinet* (Methuen, 1933), supports the supposition. It is described, in turn, as "brimming with zest for living" yet "hostile when confronted with life"; "too individual for convention" yet "not brazen enough to break convention with impunity"; "without snobbery or other ordinary pretensions and defenses" yet "breathing a different air." Arisen in King John's time, it had cut quite a swath in Tudor days, but only seldom emerged thereafter. A great-grandfather of Mary Butts was an intimate of William Blake and had acquired half of his finest graphic works. Mary's mother, the flighty widow of a Victorian Butts, had sold the collection for a fraction of its future value. One of Mary's great-granduncles had been Bishop of Ely. Rider Haggard was a distant cousin.

After a childhood lived in a corner of Dorset that is virtually Edgar Allan Poe country, Mary Butts had entered Saint Andew's

in Fifeshire, the first of the public schools patterned after the
boys' schools to knock the Dickensian sentimentality out of
British girls. Still in its experimental stage, it had subjected her to
exaggerated rigors that only served to intensify what was over-
self-reliant and erratic in her nature. The University of London,
where her education was continued, would in normal times have
provided a perfect transition out of this Spartan adolescence.
A product of the old school of Evangelical Christianity, it brought
her in friendly contact with life in various aspects, spiritual,
intellectual, and social. She left the University all of a piece,
steadied for a life of her own. But in the disillusioned tumult of
postwar England, a disillusionment not unlike that which had
given birth to Dada on the Continent, she split into several
pieces none of which fitted the others. Yet rather than suffering
from the wear of experience, her beauty, with its classic features
and Titian tone, seemed the brighter for it. Nor had her intellect
lost edge. There were few fields in which she could not discourse
with brilliance and erudition. Though without musical training, she was supersensitive to verbal sounds and aware as a poet
of the significance of words. Her manner of living had grown
haphazard, but her personal world retained its early grace. Her
flat near the Eiffel Tower was a chaotic place, but there was
much charm in the disorder. However littered with books, papers,
bibelots, and scattered pieces of a tea service or a dressing set, it
reflected a tradition of "gentle things." Had a similar disarray in
dress existed, it might have seemed as fitting in Mary Butts as
lax syntax in a peer of the realm. Even in her simple clothes
and perfect grooming she brought to mind Bacon's observation
that true beauty is not without "some strangeness in the proportion."

Her friendship was a voyage of discovery to Thomson. She
penetrated the Chinese Wall of his creative ego, took him out
of himself, opened his eyes to new values, gave him fresh perspec-
tives. She even dispelled his inveterate skepticism about romantic
attachment. Until then, a woman's attraction had lain for him
in her cerebral sparring powers. It assumed new dimensions with
his discovery of the siren that thrives in some specimens of the

sex. But after embarking upon this intellectualized love affair, he came to perceive that Mary Butts had a feminine weakness for marriage. The fact that despite an adequate income she was always short of funds pointed to reasons not wholly impractical, to which he reacted with mixed feelings. It was flattering to have his future regarded as a source of security, but it was harrowing to be confronted with the possibility that her affection was not disinterested. Even if it was, the thought of their relationship turning into a daily routine appalled him. They shared many tastes, but their views of life were antithetical. This contrast had given edge to their companionship, kept it from going stale. It was conceivable to Thomson that it might well reduce marriage to a cat-and-dog existence. She was as fatalistic as an Oriental; he believed in free will. She tended to drift; he had chosen a goal and dedicated himself to its attainment. She was quixotic; he exemplified common sense. She teetered on the brink of bankruptcy; he was a model of thrift and anything but nonchalant about his obligations. She had no sense of order; he was an old maid for neatness. She was unmusical; music was his reason for being. To have attempted to lead life in conformity with each other's psychological pattern could have driven them out of their minds.

Thomson sought out Mary Butts less often; but no matter how intently he worked on his opera, she pervaded his thoughts. He would have welcomed a trip somewhere, for he knew that memories are most successfully edged aside by fresh impressions. Providentially, at this point a throat infection, induced by an unusually clammy winter and the French theory that fifty degrees fahrenheit is an ideal indoor temperature, became so acute that his doctor ordered him south. He took his sketches and writing materials to Ascain, a village in the Basses-Pyrénées reputed to be dry, warm, and cheap. The mild yet bracing air so soon restored him that within a month he had completed the piano-vocal score of *Four Saints*. Ascain's claim to renown is the pungent Basque flavor that impelled Pierre Loti to set there his *Ramuntcho*, a novel about Basque ways. To Thomson the stronger attraction lay in its nearness to the Peninsula. He was seized with an urge to see Spain that it would hardly have been wise to gratify with his opera unfinished; further, the expense of such a journey would have exceeded the income at his disposal. But Spain was in his cards, as were innumerable pleasure trips—to Europe, Mexico, and South America in the capacity of lecturer, juryman, or conductor; to off-the-map corners of France, Italy, and Austria for "vacations" devoted to composing; to all parts of the United States for music festivals, though the basic reason for his continuous travel is a compulsion to move about, without uprooting, in search of a means of self-renewal. By the time he had finished the piano-vocal score of *Four Saints,* an American army officer and his family who were spending a leave touring the Côte d'Argent put up at Thomson's inn. A hotel friendship sprang up, and Thomson was invited to motor across the border.

It was a brief jaunt, along the coast to Santander and inland to Valladolid, Burgos, and Pamplona, but Thomson's hosts were the type of travelers who believe in poking into odd corners where the heart of a country is best discerned. Reading had prepared him for the contradictions that are Spain: the xenophobia expressed in sedulous courtesy to foreigners, the preservation of individuality through the rejection of most of Western progress; the tenuous balance of the Spanish psyche between harsh irony and tender mysticism. What surprised him was the vital role of the onlooker in Spanish collaborative activity: the discovery that the *olés* of the audience are an integral part of flamenco singing; that bullfights are kept going by the public's cheers or cut short by their roars of abuse; that Spanish children playing bullfight require a minimum of three players—two to mime the action, one to comment from the sidelines. He left Spain with a new respect for the function of the "participant observer," a phrase later to serve as his definition of a critic. And the polychrome wood carvings of Biblical scenes in the museum of Valladolid were to become as indelible a memory as the mosaics in Ravenna's basilicas and the spectacle of High Mass in Strasbourg Cathedral.

On returning to Paris, he tried out his opera on his friends. Cocteau, Bérard, Hugnet, Sauguet, and others of what was then

the vanguard heard him go through it with the multi-ventrilo-
quism by means of which he managed to project all the vocal
ranges. They were charmed by its songfulness and wily simplicity,
but they found the text too original for its own good or that of
the score. Gertrude Stein herself was skeptical about a production. However, Thomson, once again in fine fettle, was convinced that *Four Saints* would see the light. Not even the re-
appearance of Mary Butts in his life could draw his thoughts
from the neo-baroque décors he envisaged. She had written to
suggest a fresh start:

> Wouldn't it be possible to make things right again between us, to
> give the affection you had for me a chance to grow again? It brought
> me back to life. Try to think how it must feel to die again. . . . I
> came upon what Amenophis IV wrote, the beautiful Pharaoh king,
> you know: "I dig the living god out of the dead sands, the dead
> hearts. People, have mercy upon one another and you shall not see
> death." It was with some such idea that I thought of our coming to-
> gether again.

His affection for her was unchanged and unchangeable. She
was the one emotional involvement of his life that was focal
rather than peripheral, the one woman who almost succeeded in
holding the entire man. Still, he knew that the first magic of
their attachment could not be recaptured. He found an American market for her writing and helped her in other practical
ways, but saw little of her. In 1937, living in England again, she
fell ill during a stay in Dorset. A local physician mistook her
symptoms for indigestion and let her die of a ruptured appendix.
A group of her friends asked Thomson to write his reminiscences
of her for a volume of her letters. Before he could begin the
poignant task, her family, from whom she had long been es-
tranged, opposed the volume's publication. Soon afterward her
published works mysteriously went out of print. Her life had
been a series of real short stories of the kind she wrote with a
sensitivity all her own—delicately etched vignettes, rich in in-
sights, of the irony of human experience. The contrived lapse into
oblivion of her literary output was an episode made for her

pen. Thomson's persisting regret for her, despite his confirmed misogamy, would have been equally grateful subject matter.

Through Nadia Boulanger's intervention, Thomson and a few other young American composers had been given joint hearing, in 1922 and 1926, in two concerts sponsored by the Société Musicale Indépendante at the Salle Gaveau. He now felt prepared for a one-man show. Mrs. Chadbourne's subsidy had ended with the completion of *Four Saints;* but Mrs. Lasell's, which continued for several more years, enabled him to present in the spring of 1928 a program of his own works at the Old Conservatoire's Salle d'Orgue. To celebrate the restoration of the hall's eighteenth-century organ, he opened with his *Fugue and Variations* for organ on American Sunday School tunes. His *Five Phrases from the Song of Solomon,* his *Sonata da chiesa,* his *Capital, Capitals,* and songs on texts by Hugnet, Gertrude Stein, and the Duchess of Rohan made up the rest. Soon afterward he figured with Hugnet and Henri Cliquet-Pleyel, a follower and former pupil of Satie, in a *"Concert d'oeuvres musicales et poétiques"* staged in the ballroom of the Majestic Hotel. His participation included some of his early essays in musical portraiture, for which the subjects had sat for him as they would for a painter while he tone-sketched their mental or physical characteristics. Though description of character through music is an ancient preoccupation of composers, the psychological penetration Thomson brings to it has made him its outstanding exponent. These particular portraits were written for violin alone, and the imaginative handling of their monolinear structure was was not lost on the audience. Both concerts attracted an encouragingly controversial public, for if applause of a new work at a Paris concert is meaningless, a mixed reception is reassuring. It proves that the music is alive, different, provocative. The style with which Thomson fused tradition and novelty pleased. His deceptive simplicity baffled. He scored both a *succès d'estime* and a *succès de scandale,* and the latter is a first step toward fame in France. When he left for New York in December, 1928, artistic Paris was buzzing with speculation about the future of the Stein-Thomson opera.

The critics' enthusiasm for *Five Phrases from the Song of Solomon,* which with works by Walter Piston, Theodore Chanler, and Carlos Chávez opened the 1928 Copland-Sessions series, had encouraged Aaron Copland to ask for *Capital, Capitals* for the 1929 series. Before its performance in February, which Thomson prepared and accompanied, he conducted his *Sonata da chiesa* in Boston at a concert of the Flute Players' Club and lectured on contemporary music at the Harvard Musical Club. After the New York première of *Capital, Capitals,* he was hailed as the bearer of a typically French contribution to American music. The rest of the composers presented by Copland and Sessions tended to an abstruseness that the critics had diagnosed as "nostalgia for Schoenberg" or "Gershwinization of Prokofiev." Thomson's music was no less modernistic than theirs, but it was simple, tuneful, and slyly humorous. In his role of transatlantic liaison officer he was interviewed, caricatured, and fêted. A vogue for presenting all-Thomson programs at private parties set in. At one, given by Carl Van Vechten, he sang the whole of *Four Saints.* The guests included Ettie Stettheimer, youngest of the trio of sisters whose salon did much toward shaping the intellectual and artistic efforts of the twenties. Celebrated writers, musicians, and artists were drawn to it because the arts where to the Stettheimers a vital issue, practiced and patronized by them with equal distinction. Ettie wrote novels under the pseudonym Henrie Waste. Florine was one of the few individual women painters America has produced. Carrie constructed a doll house filled with miniature replicas of noted works of art made for her by the artists themselves (now housed at the Museum of the City of New York). Each achieved self-expression with her own brand of brilliance. Their salon was their common accomplishment, reflecting their fundamental agreement on the nature and purpose of art in their time.

When Thomson repeated his performance of *Four Saints* for the Stettheimers, he noticed on their drawing room walls canvases that spoke to him in an unfamiliar painting language. Their colors evoked Matisse. Their themes ranged from flowers of a Redonesque unearthliness to whimsical social satires. Their brushstroke was that of a trained draftsman, yet it took all the liberty of a primitive. Their special quality was a decorative sense of the utmost refinement coupled with a flair for the humor inherent in the merely decorative. From living in close communion with the artists of Paris, Thomson had learned to know pretty well at a glance real talent from the spurious. His admiration for these specimens of Florine Stettheimer's work was instantaneous. "Why haven't I heard about them? Why hasn't Paris seen them?" he exclaimed, unaware that she lived as withdrawn from the world as Emily Dickinson, though not for similar reasons. She circulated little because she enjoyed painting more than all else. She exhibited seldom because she held that imaginative works of art need bright white backgrounds rather than the neutral-toned walls of commercial galleries. She was even opposed to selling, on the ground that her work formed a unit, as does a poet's in a volume, and should be kept together as such. Thomson's peak-in-Darien reaction to her paintings was re-experienced when he visited her studio in the Beaux Arts Building on Bryant Square. The rooms might have sprung up at the wave of a conjuror's wand. The white walls glowed with brightly colored canvases. White cellophane with gold fringe curtained the windows, and the divans were upholstered in white linen. The chairs were white and gold, the tables glass and gold. Blanc de Chine vases held gleaming crystal flowers. Yet everything about this baroque fantasy bespoke artistic integrity. There was no pose, no preciosity, no conscious exploitation of feminine charm, but only truthfulness to a highly feminine esthetic sense. Florine Stettheimer's painted visions needed such a liaison with the actual world. Thomson, knowing that she was the inevitable stage designer for *Four Saints,* begged her to decorate the opera when and if it should be produced.

He returned to France in March, 1929, in an ultra-rosy mood. A reunion with his parents had been heart-warming. He had made new friendships. His music and his lecture-recitals had been received with interest. There was talk of producing his opera. Ideas for new compositions were stirring in his mind, and it would be spring in Paris when he set to work on them. His piano sonatas Numbers I and II were the first to take shape. As he was beginning his *Five Portraits* for a quartet of clarinets, word came to him from the Hessisches Landestheater in Darmstadt, a company of rank in Europe. The manager had heard about *Four Saints,* and growing interest in Germany in novel forms of opera had prompted him to ask to see the score. Thomson dispatched the piano-vocal score, and the manager responded by suggesting a meeting to discuss the première. Negotiations never went beyond this, however, for shortly thereafter the Hessisches Landestheater broke up. Modern works had entailed such heavy losses that the conservative wing of the house refused to consider any others. In protest, the modern wing resigned and moved on to Berlin, where they found at the Städtische Oper in Charlottenburg a public receptive to their ideas. When Hitler came to power, the individual members migrated to England, joined forces at Glyndebourne, and made operatic history. One of them, Rudolf Bing, went on from there to Edinburgh and came eventually to head the Metropolitan Opera.

After the Darmstadt episode, further interruption to the progress of the clarinet *Portraits* occurred: Gertrude Stein wrote urging a visit to Bilignin. "With nothing to do but scenery and me, you can work or rest as you choose," her breezy scrawl promised. But it was impossible to do either there. The place is insidiously distracting. Skirting the old frontier town of Belley, where the Jura Mountains penetrate the Rhône Valley, the hamlet of Bilignin views, across a valley, a hilly rural France. This view has neither the storybook loveliness of the château country nor the postcard brilliance of the Côte d'Azur. It is gentle, silvery, Corotesque. Lamartine tells in his memoirs that he developed his passion for contemplating nature while a student at the local college. Beyond the valley, checkered with planted fields, lie mountains of Alpine beauty without the overpowering grandeur of the Alps. Foothills serve as perches for white stone manor houses shadowed by poplars. Covering it all is a sky seductively constant with its cottony clouds on a Tiepolo blue.

The manor house leased by Gertrude Stein had added distractions. The proprietor was a descendant of Brillat-Savarin, inventor of modern gastronomy and Belley's native son, and had installed his ancestor's furniture on the premises. The fact that an adjacent manor house had been the scene of a murder celebrated by Balzac, who had known the key figure in the triangle, relieved the tranquillity of the neighborhood with a touch of excitement. Besides, visiting Gertrude Stein was in itself a perpetual excitement. She was never more her exhilarating self than when she was supposed to be resting. Her idea of summer hospitality was to speed her guests by Ford, which she drove with reckless ease, to the manor houses of French acquaintances, to peasant festivities of the village, to restaurants renowned for regional specialties, and to sites of natural splendor or historic significance. Of these, her favorites were the villa at Les Charmettes once inhabited by Rousseau, the pavilion at Uzès where Racine did some writing, and the Abbey of Hautecombe on the Lake of Bourget—Lamartine's lake—with the granary that Paul Claudel held to be "the loveliest building in all the world." Talk that was no anticlimax to the riches of the Rhône Valley filled the intervals between the jaunts.

But in any circumstances Gertrude Stein kindled inventiveness. Thomson took back to Paris musical ideas that were to jell as his Violin Sonata Number I, his string quartets Numbers I and II, his *Stabat Mater* on Max Jacob's miniature drama, his settings of the tirade from *Phèdre* and Bossuet's Funeral Oration for Queen Henrietta Maria, and his Symphony Number II, conceived first as a piano sonata and later translated into orchestral terms. The war bonus distributed in 1930 enabled him to present another one-man show, this time at the Salle Chopin in the brand-new Maison Pleyel. His artists were a top French string team (the Quatuor Krettly), an American pianist, a French violinist, and a soprano and tenor from the Opéra, whom he accompanied. The program introduced his Violin Sonata, *Air de Phèdre,* Funeral Oration, *Stabat Mater,* and First String Quartet. Parisians recognized a virtuoso prosodist in the settings of two supreme examples of their classic literature, but found a point of controversy in the Violin Sonata and the String Quartet, which some considered to be experimental in a dry way. Being by training a keyboard musician, Thomson had decided to amplify his musical mastery by exploring the strings. The result was a musical style derived from technical devices peculiar to strings, in no way reminiscent of his usual method of composing by placing Satie-like allusions to heterogeneous styles into his own disciplined framework.

His Second Symphony revives the system of multiple allusion with a new mastery. It is no less evocative of the American vernacular than the First, but a more fluid unfolding replaces the early squareness, the sacrifice in humor paying off in increased expressivity. After being given a few piano performances, the piece led to an incident that clearly illustrates Thomson's awareness of his growth in professional stature. The Society for the Publication of American Music, headed by John Alden Carpenter and other outstanding composers, notified him that his Second Symphony had been so warmly recommended that they wished to see the orchestral score. At no small expense he had a copy made and shipped it. Six months later it was returned by a secretary with only a "Thank you for giving our judges an opportunity to see your manuscript." Few nuggets can be mined out of Thomson's correspondence that set in with his association with Gertrude Stein, for under her influence he adopted a style of telegraphic brevity. The Society for the Publication of American Music was honored with his most expansive letter of these years:

I take it that "Thank you for giving our judges an opportunity to see your manuscript" is a phrase of general utility you consider equally applicable to solicited and unsolicited manuscripts. You use the word "judge" to designate those who decide your editorial policy, but you carry on your business through a secretary. Your decisions are secret, your gestures discourteous, your airs and pretensions such as one is used to from the committees of foundations that annually award high academic honors and large cash prizes.

I respectfully call your attention to the fact that you are an amateur and private publishing society like any other, of which there are many; that in correspondence with composers you have the prestige and the obligations of the composers whose names are printed on your letter paper; that a discourtesy from you, however banal, is a discourtesy from one musician to another, from an American citizen to his equal. My protest is that after sacrificing the use of my score for six months, not to mention copyist's fees and several dollars' worth of postage, I received a terse thank you and a vague assurance that somebody had seen the piece, though the secretary did not even know the title.

Not for nothing had he mastered at a tender age the technique of operating on a first-class professional standard. He treated colleagues of all ranks with fairness and courtesy and expected the same of them. The Society for the Publication of American Music apologized.

A brighter communication came in the fall of 1931 from Hartford, Connecticut. The late A. Everett Austin, Jr., an associate of Thomson's at Harvard, and then director of Hartford's Wadsworth Museum, reported that a new wing, representing the most advanced example of museum architecture in the world, was under construction to house the Samuel Avery Art Collection. Its projected auditorium had been designed to serve as a theater as well as a lecture hall. He would like to open it with an operatic première involving novel and distinguished décors. *Four Saints* had been recommended for the purpose by Henry-Russell Hitchcock, who had heard Thomson sing and play it in Paris. But Austin was not only a protagonist of modernity. He was equally a fervent of baroque art and responsible for the brilliant emphasis on it in his museum. Had Thomson set out to pick an ideal theater for the production he envisaged, he could have found many more commodious than that of the Avery Memorial. Nowhere else in world, however, could he have found a more understanding producer than his friend "Chick" Austin or an audience better prepared to accept artistic collaboration on the level of *Four Saints in Three Acts*.

The Mature Years

OPENING THE AVERY MEMORIAL THEATER WITH THE WORLD
première of *Four Saints* required money. Austin raised it by
mobilizing The Friends and Enemies of Modern Music, a New
England non-profit society he had founded. With a faith rarely
felt outside France in the healthy effect of controversy, these en-
lightened amateurs had already presented, with the co-operation
of musicians and artists of quality, programs of Schoenberg,
Stravinsky, Hindemith, Bartók, Satie, and others about whose
work critical opinion was still at odds. Through them and
through the distinction of its museum, Hartford had attained
for the time being something of the artistic prestige held by
Salzburg, Venice, Florence, Bayreuth, and other provincial European cities. *Four Saints* meant an extension of their financial
responsibilities, but it opened such tempting prospects of controversial discussion that despite the Depression they raised the
needed funds. Sixty-four members representing twelve New
England towns and also New York, London, and Kansas City,
contributed twelve thousand dollars, of which the society was
to recoup nearly three-quarters at the box office.

On returning to New York in the fall of 1932, Thomson re-
newed his urgent invitation to Florine Stettheimer that she
design the sets and costumes. She had obviously imagined a plan
for the first act, for her portrait of him, painted from memory in
1930 after seeing him only twice, includes a lion from Avila Cathedral and a tufted blue sky. Her next step was to construct for
herself a scale model of the Avery Memorial stage and small pup-
pets of the Stein characters. Then for weeks she combed the shops
until she found the exact colors and stuffs she wanted. Here was
the first instance in America in which a painter of rank had been
called upon to serve the stage, though this had been a growing
practice in Europe ever since Diaghilev's Ballets Russes had

begun to use the most advanced artists of Russia and Western Europe.

Among Thomson's hosts during this visit was the art dealer R. Kirk Askew, Jr. A frequent guest at Askew's house was the literary critic Lewis Galantière, then trying his hand at writing plays. Collaborating with him was a young Franco-Briton of future M-G-M celebrity, John Houseman, whose intelligent interest in *Four Saints* convinced Thomson that he was the stage director for it. After reading the scenario and hearing the score, Houseman accepted Thomson's ideas of ballet-opera treatment and of co-operative staging with a still younger Briton, Frederick Ashton, to whose subsequent choreographies the Royal Ballet (*né* Sadlers Wells) owes so much of its prestige. For lighting they engaged Feder, a Carnegie Tech-trained Midwesterner who was just beginning the reform of theatrical illumination that has since been carried out by his pupil Jean Rosenthal. To execute Florine Stettheimer's sets and costumes Kate Drain Lawson, then a member of the Theater Guild staff, was induced to act as technical expert. Thomson also invited Alexander Smallens to conduct. Meanwhile, during a visit to a Negro night club, he had hit upon the. idea of having an all-Negro cast. He was attracted primarily by the fine verbal projection of Negro singers. Their lack of intellectual resistance to a hermetic text and their noble dignity in acting out a religious theme came as later surprises, pure dividends. Austin, Houseman, Florine Stettheimer, and Ashton approved, but Gertrude Stein, back in Paris, was skeptical. "Your Negroes may sing and enunciate ever so much better than white artists, but I still do not like the idea of showing the Negro bodies," she wrote, envisaging no doubt the women as sketchily garbed and the men in loincloths. "It is too much what modernistic writers refer to as 'futuristic.' I cannot see its relevance to my treatment of my theme"—as if relevance were of the essence in her treatment of any theme. "However, it is for you to make a success of the production." So Thomson chose and cast skilled Negro singers and then coached them in their parts. Under his direction they rehearsed with a thoroughness that had no precedent on the American lyric stage.

There was a host of reasons for the historic success of the Hartford première of *Four Saints in Three Acts* on February 8, 1934. It had influential sponsors. It was part of a program inaugurating what was then the most modern of America's museum buildings. It was one of two notable features serving to emphasize the museum's baroque and modernistic orientations, the other being the first American retrospective exhibition of Picasso's painting, for which art connoisseurs from all parts of the country journeyed to Hartford. It was briefly preceded by the Literary Guild's selection of Gertrude Stein's *Autobiography of Alice B. Toklas,* in which she had Boswellized herself and, in the process, rediscovered normal syntax and word order. It coincided with Harcourt, Brace's publication of an abridged edition of her *The Making of Americans,* an early novel about her relatives, disguised as a history of mankind. Florine Stettheimer, too, had a following, and such a recherché combination of talent attracted cognoscenti and novelty-seekers alike. The audience, of a Parisian choiceness, was composed of distinguished names in the fields of music, art, and literature, and their fashionable devotees; it included also many persons eminent in other professions. Still, the basic reason for the success of the Hartford première was the fact that the production was that delectable rarity, a perfect musico-theatrical creation, forged at the white heat of total artistic co-operation. By the consistency, high quality, and painstaking preparation of all the contributing elements it showed, as only the ballets of Diaghilev had shown, that the Wagnerian ideal, divested of its Victorian erotico-philosophic paraphernalia, could still be realized. (*Four Saints* has been called a "Negro *Parsifal.*") And this close union of the arts was achieved by the most difficult means: everything in it was of contemporary design. No shade of the easy-ways-out known in lyric theater jargon as "tradition" dimmed its bright workmanship. The décor was modern art at its most imaginative. Cellophane, crystal, feathers, seashells, lace, and brilliant colors such as the American stage had never seen before—nor has seen since—went into this confection of a visionary Spain. The illumination brought to the scene, in turn, dawn, noontide, dusk, and the

white light of Heaven itself. The singers, holding their tutored
poses with an exaltation all their own, might have served as
models for El Greco or Zurbarán. The dancers blended their
native abandon with attitudes from the classic ballet. And the
score achieved the ever-astonishing feat of transcending the limi-
tations of the libretto: its tunefulness and bounce dispelled per-
plexity over the cryptic text; its gravity, glinting with blithe
overtones, evoked both the mystical strength and the naïve gaiety
of lives devoted in common to unworldly ends. The production
even created that sustained illusion of reality that is the test of
good theater.

The producer Harry Moses had been taken to a working rehearsal of *Four Saints* in the basement of Saint Philip's Episcopal
Church in Harlem. Before it was over, he had engaged to bring
the opera to Broadway. The rest is operatic history. A New York
première acclaimed by the critics and by the elect of the arts,
sixty performances in one year in New York and Chicago, a national press, the David Bispham medal to the composer "for
distinguished contribution to native American opera," two national broadcasts, an RCA recording, a New York stage revival
sponsored by the American National Theater and Academy, a
week's run in Paris as part of the Festival of Twentieth-Century
Masterpieces sponsored by the Congress for Cultural Freedom,
concert performances in many parts of America and even in such
cities as Yokohama and Cape Town—all this is something of a
record for a contemporary American opera in English, Steinian
English at that. Only its successor, George Gershwin's *Porgy and
Bess,* has received more glory.

Famous overnight, Thomson was faced with the fact that
fame was no solution to his economic problems. His royalties,
though he supplemented them with fees for lectures and magazine articles, were not large enough to live on for long. He
applied for a Guggenheim Fellowship, but the Committee of
Selection concluded from the list of grants already awarded him
that less fortunate applicants had a stronger case. With the
fashion created by *Four Saints* showing no signs of abating—shop
windows were emulating its décors, and one dared not circulate

socially without having seen it or at least brushed up on baroque
—he returned in the spring of 1934 to the simpler living conditions of Paris. A book was in his mind; but before he could put
his hand to writing it, Houseman re-entered his life and shifted
its course. Convinced that in the New York theater a commercial
spirit was defeating adventurous modernism, Houseman had
organized a non-profit-making producing company and arranged
to present at one of the lesser Broadway houses plays of the
vanguard and the older tragedies and comedies from which they
stemmed. The Phoenix Theater, as he named his venture, was
to open that fall with Countee Cullen's adaptation of Euripides's
Medea. If Thomson would provide incidental music and return
for the rehearsals, Houseman offered him travel expense in addition to a fee. Thomson found Cullen's simple prose so much
richer in direct theatrical power than the language in which
he had previously known *Medea* (the verbose pseudo-Swinburne
of Gilbert Murray's translation) that he devoted a good part of
his summer to composing its choruses. When he arrived in New
York in the fall of 1934, the project was well advanced. Austin
had sketched Cretan décors. Martha Graham had planned a pattern of stage movements keyed to their tone. Houseman, on the
theory that Medea, being of Egyptian origin, might well have
been swarthy, had chosen for her role the Negro tragédienne
Rose McClendon. Mulattoes were to play her children. The
rest of the cast would be white. But the tragédienne's sudden
illness deflected Thomson's choruses to the concert repertory.
Instead of *Medea,* Archibald MacLeish's *Panic* launched the
Phoenix on its brief career. Midway in its first season, Houseman
discovered in the Tybalt of Katherine Cornell's *Romeo and
Juliet* an unknown actor of compelling power, Orson Welles.
He took Welles on as co-producer, and both young men were,
in turn, discovered by the organizers of the theater division of the
Works Progress Administration.

  The pair's first production for the government's experiment
in show business was a *Macbeth* laid in Haiti and played by the
Federal Theater's Negro unit. For this Thomson provided a
score of such dramatic pungency that it brought him commissions

for background music from Leslie Howard for *Hamlet;* from Roland Stebbins, producer of an *Antony and Cleopatra* starring Tallulah Bankhead; from the Federal Theater for the Living Newspaper's *Injunction Granted;* from Lincoln Kirstein's Ballet Caravan for a ballet, *Filling Station;* and from Pare Lorentz, just emerged from the shooting of his government-sponsored film about soil erosion, *The Plow That Broke the Plains.* Though Thomson was unfamiliar with the requirements of cinematic drama, his Midwestern childhood had prepared him to frame this one with music. The prairie locale of the picture made the invention of accompaniment for its wheat field and grassland sequences easy for him. For episodes involving people in these surroundings he quoted the settlers' songs on which he had grown up. And the Texas period of his military training had acquainted him with all the horrors of the dust storm. The score he produced was so indigenous, so closely articulated with the narrative, that Lorentz engaged him also for his second documentary, *The River,* which treats of floods as the direct result of mishandling the Mississippi and its tributaries for private gain.

Before beginning work on *The River,* Thomson was consulted about still another documentary, sponsored by a literary group calling themselves Contemporary Historians. The Spanish Civil War had just begun, and the plight of the Spanish peasant offered these liberal-minded intellectuals a fresh outlet for their social sympathies. A motion picture, entitled *The Spanish Earth,* was organized to propagandize and raise funds for the cause. Archibald MacLeish and Lillian Hellman collaborated on a story, Hemingway wrote and spoke the narration, and the Dutch photographer Joris Ivens, just returned from a wartime journey through Republican Spain, provided portrait studies of her peasants in the face of bloodshed and disaster. Money being short for composing and recording, Thomson advised a musical montage, and with Marc Blitzstein, who had also been engaged as consultant, searched New York for Spanish folklore material. Their exploration brought to light Gerald Murphy's collection of authentic discs, which they cut and pieced to fit the picture.

The private production of this documentary excluded it from chain distribution, but it aroused considerable interest when it was shown at independent motion picture theaters in 1937 and 1938. *The Spanish Earth* is still rated highly by film experts.

The River was conceived on a more elaborate scale than *The Plow That Broke the Plains,* for by the time it was shot, Lorentz had obliged the film industry to co-operate about distribution, which they had not done for *The Plow.* The locale was the Mississippi River Valley, which Thomson knew. While studying its folk- and hymn-lore more systematically, he entered into correspondence with the late George Pullen Jackson, specialist in the field and then a faculty member of Vanderbilt University in Nashville, Tennessee. Jackson was overjoyed to help familiarize millions with America's richest vein of folk music, the so-called "white spirituals." Many of these, older than America herself, had been imported by early settlers from the rural districts of the British Isles and had become the basis of Protestant hymns, Negro spirituals, popular ballads—almost everything that America has contributed to music. After months of bathing himself in these ancient melodies, Thomson emerged with a score that sharpened the reality of Lorentz's story; a score, moreover, in every sense his own creation. For the human episodes he drew on folk tunes, but his idiom was modern and individual. For the landscape sequences he invented material that captures the Mississippi's changing moods with electric immediacy. *The River* brought to the American cinematic world conciseness and restraint. After its release, Hollywood itself tended to depend less on instrumental lushness and impressionistic haze, and the term "movie music" began to lose its pejorative meaning.

Meanwhile, Aaron Copland had formed with Thomson, Roger Sessions, Roy Harris, and Walter Piston what can best be described as a composers' commando unit. They had written about one another in magazines, organized concerts of their own works, and made a place for themselves in the programs of contemporary music presented by the Library of Congress and the New School for Social Research. This militancy had brought commissions, including one from the League of Composers for Thomson's *Missa*

Brevis for Women's Voices and Percussion. It had also alerted publishers to the raiders' marketability. William Morrow, W. W. Norton, and several others had invited Thomson to write a book. In short, he could be said to have arrived. And it was typical of him, as it still is, on achieving a rounded professional success, to leave the scene of the achievement. His reason for resettling in Paris in the spring of 1938 was that success provided freedom to do what to him is most satisfying and worthwhile: to devote himself to composing in the esthetic climate in which he feels most at home. France was still such a climate for him. Though music there is neither the universal talent nor the national pastime it is in some other countries, the Frenchman's clear understanding of the fact that all the faculties are involved in the creative process provides an atmosphere in which creative talent of any kind may find fulfillment. Added impetus to this second hegira was disillusionment with Houseman and Welles. The censor's withdrawal of the most challenging of their productions for the Federal Theater, Marc Blitzstein's left-wing *The Cradle Will Rock,* had emboldened them to found their own producing company, named the Mercury after Ashley Duke's smart London playhouse. In their efforts to live up to what they believed was expected of the Mercury, they had become instruments of their own aggrandizement. The fiasco of a particularly ambitious production, *Five Kings,* for which Shakespeare's two *King Richards* and three *King Henrys* were telescoped, led to a fling in radio. This last was climaxed by their now famous *The War of the Worlds,* a broadcast that created a civil emergency in New York, when many listeners really believed we were being invaded by Martians. Then the pair went to Hollywood, where they produced the historic *Citizen Kane.* Meanwhile tensions engendered by their vicissitudes had begun to snap.

Writing Thomson from Hollywood, where he remained after the rupture of the partnership, Houseman poured out ruminations rich in hindsight's wisdom. He held that Thomson's integrity, sound judgment, and deflating wit had been the soil in which his—Houseman's—directorial talent had been able to grow; that producing *Four Saints* had given him his first taste of work-

ing in the theater for no reason but faith in it and love for it,
had taught him that neither creative work nor values of any kind
can bear up under the compulsion of ambition; that the price he
had paid for ignoring the lesson was beyond reckoning. All of
which was a preamble to the plea that Thomson return to New
York and resume his role as a dispenser of esthetic catharsis.
But Thomson, who normally extended the helping hand with
abandon, had to restrain the gesture. He was harnessed to a
contract from Morrow, and his Pegasus was running away with
him. "The book races on in its own chaotic fashion no matter
how hard I try to force it into other fashions," he notified Morrow's Thayer Hobson in the fall of 1938. To Hobson, this head-
long course was a promising sign: he was skeptical of things that
"come out like a ribbon and lie flat on the brush." So Thomson
gave rein to his project. In his next report it had become "a
complete account of the present-day musical world. . . . Not an
encyclopedia, of course. Just my opinions about that world. But
I must do lots of explaining to have my opinions make sense.
I've written nearly twenty thousand words, and that is practically
all introduction. I haven't yet touched the meat of the book,
which is my economico-esthetic theory."

Critical opinion held *The State of Music,* as this treatise was
entitled, to be the most informative and least conventional book
about music America had produced. Its reader appeal was as
potent in intellectual as in musical circles. Some reacted to it
with passionate agreement, some with angry dissent, but all
found it full of brio and brilliance. Spearing a host of popular
fallacies, it explored the problems of composing for different
media, defined the composer's status in sociological terms, and
shed light on the economic pressures to which he is subjected.
With sweeping over-simplifications, but a crusading fervor, it
advocated professional solidarity: a united front *vis-à-vis* publishers, producers, and consumers; a complete assumption of authority over the nation's musical standards. The composer *qua*
composer bodied forth from its pages as a highly desirable solid
citizen, no less expert at his craft for being not wholly oblivious
of money and prestige. Thomson himself emerged as that rarity

among those whose natural means of expression is music, a born
writer, and that still more infrequent phenomenon, a musician
with an acute but undoctrinaire sense of the social, political, and
economic aspects of his art.

No sooner had *The State of Music* appeared than a second
book, treating English musical prosody, sketched itself in his
mind. He had lectured widely on the subject and demonstrated
that it is anything but the dry affair it sounds. But Morrow, after
prodding him to pursue the project, suddenly cabled they could
offer no contract. Like all practitioners of their barometric trade,
they had sensed a need of retrenching. Nor was Thomson over-
disposed at this point to chew on another literary cud. With the
Nazi occupation of Austria, a second World War ceased to be
inconceivable. With the Munich crisis, it became clearly inevitable. Until its outbreak he wanted a modicum of freedom with
which to savor Paris life. Originality was still practiced there.
One was not expected to be one of a kind, but oddity still had
to be achieved with style. The thoroughness and breadth of
interest with which Thomson had always thought for himself
shaped him early into a pundit on any theme about which he
elected to discourse. This authority and precision in his opinions,
supplemented with wit, fluent French, and a gift for knowing
eminent talented people, gave him an important place in the
intellectual life of Paris. He circulated among the musical, literary, and artistic great, and he received them in his studio on the
Quai Voltaire. His Friday evenings were, in fact, among the most
recherché on the Left Bank. Scores were tried out, poems read,
theories debated. And the food was good. The wine cup and
pâté were formulas of Alice B. Toklas, a culinary expert. In
winter the specialty was fruit cake made in Kansas City by
Thomson's mother from an old Scotch recipe. Hugnet, in a mem-
oir written for the *Figaro littéraire* (May, 1954), describes a typical evening. Among the guests were Gide, Picasso, Cocteau, Hemingway, Scott Fitzgerald, Sauguet, Bérard, Christian Dior (then
an art dealer), Gertrude Stein, stars of the avant-garde theater,
editors of avant-garde magazines, and that insatiable novelty-
seeker, the Duchess of Clermont-Tonnerre. Cliquet-Pleyel went

through the score of his latest *opéra-bouffe,* soon afterwards heard at the Théâtre de l'Atelier, and Thomson "unveiled" his Portrait of Picasso, entitled *Bugles and Birds.* (Could this have been because it stresses the militant strain in the man and at the same time conveys the heterogeneity of his art by the sound of birds of diverse feather flocking together?) Picasso's satisfaction, which he proclaimed from the Café de Flore, spurred Thomson to compose a whole gallery of likenesses of his Paris friends.

Though some of the guests were mobilized, these evenings continued until the Germans were nearly in Paris. Not until Hitler had conquered France did Thomson decide to leave. In the summer of 1940 he shipped his paintings to a friend's château, and with his manuscript scores and his Lanvin suits made his way, after summering in that same château, via Lisbon to New York. He had no more money; staying in France during the first year of the war had used up his reserve. Nor had he plans, for in the nascent turmoil that greeted him in an America moving toward war, no easy means of breadwinning seemed feasible. His royalties from *The State of Music* had dwindled, and he felt no impulse to write another book. Teaching, which then barely kept one at an existence level, he had had his fill of. Commercial film contracts offered composers too little margin for freedom to interest him, and he could not expect more commissions for documentary film music, for he had quarreled with Pare Lorentz in making *The River.* Nor could he, as a composer with clear allegiances to certain styles and schools, consider himself fitted for reviewing music in the daily press. To his friends it seemed that his competence in the practicalities of life had failed him, until on October 11, 1940, they learned from the New York *Herald Tribune* that he had succeeded the late Lawrence Gilman as its music critic. By then, Janet Flanner, the Paris correspondent of *The New Yorker,* had recommended him to the editor of the magazine. The editor's lack of prompt action on her recommendation resulted, in her opinion and before long in his, in "the greatest loss in the non-capture of a born columnist and consummate critic we have ever suffered."

A reading of *The State of Music* had convinced Geoffrey

Parsons, then chief editorial writer of the *Herald Tribune,* that he had found his man. Ogden Reid, the editor, had agreed. Thomson had pointed out that he was untrained in journalistic routines, that his views would offend vested musical interests, that his approach to criticism would sweep the *Herald Tribune* into the tempest of music-as-it-really-is. But his employers were encouraged rather than alarmed by his admonitions. Their principles proved to be, in essence, identical with his: neither to back nor to attack personally the directors of established institutions and commercial associations engaged in concert management; simply to inform the public clearly and fully about the nature of their operation and the products offered. He made his bow in the paper with a review of the concert with which the Philharmonic-Symphony Society opened its ninety-ninth season. Headed "Age Without Honor," the piece ended thus: "The concert . . . was anything but a memorable experience. The music itself was soggy, the playing dull and brutal. . . . As a friend [his guest, Maurice Grosser] remarked who had never been to one of these concerts before, 'I understand now why the Philharmonic is not a part of New York's intellectual life.' " The rocking Thomson gave to complacency in high quarters had beneficent impact. Overblown reputations were deflated, those unfairly grown dim were burnished. The musical scene lost some of its German, Slavic, and Italian patina. Unfamiliar masterworks, both ancient and modern, were increasingly programmed. The radio assumed a few of its cultural obligations. And last, but not least, the Philharmonic regained some of its earlier prestige.

Thomson's blasts also loosed a torrent of reader wrath. Critics of the critic held that his opinions sprang from passing psychological states rather than from a reasoned philosophy of music. They read into them a peculiarly Thomsonian perversity that liked to leave no turn unstoned. As proof of his irresponsibility they pointed to his cat-napping at concerts. And New York soon learned that the habit was not restricted to the concert hall or the opera house; that it is an undisguised defense against boredom. Any form of entertainment has a soporific effect on him when it tends to sag, and he makes small effort to combat the effect, to the exasperation of even his closest friends. But at musical performances he seems to have listened with what psychologists describe as "the third ear." Nothing escaped him, and programs at which he was known to have dozed resulted in some of his most penetrating reviews. Even his praise, which he lavished on events having interest, beauty, or novelty for him, was challenged. Personal friendships, the furtherance of his own career as composer, and similar motivations were ascribed to him.

Taking all expressions of hostility with a laugh, Thomson held to his line, to which his employers at the *Herald Tribune* gave their full support. That line assumed that a critic should battle against the traditional American apathy to an intellectual consideration of music; that he should uphold everyone's right to immersion in the living stream of modern music, even at the expense of the classics; that he should treat as real news every experimental, off-beat, or novel idiom that prepares music for going forward in new ways. The self-confidence and verve with which Thomson applied these assumptions made the *Herald Tribune* music column the most discussed in the country. To words of admiration for his courage his reply was: "There's no such animal as a courageous critic; when you have something to say you don't need courage to say it." Letters of protest, which poured into his office, were acknowledged in a manner that conveys something of the ambiguous charm of the man—that combination of amiability, innocence, and guile, to say nothing of the steel in him. Each complainant was thanked for his "delightfully indignant outburst" and cordially reminded that "difference of opinion is the life of art." Typical of his no less abundant "fan mail" is this tribute from an eminent colleague:

I'm simply forced to write you a letter of homage. Your review this morning hits off to utter perfection the exact character of the performance and of the music. I've read it half a dozen times and realize that in spite of the ease with which it was evidently thrown off, one wouldn't change a word or add or subtract a sentence. . . . What a blessing that you have come to town! The whole bumbling business of music criticism as it is written today has been perked up by your arrival. Life is the better for it, less stupid, less logy, less bumptious. You will do everybody in our line a world of good, provided none of us is fool enough to try to imitate you.

Olin Downes

Other qualities besides modern-mindedness set Thomson's criticism apart from the passing run of New York musical journalism. Like his predecessors in the shining era when the confrèrie included a Weber, a Berlioz, and a Schumann, he is a musician-composer and as such brings to bear on his appraisal of a composition an absolutely professional knowledge of all its elements. In his intensity, though to a lesser degree of ferocity, he suggests another pre-eminent composer-critic, Debussy. His viewpoint, by virtue of his personal creative experience, has therefore little in common with those of Hanslick, Newman, or Shaw, none of whom was a composer or even a professional performer. And if his poetic expression is less profound than that of Hale, less sensitive than that of Gilman, his analytical acumen has the deeper thrust, his wit the brighter edge. The rise of his writing from the level of his pieces for *Vanity Fair* is documented in the many articles he contributed during the thirties to *Modern Music,* the quarterly edited by Minna Lederman and published by the League of Composers from the middle twenties to the middle forties. Written chiefly by composers, often by composers of world prestige, this excellent magazine told the story of music straight from the creative laboratory. The promising young who were a part of the contemporary movement were also given a voice sometimes in its forum. Horizons widened, perceptions were sharpened in the atmosphere of esthetic controversy pervading its pages. Not the least of Miss Lederman's achievements was the fact that, in addition to discovering and forming such gifted contributors to musical letters as Aaron Copland, Roger Sessions, and Henry Cowell, she brought to maturity Virgil Thomson's critical powers.

In the foreword to his *Gesammelte Schriften über Musik und Musiker* (Leipzig, 1854), Schumann indicates that before permitting his accumulated writings to appear in book form he had subjected them to close scrutiny, but found little that had been invalidated by time. The wide selection of Thomson's reviews and Sunday essays reprinted in *The Musical Scene* (Knopf, 1945), *The Art of Judging Music* (Knopf, 1948), and *Music Right and Left* (Henry Holt, 1951), and others awaiting a fourth volume show that he, too, weighed his judgments. With few exceptions they are as sound and as relevant today as when he committed them to paper. That they were to be among the most readable in any language was evident from the first, for his literary style had become the counterpart of his musical style: clear, precise, full of bite and pace, free of esoteric verbiage, adapted to treating the most abstruse topics in terms of everyday speech, yet shimmering with edge and elegance. The flashing phrase that illuminates—and debunks—was his signature.

These volumes invite endless quotation. A typical instance of critical open-mindedness deals with dodecaphonism at is most hermetic:

> [Anton Webern's Symphony for chamber music] offends, as it delights, with its delicacy, transparency, and concentration. The first movement, for all its canonic rigor, is something of an ultimate in pulverization—star dust at the service of sentiment. . . . One note at a time, just occasionally two or three, is the rule of its instrumental utterance. And yet the piece has a melodic and an expressive consistency. It is clearly about something and under no temptation to fidget. . . . The sonorous texture becomes even thinner at the end. . . . A tiny sprinkle of sounds . . . and vaporization is complete. There is every reason to believe the Philharmonic's reading of this tiny but ever so tough work to have been correct. . . . The rest of the program, standard stuff, sounded gross beside Webern's spun steel.

In nearly as few phrases Thomson contributes more to our understanding of Bartók's difficult idiom than others have done in whole books:

> The despair in his quartets is no personal maladjustment. It is a realistic facing, through the medium of pure feeling, of the human condition . . . as this was perceptible to a musician of high moral sensibilities living in Hungary. No other musician of our century

has faced its horrors quite so frankly. . . . It is this intense purity of feeling that gives [these works] warmth and makes their often rude and certainly deliberate discordance of sound acceptable to so many music lovers of otherwise conservative tastes. Nobody, as we know, ever minds expressive discord. The "modern music" war was a contest over the right to enjoy discord for its own sake, for its spicy tang and the joy it used to give by upsetting apple carts. Bartók himself, as a young man, was a spice lover but not at all an upsetter. He was a consolidator of advance rather than a pioneer. As a mature composer he came to lose his taste for paprika but not for humanity. His music approached more and more a state of systematic discord, rendered more and more truly and convincingly the state of European man in his time. His six string quartets are . . . the essence of his deepest thought and feeling, his most powerful and humane communication. They are also, in a century that has produced richly in that medium, a handful of chamber music nuggets that are pure gold by any standards.

Like Huneker, Thomson has the gift for characterization in a phrase, a sentence, or a brief paragraph. To quote at random:

[Strauss's *Salome*] is like modernistic sculpture made of cheap wood, glass, rocks, cinders, papier-mâché, sandpaper, and bits of old fur. The material elements of it are without nobility; but the whole makes a composition, and the composition speaks.

[Bruno Walter's Mozart] is noble in proportion but careless of detail. . . . It resembles more the whipped-cream-in-stone aspect of Austrian baroque architecture than it does the firm workmanship of Mozart's music.

[Martinů's florid textures] suit best exotic and fanciful subjects. Applied to straightforward melodies of songlike character or to the semi-abstract motifs that are the basis of symphonic continuity, they create a dichotomy of style that suggests a photograph of your Aunt Sophie in front of the Taj Mahal. Neither the subject nor the background appears to advantage in such an arrangement. The background goes a little tawdry, the subject does not completely express itself.

[Reynaldo Hahn's Three *Etudes Latines*] gave us Martial Singher at his most charming. A concert version of the salon style is not an easy

note to achieve, but Mr. Singher observed it with all the grace (and
some of the unction) of a French restaurateur. If Hahn's songs are
not quite first-class provender, they are none the less delicate cui-
sine; and no public's taste for them can be reproached. They are hot-
house Parnassian poetry blended to suave melodies and set off by
delicate accompaniments, bland nourishment, a little monotonous
each. Sung in anything but half-tints and perfect French, they are
unendurable. Impeccably presented, they become, if not works of
art, a luxury product of distinction.

[Alexander Uninsky's pianism] always sounds like piano playing,
never like singing or trumpets or harps or wind or quiet rain. It
evokes no orchestra, no landscape, no dancing, no meditation, and no
fury. The notes are there, and the sound of them is good. But they
carry one nowhere save right back to the printed page they came
from. Perhaps also a bit to Russia . . . because there is a kind of Mus-
covite crudeness beneath all his studied imitation of flexibility.

[A Heifetz recital] was luxury expressed in music. . . . His famous
silken tone . . . his well-known way of hitting the true pitch squarely
in the middle, his justly remunerated mastery of the musical marsh-
mallow, were like so many cushions of damask and down to the musical ear. . . . [He] is at his best in the lengthy chestnuts . . . where every
device of recitative style, of melodic phrase-turning, of brilliant passage work is laid out, like the best evening clothes and the best jewelry,
for Monsieur to put his elegant person into. No destination, no musical or emotional significance is implied. . . . Four-starred super-luxury
hotels are a legitimate commerce. The fact remains, however, that
there is about their machine-tooled finish and empty elegance something more than just a trifle vulgar.

[Mitropoulos, in an access of egocentrism,] for the most part did
everything to the orchestra but conduct it. He whipped it up as if it
were a cake, kneaded it like bread, shuffled and riffled an imaginary
deck of cards, wound up a clock, shook a recalcitrant umbrella,
rubbed something on a washboard and wrung it out. There were few
moments when a film taken of him alone, without sound, would
have given any clue to the fact that he was directing a musical composition. . . . Vehemence, self-absorption, an urgency toward commu-
nicating something, though not necessarily the music's own meaning
—only the personal intensities were there.

About what he believes to be artistically valid and valuable Thomson is lyricism itself. Landowska playing the harpsichord summoned this stroke of imagery:

[Her] recital was as stimulating as a needle shower. Indeed, the sound of that princely instrument, when it is played with art and fury, makes one think of golden rain and of how Danaë's flesh must have tingled when she found herself caught out in just such a downpour.

Ansermet's care for aural exactitude evoked these shining similes:

Smooth as a seashell, iridescent as fine rain, bright as the taste of a peach are the blends and balances of orchestral sound with which he renders, remembering, the lines, the backgrounds, and the tonal images of the great painters who worked in France round the turn of the century. Mozart he plays with love and light, too; and he began last night with the Prague Symphony, just to show us how a classical rendering can be clean and thoroughly musical without being dry or overcrisp.

Hofmann's playing prompted this Protean metaphor:

The pillars and buttresses of its architecture are thin and strong. The rooms above are high, airy, clean, eminently habitable. His forms, to change the figure, grow like trees. No leaf but is attached to stem and branch; no branch but leads us downward to the root. All is organic, orderly, straight-grown toward the light. The word pedagogic springs to mind as one listens. Not pedagogic in any pejorative sense, but pedagogic as if each execution were an example to be preserved of how incredibly right piano-playing can be when it is right.

A Flagstad recital brought forth comments lighted with insight and sensibility:

Straightforwardness on the concert platform is something rarely encountered except on the part of children and of the very greatest artists. Straightforwardness in musical execution is met with practically only on the part of great artists. Madame Flagstad is straightforward in her platform manner and in her musical interpretations. She is not, for that, an unsubtle musician. Nor is her splendidly majestic voice an unsubtle instrument. . . . But such an assured mistress is she of her voice, and so clear is her comprehension of the songs she sings, that she is not constrained to seek to please listeners by any trick of willful charm or feigned emotion. . . . By eschewing exploitation of her personality, she warms all hearts to that personality. By not feeling obliged to give her operatic all to every tender melody, she offers us each a song as if it were a living and fragile thing in our hands, like a bird.

But it is in his tributes that Thomson most forcefully—and poetically—voices his love and respect for the masters closest to his heart. Of Casals playing at a session of his classes at Zermatt in 1954 (the artist's seventy-second year) he wrote:

> It was with Beethoven's last cello concerto that the Casals qualities of sensitivity, of sadness, and of resignation seemed most perfectly paired. One understood both in the work and in its performance the meaning of the poet's phrase "all passion spent." And the whole presence of both was the more vibrant since every other vigor had remained intact. Vibrancy in resignation is what makes of Casals today a sort of musical saint. But the miracle that he performs . . . is to make familiar music flower and a familiar instrument sing. For doing this he has, like any saint, both inspiration and technical methods. And if the result seems at times almost supernatural, that effect comes from an interpenetration of ends and means so complete that we wonder however it could have been achieved. One can name the elements in it, but not explain their fusion. . . . But let no one forget that when Casals plays the classical masters he is also playing the cello, an older and possibly grander creation than any piece ever written for it. I suspect, indeed, that the instrument itself, even more than Bach or Beethoven, is his true love. . . . The way he plays it is surely the way the cello should be played, can be played, wishes to be played. As I once heard a Spaniard cry out at a bullfight, "Así se mata el toro!" ("That's the proper way to kill a bull!") Naturally, the bull had to be a high-bred one. The great techniques were never made for poor material.

Ravel's work, to him,

> represents the classic ideal that is every Frenchman's dream . . . the dream of an equilibrium in which sentiment, sensuality, and the intelligence are united at their highest intensity through the opera-

tions of a moral quality. That quality, in Ravel's case . . . is loyalty
to the classic standards of workmanship, though such loyalty obliges
its holder to no observance whatsoever of classical methods. It is an
assumption of the twin privileges, freedom and responsibility. The
success that Ravel's music has known round the world is based, I am
convinced, on its moral integrity. It has charm, wit, and no little
malice. It also has a sweetness and a plain humanity about it that
are deeply touching. Add to these qualities the honesty of precise
workmanship, and you have a product that is irresistible. All French
composers, whether they care to admit it or not, are in debt to
Ravel. It was he, not Gounod nor Bizet nor Saint-Saëns nor Massenet, nor yet César Franck nor Debussy, who gave to France its contemporary model of a composer. That model is the man of simple
life who is at once an intellectual by his tastes and an artisan by his
training and by his practice. He is not a bourgeois nor a white-
collar proletarian nor a columnist nor a priest nor a publicized
celebrity nor a jobholder nor a political propagandist—but simply
and plainly, proudly and responsibly, a skilled workman.

Debussy is hailed for having "freed" harmony:

He gave everything to expression, even structure. He did not
sculpt in music or build architectural monuments. He only painted.
And no two of his canvases are alike. . . . [All forms] receive from his
hand a new liberty, say things and mean things they never said or
tried to mean before. . . . That France, classically the land of freedom, should have produced a model of musical freedom is only natural. All the same, Debussy, even for France, is something of a miracle. . . . His music is not only an ultimate, for our century, of sheer
beauty. It is a lesson to us all in how to make use of our liberty.

A hardy misconception of the composer whose influence was
strongest in Thomson's own musical life is set right with a
bridled urgency that has its own eloquence:

[Satie's works] are as simple, as straightforward, as devastating as the
remarks of a child. To the uninitiated they sound trifling. To those
who love them they are fresh and beautiful and firmly right. . . .
French music in all centuries has been rather special, not quite like
anything else. In our century it has . . . eschewed the impressive, the
heroic, the oratorical, everything that is aimed at moving mass audi-

ences. Like modern French poetry and painting, it has directed its
communication to the individual. It has valued, in consequence,
quietude, precision, acuteness of auditory observation, gentleness,
sincerity, and directness of statement. Persons who admire these
qualities in private life are not infrequently embarrassed when they
encounter them in public places. It is this embarrassment that gives
to all French music, and to the works of Satie and his neophytes in
particular, an air of superficiality, as if it were salon music written
for the drawing rooms of some snobbish set. To suppose this true is to
be ignorant of the poverty and the high devotion to art that marked
the life of Erik Satie to its very end in a public hospital. And to
ignore all art that is not heroic or at least intensely emotional is to
commit the greatest of snobberies.

And there are sheer "charm numbers," like the piece that
lured even tone-deaf people to the New Opera Company's production of *La Vie parisienne:*

> Paris has always been good for foreign musicians and sometimes
> good to them. To none was it ever more generous than to Jacques
> Offenbach, *né* Levy, from Offenbach-am-Main. And no musician,
> foreign or French, not even the Gustave Charpentier of *Louise,* ever
> placed at the feet of his mistress a fresher or a lovelier tribute than
> *La Vie parisienne.* It is a crown of waltzes picked out with polkas
> and quadrilles and interwoven with melodies that distill the tender
> sentiment, the whole tied up with a great big lacy ribbon in the form
> of a cancan. And the melodies are as fresh as the day they were picked;
> the rhythm pops like champagne. . . . Every company that acts this
> operetta has the time of its life and communicates its effervescence. . . .
> The grand quadrille and cancan that end the third scene are a very
> ocean of lace and legs. As Jean Cocteau, himself no mean lover of the
> Lutetian strand, once said of such an occasion, "Venus herself, nascent,
> could not have kicked up more foam."

Many of Thomson's articles on more general subjects grew
into lectures in summer seminars that he has conducted at universities in Europe, South America, and the United States.

He had his faults as critic. His approach to music is so professional, so practical and matter-of-fact, that some of its com-
municative aspects elude him. He listens to it as an intellectual

exercise, and he expected his readers to do the same and to consider the exercise as entertainment in the fullest sense. He did not always develop an idea sufficiently, but sometimes darted instead from point to point, though at each point he inevitably set his readers thinking. Even his style was erratic; he was not above spicing it with vulgarisms for shock purposes. As could be expected, he was biased in favor of the influence that had been strongest in his own musical career, that of Paris of the twenties. However, he avowed the orientation and was not afraid to change his mind. "I hope," he states in the Introduction to *The Musical Scene,* "that a clear attitude has been expressed. . . . This does not mean that I hold my opinions to be all true. Nor do I consider them to be permanent. I am both submissive to facts and amenable to argument. And I consider my personal biases to be facts, not opinions. I will not hold, therefore, that these do not carry some weight in the balance of my judgment. But if my opinions are not wholly unbiased, neither are they irresponsible. They are the opinions of a man from Missouri who is also a workman."

There was no nostalgia in this allegiance. It was rather a tendency to fit subsequent issues into the intellectual framework he knew best, to view New York in the forties as an extension of Paris in the twenties. But he did so in full awareness of the issues of the day. His sensitiveness to new talent was unique in American criticism, as was his wide coverage. Leaving standard repertory and standard soloists largely to his staff, he devoted himself primarily to alerting the public to fresher trends. This kept him panning for gold. He examined experiments in the universities, visited cities with a non-standardized musical life, attended festivals where novel esthetic positions were tested. He was always the first, and sometimes the only one, to discover the merits of new works, and in his own column discussed them in terms the layman could understand. With the aim of stimulating in the public mind, and among reviewers themselves, an awareness of composition as a contemporary activity no less interesting than the musical performing arts, he founded in 1941 the Music Critics Circle of New York. The organization makes an annual award for excellence, in much the same way that the Drama Critics Circle and the Film Critics do, to one or more works that have received their first New York performance during the year. The categories recognized include symphonic works, dramatic works (ballets and oratorios as well as opera), and, in the early years of the Circle, chamber works. None of these need be of American authorship.

By carefully budgeting his time, Thomson was able to compose as much after becoming a critic as he had before. His documentary films *Tuesday in November* and *Louisiana Story,* his opera *The Mother of Us All,* his orchestral pieces *The Seine at Night, Wheat Field at Noon,* and *Sea Piece with Birds,* his *Five Songs from William Blake,* his *Four Songs to Poems of Thomas Campion,* his Cello Concerto, Flute Concerto, two books of Piano Etudes, and fifteen Portraits date from the fourteen years that were his *Herald Tribune* period. He also supplied incidental music for the production of Euripides's *The Trojan Women* by the CBS Radio Workshop in 1940, for that of Sophocles's *Oidipous Tyrannos* at Fordham University in 1941, for that of *King Lear* by the TV-Radio Workshop of the Ford Foundation in 1952, for Truman Capote's *The Grass Harp* in 1953, and for an English version of Giraudoux's *Ondine* in 1954.

Tuesday in November, picturing a Presidential election, was commissioned in 1945 by the Office of War Information for use as propaganda outside the United States. John Houseman provided a script that was "dubbed" in twenty-two languages, and Thomson captured in music much of the color and vigor of our political battling. To date his highest achievement in this medium is the score of *Louisiana Story.* He had always been discerning in his choice of collaborators. Now it was Robert Flaherty, who had perfected a method of filming that dramatizes untraveled man against his own landscape, with both actors and setting taken from life and the studied suavity of the usual travelogue left far behind. While exploring uncharted stretches of the Arctic for a mining company, Flaherty had encountered a philosophy for meeting the challenge of existence that found its way, with backing from Revillon Frères, into the film classic

Nanook of the North. After the picture met worldwide acclaim, Hollywood belatedly took notice of it and signed Flaherty to chronicle Samoan life. *Moana of the South Seas* followed. His refusal to fake effects cooled Hollywood's interest. British producers subsidized his *Man of Aran,* shot on surf-lashed islands off the Irish coast, and his *Elephant Boy,* based on Kipling's "Toomai of the Elephants." Both pictures won awards, but their lack of mass-appeal made it increasingly difficult for Flaherty to find sponsors. He had transferred his energies to writing travel books when Standard Oil engaged him in 1946 to disclose to the public the drama inherent in drawing petroleum from the earth.

He surveyed the American oil country for weeks, but the boom towns and derrick-dotted plains suggested no pattern for a picture. He had begun to suspect that the drama in oil takes place beyond the camera's casual reach—in the very depths of the earth where oil accumulates. The bayou region of Louisiana was a locale beyond his dreams, but he could not visualize its moss-draped cypresses and gentle Acadian inhabitants in terms of petroleum. Finally, he happened upon a derrick in motion. With marsh grass concealing the barge that towed it, the giant steel web suggested a story about industry's encroachment on rural existence as seen through the eyes of a boy of the bayou. Flaherty combed the countryside for his 'Cajun characters, recruited his animal actors from a wild-life preserve, cast an oil-prospecting crew, and for two years shot, screened, and processed. His kind of filming was a course in survival techniques. It had exposed him to death by freezing, to drowning, to tropical fevers, to cobras, to man-eating tigers. These perils pale beside an experience involved in the making of *Louisiana Story.* To convey the danger of drilling for oil in a bayou, he and his cameramen boarded a derrick during a violent escape of gas from a well. By looking directly down into the discharge they got some fine footage, but if the motor of their camera had generated a spark, they and the bayou would have been blown to fragments.

Flaherty took his completed film-footage to New York to be cut and pieced. Knowing and admiring *The Plow That Broke the Plains* and *The River,* he invited Thomson to a studio showing of the oil saga. Thomson was ravished by its beauty and engaged himself with joy to compose music for it. Written early in 1948 and recorded for the sound-track that spring by the Philadelphia Orchestra, the score of *Louisiana Story* was in 1949 awarded the Pulitzer Prize for distinguished musical composition, the first, and still the only, Pulitzer award ever granted to a film-score. By turning impressionism to uses that touch both Dada and the twelve-tone system, Thomson had captured every inflection of Flaherty's Acadian idyl. He had worked out his tone-painting in terms of baroque form, framing the dramatic episodes with a twelve-tone chorale, a chromatic passacaglia, or a chromatic double fugue. For the genre scenes, he had evoked rustic fiddle sonorities and observed the naïve rhythmic freedom of the 'Cajun airs. He had also known when to mute his orchestra: the oil-drilling sequences are accompanied only by the sounds of the machinery—throbbing engines, ringing pipes, clattering block and cables.

The Thomson formula for incidental theater-music is one that most composers would hold on principle to be unworkable. He chooses a small number of instruments of bright timbre, gives each a melodic part, and maintains a sonorous balance between them all. In other words, he writes chamber music, accented with percussion, to accompany full-scale theatrical productions; and his ensemble, with its simultaneous play of timbres and thematic ideas, is more effective than many a pale imitation of orchestral sonorities performed by the limited number of musicians that theatrical producers impose on composers. Scored without unnecessary weight or stridency, his background music for *The Grass Harp* (1952) and for *Ondine* (1954), both of which plays are fantasies rich in psychological truth, is suitable and sumptuous in every way. When the French actor-producer Louis Jouvet planned a revival of Claudel's *L'Annonce faite à Marie* for Rio de Janeiro in 1943, he invited Thomson to be his musical collaborator. Many leading composers of France were available, but Jouvet sensed that he could count on Thomson to match in sound the imaginativeness of Tchelitchew's décors for the production. Previous commitments prevented Thomson from accepting, and his reply stressed the hope that a similar opportunity would arise, "since there is no other director with whom I would esteem it such a high artistic privilege to be associated." Jouvet died before a later collaboration could be realized.

In the spring of 1945, the French Embassy in Washington offered Thomson a mission to make a summer's survey of postwar French musical life with a view to re-establishing French cultural relations with the United States. At the same time, he received from the Alice M. Ditson Fund Committee a commission for an opera to be produced in 1947 at Columbia University. An article written years later for the New York *Times* (April 15, 1956) sheds light on his choice of theme for the commissioned work:

> The nineteenth century was a time rare in history, when great issues were debated in great language. As in the Greece of Pericles and Demosthenes, in the Rome of Caesar and Cicero, in the England of Pitt and Burke, historical changes of the utmost gravity were argued in noble prose by Webster, Clay, and Calhoun in the senate, by Beecher and Emerson in the pulpit, by Douglas and Lincoln on the partisan political platform. These changes, which became burning issues after the Missouri Compromise of 1820, dealt with political, economic, racial, and sexual equality. And the advocated reforms —excepting woman suffrage—were all embodied in the Constitution by 1870. In fifty glorious and tragic years the United States grew up. We ceased to be an eighteenth-century country and became a twentieth-century one. Surely, it had long seemed to me, surely somewhere in this noble history and in its oratory there must be the theme, and perhaps even the words, of a musico-dramatic spectacle that it would be a pleasure to compose.

It would be an added pleasure to revive his collaboration with Gertrude Stein, and the coincidence of the order for the opera with the French mission, which provided air transport, enabled him to do both. Letters dashed off to Maurice Grosser amid concert-going, lecturing, broadcasting, and revisiting old friends in Paris report that there is much new French music, "most of it tops"; that the postwar Parisians are "astonishingly fit and only a little older"; that Gertrude Stein is in "high spirit though forced to live on the proceeds of her Cézanne"—a portrait of the artist's wife, which she sold when the Occupation cut off her access to her funds in America. But Gertrude Stein was far from fit and more than a little older. Organizing morale-building art exhibits and helping GI's, as she had helped dough-boys, to come to terms with their world had sapped her strength. Illness had set in which was to prove fatal within two years. Still, she was savoring life with a new zest, for she had finally been rewarded by the recognition as a serious artist for which she had so long hungered. Critical consensus had granted that her influence on contemporary literature had been vicariously potent in its effect on younger American writers. Far-sighted Steinists had given her a handhold on immortality by arranging for the deposit of her papers at Yale University. Plans for the posthumous publication of her mass of unsold manuscripts were under way. She was eager to collaborate when Thomson broached the matter.

After steeping herself in nineteenth-century American oratory through the American Library in Paris, she decided to make feminism her central theme and Susan B. Anthony her heroine. Ever since the end of the first World War she had looked for the emergence of a movement in painting capable of offering intellectual stimulus such as cubism had provided. Instead of another Picasso, she had found a fresh range of poetic painting in the works of Bérard, Tchelitchew, Berman, and other neo-romantic artists. Under their influence the direct communication of personal sentiment became her goal. The fantasy she based on the battle for women's rights blends historical and topical figures with her usual disdain for chronology, but the figures express themselves lucidly and with vehemence. The portrait of the heroine has a compelling rightness to which the parallels between her career on the political plane and that of Gertrude Stein on the literary add poignance. The dialogue is a reflection of personality rather than a vehicle for advancing a plot. The people of the play neither answer one another nor even listen; they simply say what is most on their minds, turning the text into a bright confusion of insistences, each clear and reasonable in itself.

No less deceptively simple than *Four Saints*, the musical setting of *The Mother of Us All* marks an advance in range of characterization. The intoned sermon, the political rallying song, the sentimental ballad, the parlor solo on the piano, the Gospel tune in Salvation Army band style, together with original tunes with a nineteenth-century American flavor, are all put to psychological uses. At the same time they give the score an irresistible remembrance-of-things-past appeal, and this is kept alive and fresh by means of continually shifting tonalities. Fragmentation of instrumental support provides an added form of expressiveness. Susan B. Anthony's funeral oration, which might have served for Gertrude Stein's as well, is thrown into such piercing relief by its tenuous accompaniment that the spirit of both women seems to live in the lone vocal phrase on which the opera ends. Had *The Mother of Us All* achieved as nearly perfect a mating of cast and décors as *Four Saints*, Thomson's experiment in bombazine might have become as familiar a piece as its cellophane predecessor. He wanted it to be a visual evocation of a Victorian parlor album, with a curtain designed like the cover of such an album, costumes recalling the hand-tinted photographs of the period, and stage movements choreographed to suggest photographic poses. The visual production at Brander Matthews Theater at Columbia University in May, 1947, though it had quality, did not follow these ideas. The staging was far from undistinguished. The professional singers cast in the major roles were first-class. It was no counterpart of *Four Saints*, however, and no Harry Moses arose to transplant it to Broadway. Student performances have been given at Tulane University, Western Reserve, the University of Denver, and Harvard. An off-Broadway New York revival (at the Phoenix Theater) in April, 1956, marked the first performance by a wholly professional cast. But Thomson's visual conception of *The Mother of Us All* has yet to be fulfilled.

In musical landscape-painting, which he now began to take up, Thomson aimed to create canvases that resemble nature rather

than to depict his own states of ecstasy about her. It occurred to
him that the endeavor could be made more challenging by the
choice of subjects as nearly immobile as it is possible to represent
in tone. *The Seine at Night* was written for the Kansas City Orchestra, to which Thomson dedicated it in a program note:

> During my second twenty years I wrote in Paris music that was
> always, in one way or another, about Kansas City. I wanted Paris to
> know Kansas City, to understand the ways we like to think and feel
> on the banks of the Kaw and the Missouri. Writing for Kansas City,
> I have no such missionary justification. I cannot teach my grand-
> mother to suck eggs. And so I offer to the other city that I love, and
> the only other one where I have ever felt at home, a sketch, a sou-
> venir, a post-card of the Seine, as seen in front of my own house, a
> view as deeply a part of my life and thought as Wabash Avenue,
> where I spent my first twenty years.

The "post-card" evokes, in turn, the Seine's imperceptible flow,
the flare of skyrockets over distant Montmartre, and the music of
fine rain that hangs in the evening air. *Wheat Field at Noon,* commissioned by the Louisville Orchestra, is more than an impression of a wheat field; it is the wheat field recounting its transition
from a state of motionless calm to one of yeasting exuberance.
No less resembling a portrait, *Sea Piece with Birds,* composed for
the Dallas Symphony Orchestra, suggests the tension of waves,
the tug of undertows, the back-and-forth flight of gulls. A veil of
effortlessness is thrown over the skillful construction of each
canvas.

Five Songs from William Blake for Barytone and Orchestra,
also written for the Louisville Orchestra, fulfilled a long-re-
flected desire to convey in music the philosophy of that most
humane of mystics. S. Foster Damon's research and analysis in
William Blake: His Philosophy and Symbols had made it clear
to Thomson that the essence of Blake's thought is contained in
the poems *The Divine Image,* which postulates that God abides
within the human form, *Tiger! Tiger!,* which ponders the
problem of evil in creation, *The Land of Dreams,* which ex-
pounds the futility of evading reality, *The Little Black Boy,*

which pleads for universal friendship, and *And Did Those Feet,*
which affirms the will to help to re-establish Heaven on earth. His
settings capture this essence in all its freshness and fervor. Rarely
in this century have instruments or vocal writing been turned to
expressive channels that penetrate so deep. Here music becomes
more than the handmaid of poetry; it is also at the service of
metaphysics.

Thomson has been asked to conduct the premières of many of
his orchestral pieces. The clean style and intellectual thoroughness
with which he projects these scores have established him as an
interpreter of American music capable of searchlighting its substance. His vacations from the *Herald Tribune* became filled
with concert activity in many parts of the country. In the summer
of 1954 he began to conduct in Europe, introducing works by
Copland, Cowell, Barber, and other Americans, including himself, to such far-apart music centers as Barcelona, Vienna, Rome,
Zurich, Venice, Luxembourg, and Paris. His stanch Americanism
and ebullient good will made him a welcome musical ambassador. To the foreign symphonic groups he was no Franco-American, despite his excellent French and the rosette of the Legion
of Honor in his lapel. Nor was he a New Yorker, despite his
Herald Tribune post. He was a "man from Missouri who is also
a workman," collaborating with them rather than dominating
them, rejoicing in their technical aplomb as he rejoiced in the
vigorous American music he was disseminating through Europe's
halls and over her airwaves. He was an equally successful envoy
as composer, for his music pictures an America very unlike
Lewis's Babbitt warren, or Faulkner's rachitic Southland, or
Eliot's cultural Sahara. It shows an America of exuberant indi-
vidualism, of zest for living, for art, for absurdity, for the latest
thing and the oldest—a land of irreducible euphoria.

By now Thomson had become a prime moving figure in the
realm of musical politics. When he settled in New York in 1940,
the artistic policies of the League of Composers, America's foremost avant-garde group, were largely guided by Aaron Copland.
Continual activity on behalf of vital new music—American music
in particular—had contributed to Copland's fitness for this leader-

ship. In addition to presenting with Roger Sessions series of concerts in New York, he had originated music festivals at Yaddo, organized a young composers group modeled after *les six,* and helped to found the American Composers Alliance, a fee-collecting society for professional composers of serious music who do not operate on the broader scale of members of the American Society of Composers, Authors, and Publishers. In 1938 Thomson was elected a member of the board of the American Composers Alliance. The following year he embarked on organizational pursuits of his own, initiating with Copland and a few others the Arrow Music Press, a co-operative project that still flourishes. In 1941 he founded the Music Critics Circle of New York and became its first chairman. In 1942 he varied New York's programs of contemporary music by introducing a neo-romantic series. Owing to insufficient subsidy, these memorable "Serenade Concerts," staged at the Museum of Modern Art, ended after one season. But Thomson's participation in the shaping of musical policies continued. Singly, together, and with others, he and Copland currently sit on music panels and on the boards of benefactory foundations. Respected as musicians, liked as individuals, both are consulted at home and abroad about the distribution of funds, commissions, and honors.

Thomson carried off this multiple activity with the professional ease of an acrobat balancing several people on his shoulders. Nevertheless, he was increasingly aware of its weight. Though his years on the *Herald Tribune* had been rich in musical pleasure, peppered with good fights, journalism was beginning to bore him. As no amount of prestige could compensate him for ennui, and as he was now able to live by composing, he notified his employers in the spring of 1953 of his intention to resign in the fall of 1954. The *Herald Tribune* chose a distinguished successor, but they knew that a unique era in music criticism would close. For nearly a decade and a half Thomson had brought fresh air into the musical scene. By fighting for a musical life of broader intellectuality, by upholding everything that might help to launch music on a fresh phase, by rocking tradition and puncturing pretense, he had established the climate of esthetic controversy that invigorates art. Dazzlingly readable, his column had for many been a source of illumination and of sheer delight. From as many others it had summoned protest, but never before had there been so alert an American audience for music criticism or for American music.

In way of life Thomson is as individual as in thought. Ever since settling in New York he has lived at the romantically unfunctional Hotel Chelsea, the last of Manhattan's plush inns of the hansom cab era. William Morris designed the ironwork of its sweeping stairways and innumerable balconies. Pre-Raphaelite carvings embellish the mahogany mantels and wainscots of its high-ceilinged rooms. Since its heyday, when West Twenty-third Street was uptown, it has held a special attraction for writers and artists. The roster of its departed tenants includes O. Henry, John Sloan, Edgar Lee Masters, Thomas Wolfe, and Dylan Thomas; among living alumni are Tennessee Williams, James Farrell, Ben Lucian Berman. To the Victorian furnishings of his flat in this amiable anachronism Thomson has added paintings by Bérard, Florine Stettheimer, Leonid Berman, Maurice Grosser, Inna Garsoian, and Roger Baker; also sculptures by Hans Arp, a collection of timpani, a library of books and music. Its stone masonry walls, three times thicker than modern partitions, are so soundproof that he learned only by chance that piano lessons had been going on in an adjacent flat for some years. In these surroundings, and behind the telephonic Maginot Line of the Chelsea's answering service, he works in splendid isolation. Recent scores written here include his transcriptions for orchestra of the Eleven Chorale-Preludes for organ by Brahms, his *Old English Songs* on Tudor texts, his *Tres Estampas de Niñez* on Spanish poems by Reyna Rivas, his music for Paddy Chayevsky's motion picture *The Goddess,* and his music for the Stratford, Connecticut, productions of *Measure for Measure, King John, Othello, The Merchant of Venice,* and *Much Ado About Nothing.* But now and then Thomson entertains in a typical fashion. At his dinners, which are prepared by a Negro cook whom he has taught out of Escoffier, the art of good talk comes alive. His evenings of chamber music have a pre-war Viennese authenticity. His guest list reads like a distillation of *Composers of Today, Twentieth-Century Authors, Dictionary of Contemporary Painters,* and *Who's Who in the Theater,* plus lay friends, who are literally past counting, though his zest for needling smugness continues to harvest foes. In the summer he resumes his musical evangelism by means of which he has made American art music almost as exportable as jazz to music centers throughout Europe and South America. An international figure in music and letters, he is an officer of the Legion of Honor, a member of the National Institute of Arts and Letters, a trustee of benefactory foundations, the holder of honorary degrees. Under this cosmopolitan exterior he remains a solid Midwesterner—sensible, genial, beaver-busy, tolerant of all things but snobbery and sham. Packaging these qualities is a finely evolved standard of values that makes success lie lightly upon him. And if youth can be equated with enthusiasm, he is still one of the youngest composers around. Nevertheless, beneath these clear facets of his nature the central enigma persists: he is more than ever the "harmonious human multitude" that falls into no pattern.

The catalogue of his compositions so far points up a creative output of remarkable diversity. It lists orchestral works, music for solo instruments and orchestra, music for voices and orchestra, choral works, operas, ballets, songs, piano music, film music, incidental music for the theater. It varies in merit, but the major portion is of high distinction, its indigenous aspects being in themselves an achievement in American culture. Long a subject of controversy by reason of the paradox of its unidiosyncratic style and highly individual content, it has entered the main stream of world music. At home and abroad it is standard repertory. At international conferences on contemporary music it bulks large. American universities build festivals around it. Conservatives as well as avantgardists have come to subscribe to the Thomson theory that the purpose of music is to refresh rather than to impress; that there is room for a more relaxed art than that which strains for the maximum complexity, room for a simplified music based on a severe but fluent technique and adhering to the most fastidious standards of taste and imagination. Thomson has applied the theory to many forms, but it is in theater music, particularly in films and in the opera, that he has had the most to say. The public is waiting for him to exercise again his gift for creating through the tone-setting of language a verbal excitement that carries operatic prosody to a new dimension. His preferred type of libretto—so tenuous in surface meaning that he may concentrate his whole attention on the linguistic content—probably expired with Gertrude Stein. But Thomson is known for his ability to surprise. The basis of his next fling in lyric drama may observe the unities, have point and passion, be lucidity itself.

The befogged trends of modern music cannot shake his conviction that the art will continue to advance. He does not hold with the radicals who insist that its only new path lies the atonal way, or that the twelve-tone serial style, if it is to survive, must kill off all other styles. He believes that the war about modernism has benefited all contestants; that the neo-classical center, having penetrated the orchestral repertory and seized the teaching posts, is entrenched; that the twelve-tone forces, currently the attacking wing, are attaining a status close to co-dominion; that each, by absorbing something of the other's methods, is invigorating its own expressive powers and giving a measure of stability to the amalgamated idiom. The situation, for him, promises expansion, enrichment. It is his conviction that the modern techniques are now being fused into a twentieth-century classic style; that when this fusion is complete, the art of composition will regain its former powers of communication. If a dual loyalty—to his American heritage and to the culture of France—and a personal idiom clear in thought and terse in statement are his contribution to the music of this century, faith in the power of this music to carry on in a world out of joint is his special tribute to it. One of the century's most bounteous dispensers of mental champagne, Virgil Thomson, composer, critic, esthete, and humanitarian, has truly lived by the maxim of Baltasar Gracian, the La Rochefoucauld of Spain: It is not enough to do good; one must do it with zest, originality, style.

Virgil Thomson

HIS MUSIC

by

John Cage

Foreword

NOW AND THEN, HEARING AT A CONCERT MUSIC BY VIRGIL THOMSON, one finds that many in the audience are noticeably shocked either by an entire piece or by some part of one. On the other hand, one has listened and watched others listen through numerous performances of his works, never once disturbed, often deeply moved. The *Sonata da chiesa* for five disparate instruments usually produces a scandal, all of it, the audience becoming during its performance nearly as noisy as the musicians. And were it not for the fact that one is in church when listening to the *Pastorale on a Christmas Plainsong* (for organ), its polytonal chromatic parts would tempt almost anyone to create an uproar. Yet neither another early work, *Tribulationes* (for a capella choir), nor a later one, *A Solemn Music* (for band) is in any way disturbing.

Several critics, among them Frederick Goldbeck, have referred to Thomson as "an American Satie." Satie's music is little enough understood anywhere, and this lack of understanding is sanctioned by Rollo H. Myers in his book *Erik Satie,* when he concludes that Satie's music is less interesting than was Satie the man, particularly Satie the humorist. Thomson's wit as expressed in his books and newspaper articles being a matter of household information in America, it would be easy to content oneself with Goldbeck's estimate. However, this would only add to the mystery associated with Thomson's music, as it does to that associated with the music of Satie. To regard Satie as essentially a comedian with a taste for mystifying is an opinion I long ago convinced myself was untenable by examining his music, all of it. In the same spirit I undertook a study of Thomson's work. Though I had heard much of it, I decided to remake, insofar as possible, the adventure he himself had actually experienced. What follows is a report of what I found outstanding in the course of that expedition. I am grateful to Thomson for having given me the use of his unpublished manuscripts and his private recordings, for answering questions, and for offering opinions about certain of his works that more often than not differed refreshingly from those I was entertaining.

I followed the general plan of beginning at the beginning and going on until I got to the present. In studying each work I asked myself four questions: What is its structure (how is it divided into parts)? What is the method employed (by what means does the composer proceed from note to note)? What materials are used (what instruments, what sounds and silences)? and finally, What is the form of the piece (its morphology of feeling, its expressive content)? I asked myself these questions with an "open" mind, an empty one, as if his music were the only music in existence. At the same time, I wished to encounter it with a "closed," or objective mind, to view it in relation to that of other composers. Such a procedure should provide the answers to two further questions: What is the nature of Thomson's music? and What position has it in the field of contemporary music? Another set of opposites I took as existing in Thomson himself, as indeed it exists in anyone: namely, that between what is spontaneous and free and what is law-abiding and rigorously ordered. With both pairs of opposites in mind, one might estimate what Thomson's attitude toward life is, answering the final question: What is he "saying" in his music? It would be pretentious of the writer, and naïve of the reader, to expect all these questions to be answered to everybody's satisfaction. Nevertheless, they do situate my point of departure in setting forth on this surprising journey.

JOHN CAGE

New York

1

"IT WILL SURPRISE READERS THAT MY EARLIEST MANUSCRIPT IS FROM 1920, when I was already twenty-four years old," Virgil Thomson has written. "The reason is that, though I was already a trained pianist, organist, and choirmaster with a long professional experience, my training in composition was almost non-existent when I went to Harvard. Kansas City had had little to offer in that branch. Also, I had been in the Army for nearly two years. Consequently, when I set about building up a composer's technique (I arrived at Harvard in the fall of 1919), I had to work fast in order to master the classical disciplines before my rapidly maturing manhood should come to dominate my powers of receptivity with its ever-increasing demand of expressivity. This circumstance explains why:

"Though musically precocious and trained in execution, I came late to composition.

"My twenty-four year pieces are so tentative about materials.

"My progress in mastering techniques was so rapid.

"My early pieces are almost painfully urgent in their expression.

"My personality appears fairly early in my music.

"My impatience with the techniques appears constantly until about 1927. After that, very little."

The first extant piece, dated at Cambridge in July, 1920, is a song with piano accompaniment, *Vernal Equinox*. The words are by Amy Lowell, the feelings described those of a lonely lover. One can only regard the manuscript tenderly: it is the first work by a man who was to devote his life to music. The appearance of the notes indicates that writing them was difficult for the young musician. His hands were accustomed not to the pen, but to the stops and manuals of the organ and to the gestures in thin air with which he conducted the Harvard Glee Club. This

VERNAL EQUINOX
Amy Lowell
Rather slowly

1920 (July)

song, however, does not suggest either organ or choral music. Intimate in character, suitable for private recital, it reflects his experience as a vocal coach. The melody is diatonic, with many repeated tones. Where the word "wind" occurs this event is imitated in the vocal line. Though there are four measures of introduction in 3/4 time, the song itself is in 2/4. The rhythm presents many *grupetti* (triplets, quintuplets, and the like) used not to create complexity, but to render the rhythm of spoken English. The accompaniment adds color and support to the melody. When it is alone, it announces the vocal line to come. The tonality changes not by the customary shifts of a fourth, a fifth, a major or minor third, but by the very "modern" one of a half-step. The choice of chords, many of them altered, is sensitive, though not of a taste acceptable today. There are no tone-clusters but many open parallel fifths. The variety of materials suggests that no conscious method was used in their selection: they seem to have corresponded to the young composer's feelings, which in their turn corresponded perhaps a little to Debussy's, but still more to those strainings toward the unattainable found in many parlor songs.

The piece *De Profundis* (Psalm CXXX), an unaccompanied chorus in English for mixed voices, was written in Cambridge the same month. It exists also in a recently revised version. At the head of the score are the words "slowly, with mystical expression." Both versions contain many changes of meter. In the revision, Thomson has simplified some of the chords and clarified the movement of the parts. Where in the original one line diverged from the others, its divergence in the revision is sup-

ported by the parallel movement of a second line. He has further
elaborated an alto line that in the original suggested a certain
floridity. Other revisions concern the phraseology, some phrases
being extended for declamatory emphasis, others contracted, and
spaces of silence being introduced between phrases. However,
the main outlines, the harmonic structure, and most of the
melodic detail are preserved in the recent version, indicating an
unusual acceptance on the part of the mature man of his youthful feelings and their expression.

Among Thomson's friends at Harvard was the composer, poet,
and Blake scholar S. Foster Damon, who introduced the young
composer to the music of Erik Satie and showed him how far
from naïve was its apparent simplicity. He also clarified for him
many of the obscurities found in the poetry of William Blake. In
September, 1920, Thomson set Blake's *The Sun Flower* as a song

with piano accompaniment. The poem expresses Blake's conception of America as a "golden clime," where Europeans, freed
from oppression, could live more fully. The choice of these
verses points to a reaction on Thomson's part against Amy
Lowell's poem about erotic inhibition. The song itself, by being
more conservative musically, turns out to be less of a parlor song
and more like a recital song. The same meter is maintained
throughout, and the phraseology is in conventional four- and
eight-measure lengths. The pianist's right hand plays triplets
almost throughout, while his left and the voice move more slowly.
The frequent octave or quintal relation of these outer voices at

major points, plus the fact that when the singer is not singing, the pianist, instead of trying to get a personal word in, continues his simple accompaniment, gives this work a charming unpretentiousness. Though the harmony is based on a repeated transformation of A flat Minor into A flat Major, the texture is largely diatonic except for two brief passages where chromaticism, rising scale-wise, is prompted by the words "desire" and "aspire." The final chord, now out of fashion but current in 1920, is a tonic major seventh with added sixth in the upper voice.

A silence of fourteen months follows.[1] Toward the end of that period, in October, 1921, Thomson began his first period of study with Nadia Boulanger, which continued for a year. He had previously taken all the courses in theory offered at Harvard, supplementing them with the practice of choral direction under Archibald T. Davison and organ lessons from Wallace Goodrich. Later (1922–1923), he studied advanced orchestration with Edward Burlingame Hill and orchestral conducting with Chalmers Clifton (1923–1924). He also went through counterpoint all over again with Rosario Scalero (1923–1924). His notebooks of counterpoint exercises submitted to Nadia Boulanger contain very few errors, and the voices move well. Any inclination to dismiss the peculiarities of many of Thomson's later works on the grounds that he was musically uninformed or lacking in skill is therefore wholly unjustifiable.

One evening in Paris, on his twenty-fifth birthday, November 25, 1921, Thomson found himself strolling alone, his anniversary uncelebrated. Returning to his furnished room, he poured out his feelings by composing a *Prelude for Piano*. This piece is definitely thematic, a six-measure theme being put through variation, contraction, transposition, and recapitulation. This insistence on a theme in so short a piece gives the effect of something that will out—a cry from within that is either not completely heard or not quite understood. Even more interesting than these aspects is the ecclesiastical character of the piece, brought about by the melodic use of parallel open fifths. One could trace Thomson's interest in organum to his long history

as a church-goer (paid and unpaid), to his familiarity with pre-
Renaissance choral works gained at Harvard, and to Nadia
Boulanger's interest in modal counterpoint. The last may have
acted as a final straw, since the fifth without the third is a
Catholic and European experience far more than a Protestant
and American one. At any rate, during the period of his study
in Paris, Thomson familiarized himself with the standard trea-
tises on the music of the Middle Ages, paid a visit to the monks
at Solesmes, and omitted the third from most of his fifths.[2]

A *Sanctus* for male choir (later incorporated into the *Missa
Brevis* No. 1) was written in December, 1921. A note on the
manuscript indicates that "the effect should be that of the ac-
clamations of an enormous crowd, heard at some little distance."
To produce this impression, Thomson built up, adding the voices
one by one, a diatonic tone-cluster (G, A, B, C, D) the root of
which remains as a pedal point throughout this very short piece,
moving only in the last three measures plagally to D, upon which
a somewhat more incisive tone-cluster (D, F, G flat, G, A) is
built.[3] This piece should sound bright and vigorous. However,
one should hear it "at some little distance," twice-removed from
the imaginary crowd, for the dynamics indicated are of the loud-
est.

A Christmas vacation in Capri (1921–1922) brought forth a
bouquet of organ works: *Fanfare, Pastorale on a Christmas Plainsong,* and *Prelude,* also an *Antiphonal Psalm* for chorus. It was
there, too, working without a piano, that Thomson emancipated
himself from dependence on the instrument. The *Fanfare,* an

PASTORALE on a CHRISTMAS PLAINSONG

1922

allegro brillante, in D Major, opens with a pedal solo suggesting Bach, a deceptive opening for a piece that so strikingly suggests Thomson. It is the first of his works to fulfill this resembling function unequivocally. The lines move in absolutely academic ways: by alternations of the tonic and leading tone; by steps in the opposite direction following a leap; by oblique expansion and contraction of intervals; by sequence; by imitation, mostly scale-wise. But the result does not fulfill academic expectations. This is partly owing to the parallel fifths that frequent the pages of an otherwise baroque- or tertial-sounding piece, and even more to the nature of the continuity, which now and again cuts off relatively important passages in order to express an academic cliché in its most naked aspects. A dissonant passage is obtained by placing the augmentation of the third and fourth measures of a four-measure passage on top of the first two measures and their repetition, both hands playing in parallel fifths. The result stands out with quite shocking effect. The composer was evidently pleased with what he had done, for he follows it with a momentary return to the Bach pedal cliché that opened the piece, only to repeat the dissonant passages twice, the second time over a pedal trill in octaves, obviously intended to give the organist some exercise. The rhythm throughout is simple and square, sometimes wooden in character because of the abrupt juxtaposition of the shortest and longest durations. A 4/4 meter is maintained throughout, and the phrases are always in two-, four-, or eight-measure lengths, for which rhythmic situation the conventional tonality shift to the dominant and back again seems highly appropriate.

The *Pastorale* is built around a beautiful plainsong of flowing character, which has a rhythmic structure (not counting extra beats for the holds) of 10, 9, 10, 9, 20 (6, 6, 8) 9. This plainsong is methodically composed (except for its cadential phrase) on the basis of three tetrachords (two whole steps and a half-step; a half-step and two whole steps; whole step, half-step, and whole step). In Thomson's treatment of it a preliminary statement, monolinear, is followed by five variations in which it appears as a *cantus firmus* for contrapuntal variation, always in the same octave and on the same tones, but in the middle voice the first, third, and fourth times,[4] the upper voice the second and fifth times. Except for one chromatic and polytonal variation (the third one) and the last measure of the piece, the composer has respected the character of the plainsong used. And if one accepts the advisability of giving the Devil his due, Thomson may be said even in these outlandish parts to have understood and faithfully expressed the nature of the material.

It is interesting to note that neither the rhythmic structure nor the tetrachordal method of the original plainsong has been followed. In the first variation the phrase relations mentioned become 12, 10, 12, 13, 24 (6, 8, 10), 11; in the second, 12, 11, 14, 13, 25 (6, 9, 10), 10; in the third, 14, 13, 12, 11, 25 (6, 8, 11), 18; in the fourth (given an upbeat) 12, 10, 12, 12, 20 (6, 6, 8), 14; in the last, 15, 14, 15, 13, 31 (6, 12, 13), 22.[5] It would be stretching a point to say that in inventing his counterpoints Thomson followed any tetrachordal method at all; for the most part they fall within every interval but the fourth—namely, the third, the fifth, the sixth, the seventh, and sometimes the octave (this last appearing near the end of the fourth variation). However, in order to create a medieval impression, he sometimes (in the cadence of the first variation and frequently in the last one, in this case supported by parallel fifths) makes use of tetrachords, but out of position and toward different ending tones than they possess in the original plainsong (e.g., the tetrachord in the original, the whole step, half-step, whole step, B, C sharp, D, E, which ends on D, its third tone, appears in the cadence of the first variation as A, B, C, D, and ends on D, its fourth tone). In this way, not to mention the impish chromatics of the third variation, tones foreign to the mode are introduced.

The interval relations throughout appear on first glance to represent what Lou Harrison calls secundal counterpoint, diatonic or modal for the most part. Harrison describes possible contrapuntal situations thus: counterpoint is either formal or informal; that is, it observes or does not observe consistent intervallic relations; if it is formal, it can be quintal, tertial, or secundal (according to which of these intervals is taken as consonant); in both cases it can be either imitative or non-imitative—and differentiated or non-differentiated, as Thomson holds, referring to whether each separate voice has special characteristics or not. The first four measures of Thomson's first variation yield the following intervallic chart:

	1st measure	2nd measure	3rd measure	4th measure
octave	**			**
2nd	/*	**/	*	***/
3rd	//	/*/	/*	
4th	**	*	/*	*
5th	/		*/	
6th	/	*	**	**
7th	/*	/*	//	*
tritone			/	

(The asterisks indicate sounded intervals and those occurring on strong beats; the slanting lines indicate those that are the result of oblique motion.) Out of a total of 27 sounded intervals, 10 (the 4ths, 5ths, and octaves) are quintal consonances; 12 are tertial (3rds, 6ths, 5ths, and octaves); and 13 are secundal (the 2nds, 7ths, and 4ths). The *Pastorale* is therefore an example of informal, non-imitative, differentiated counterpoint.

Whereas in *Fanfare,* following the rules and contradicting the spirit, Thomson obtained an unexpected result, in this *Pastorale,* by observing the spirit but disregarding rules, he achieved an even more shocking effect. The *Fanfare* follows essentially only the letter of the laws, not the principles underlying them, and it ignores the spirit associated with them. This work, reversing the procedure, follows the spirit of medieval church music (but without the laws present), and brings into sight gargoyles ordinarily concealed from immediate view.

The *Prelude for Organ* is both strange and attractive. Emphasizing seconds, fifths, and fourths, and distinguished by the presence of a chromatic scale which, being immediately continued as a diatonic one, seems to have changed before one's very ears, as in fairy tales a monster turns into a princess. This brief work exhibits Thomson's gift for letting one hear things both in and out of focus. The piece is generally modal in character, but, as in the *Pastorale,* no evident tetrachordal method is employed.

Four months later Thomson wrote another *Prelude ("pour Orgue")* subtitled *Passacaglia.* The piece is in C Minor. A long subject (expressed in the soprano melody) in five parts having the proportions 44, 38, 27, 28, 19 is followed by a first variation that carries the subject through only its third part. An episode of 27 counts overlaps by A the beginning of the second variation. The last presents the subject in the bass, distorted in its sixth note and at the end of the first part, where the dominant is substituted for the tonic, and continues through the fourth part of the subject. An overlapping episode of 27 counts is followed by the third variation, which continues for only seven notes (the sixth being again distorted), and this overlaps a forty-three measure "interlude" toward the end of which the seven notes in their distorted version appear both in augmentation and diminution (giving the effect of a recording in which some mechanical mishap causes one to hear the same thing over and over). The piece concludes with a repetition of only the first part of the subject, again placed in the soprano, but this time made grandiose by means of chords and a plethora of descending scale passages. It is clearly not a passacaglia in any strict sense. It may have begun as a short work for the extension of which Thomson bethought himself of diverse composing means offered in the C Minor *Passacaglia* of Bach. But he found himself growing impatient, and in a spirit of irresponsibility proceeded as outlined above. It was understandable that after his many years of organ-playing, any love he may have once had for the instrument had been tried beyond endurance. But with his impatience with the art of composition itself it is more difficult to sympathize. He knew all about organ-playing and a great deal about composition, but in this *Prelude* he expresses boredom with both; that is, with anything resembling law and order as associated with either. He both accepts and rejects the piece: it appears in all lists of his works, but he has never encouraged its performance nor allowed its publication.

The same reversal of procedure that took place between the

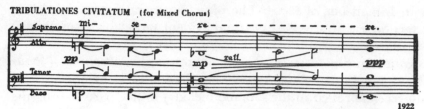

Fanfare and the *Pastorale* takes place again between the *Passacaglia* and the next work, *Tribulationes Civitatum* (motet in Latin for mixed voices, of which a version for men's voices also exists). However, this time, in turning his attention from the rational aspects of music and concentrating on the expression of feelings that he actually had, Thomson felt no need to highlight his awareness of the paradoxical nature of truth. This awareness had led him in the *Pastorale* to the use of shock tactics. True, in his *Tribulationes* the Devil in the form of his tritone appears, but only in the final cadence, a musical area hospitable to any elements, even those foreign to the main body of continuity.

Thirteen measures of quintal, non-imitative, undifferentiated counterpoint of simple grandeur open the piece. This gives place to a twelve-measure section of informal, imitative counterpoint having a quintal cadence. Fifteen more measures follow, similar in character to the opening section. Their cadence overlaps the beginning of a seven-measure antiphonal interlude of a dramatic nature, the word *domine* being repeated three times, each time louder, always on the same tone (F), the durations of the individual syllables being increased each time, and the pianissimo responses *liberos* and *nostros* appearing on a stable and dissonantly related fifth (A, E). The end of this interlude also overlaps the beginning of another imitative section that is followed by a cadential phrase of nine measures, the first five of which are antiphonal. The entrances in the two imitative sections are beautifully handled: in the first, they follow an ascending diatonic tone-cluster, C, D, E, F; in the second, the same cluster, descending, F, E, D, C. Handsomely balanced relations may be observed in the shifts of tonal emphasis, one being that between the very first phrase, opening on A, ending on B flat, and the very last, which opens on E flat and ends on D, again an opposition of ascent and descent. The Devil's appearance is first horizontal (melodically from A to E flat) and then in full stature as the chordal aggregate A, E flat, A flat, B flat. He vanishes, however, before the peaceful and noble open fifths on D with which the motet closes. Whereas in the *Passacaglia,* focusing his attention on music alone, Thomson produced an unmusical result, in the *Tribulationes,* removing his mind from purely musical matters, and writing in relation to a text, he produced a result thoroughly and beautifully musical.

In his next work, *Two Sentimental Tangos* (originally three in number and for piano solo), Thomson removed his mind farther from purely musical matters, not only from their aspects that might have interested him—he had already done that—but also from those aspects that are the life of the intellectual musical world. He had so far contributed nothing to the advance of music. He had made no technical contribution worthy of note, nor had he solved any problem of that music which for him was contemporary. He had simply expressed his feelings. Other composers of that age, Stravinsky and Schoenberg for example, had managed to do both. Thomson had up to this point kept his musical self-respect by surrounding most of his work with the aura of the Church. He had on occasion entered the parlor. In *Two Sentimental Tangos* he ventures for the first time into the public dance-hall. Here, the reaction from modernism exemplified by *The Sunflower* is unashamedly evidenced. The thirds that had vanished from his fifths are reinstated. Modulations are sometimes slightly out of focus—that is, accomplished in the melody faster or slower than in the accompaniment. Otherwise, these pieces do not evoke the 1920's. The bravery exhibited in them is esthetic, not musical, the bravery of a church-goer who, having confessed himself, proceeds to spend his weekdays on the town. The implied decision may have resulted from admiration of such works of Satie as *La Diva de l'Empire* and *La Belle Excentrique,* or for Milhaud's *Saudades do Brasil* or Chabrier's

Habanera. But in coming to this decision Thomson had to accept in himself two things that neither Satie nor Milhaud had been obliged to face: an absence of the faculty for innovation and an attachment to the music of the middle and late nineteenth century, whether sacred, secular, or popular. And like Satie, though unlike Milhaud and Chabrier, he saw no need to clothe his love in an exotic dress, but responded directly to whatever popular music he found closest to home. At the suggestion of Edward Burlingame Hill, with whom he was studying advanced orchestration at the time, an orchestral version of the *Sentimental Tangos* was made. Toward the principles of orchestration, particularly those aiming toward luminosity rather than weight (French school rather than German), he evidenced a docility he had not always shown toward other rules. These scores are colorful and admirably balanced.

A rebuff from a publisher sent Thomson back to the arms of "Mother Church." [6] Lonesome in New York and possessed of feelings not unlike those that had inspired the *Tribulationes,* also in a more ambitious mood, he undertook as his next project the writing of an a capella Latin Mass. He also wrote at this time "Return, O Shulamite," later incorporated as the second in *Three Sentences from the Song of Solomon.* The Mass, variously entitled *Missa Tragica,* Mass in G Minor, and *Missa Brevis* No. 1 (for men's voices), remains a project, not because it was left unfinished, but because it was finished twice, and of each of these versions subsidiary revisions exist. With the Harvard Glee Club in mind, Thomson wrote the first version in the winter of 1923. He submitted this with an application for the Prix de Rome, which was refused. In the fall of 1924, in Boston, he showed the work to Nadia Boulanger, who suggested revisions with a view to purer use of modal material. In the course of the next few years Thomson wrote a number of revisions, among them an *Agnus Dei* and a *Sanctus* with the addition of children's voices. Given as he was to relying on his feelings rather than on a rational control of either structure or method, he was unable to follow Nadia Boulanger's suggestions in a manner satisfactory to himself: on being revised, his original feelings came out as other feelings.

Of the versions of the *Missa Brevis* No. 1 a rounded one and a squarish one may be distinguished. One of the *Kyries* (there are four) opens nobly, suggesting the swinging of censers. The thirds and fifths that had controlled much of the melody writing in the *Pastorale on a Christmas Plainsong* here control many of the vertical relations, so that at one point a dominant seventh is suggested which must have displeased Nadia Boulanger. Another version of the *Kyrie* is similar, but harmonically more complex. A third (and different) *Kyrie* is more canonic and more quintal, has more dissonances, and is on the whole simpler, more primitive in expression. A fourth resembles the third, but is more dissonant.

One *Gloria in excelsis* is quite somber, opening after the intonation with a long unison passage. The counterpoint after this is imitative and non-differentiated. Another version is non-imitative and seems more directly felt. Two more versions derive from the latter, but one is incomplete. A fifth *Gloria* resembles the first, but is also incomplete. There are three *Credos:* one is stronger, more medieval, and at the same time more personal in feeling than the others. In the first version of this Mass, Thomson incorporated the *Sanctus* he had written in 1921. Another version using children's voices suggests coming-of-age, for at the beginning the children sing flowingly over dissonant quintal counterpoint in the men's part, but in the final cadence they lose this differentiation. One *Benedictus qui venit* is very much like the early *Sanctus,* but the entrance of the tone-clusters is inverted. Another *Benedictus* has long lines in tertial four-part canon followed by a free cadence. One *Agnus Dei* recapitulates its *Kyrie,* the noble, swinging one. A second has a tenor solo that dramatically holds a high A flat for four measures fortissimo and then three measures pianissimo. The chorus that accompanies this solo has an ostinato on the word *miserere,* two eighths and two quarters, recalling a similar ostinato in the *crucifixus* section of the *Credo* (this relation suggesting more than anything else in the Mass the rightness of the original title, *Missa Tragica*).

After writing (in 1934) a *Missa Brevis* No. 2, for women's voices, Thomson called a halt to the revisions of this earlier Mass, under the impression that he had used parts of the first work in the second. However, even superficial examination shows that the Mass for Women's Voices differs from the other both in conception and in detail.

An independent *Agnus Dei,* a canon at the unison for three equal voices, was composed in the spring of 1924. Beginning with the *Tribulationes,* more and more of Thomson's counterpoint is imitative, and canons are not rare, nor, later on, are fugues. The supposition that this development reflects greater use of the rational faculties is not tenable; for so thoroughly trained a musician writing a canon or a fugue is much like putting the right foot in front of the left. Most modern canons are wooden; not so this *Agnus Dei.* It flows beautifully in tertial triple counterpoint, two open octaves and a modal cadence coming as a surprise toward the end of each of the three sections, which are identical, except that the voices exchange entrances.

Three Antiphonal Psalms for chorus of women's voices was completed this same year. Only the third, strictly speaking, is antiphonal. The other two present single lines, the one exception being a passage in organum in the first. The antiphonal entrances in the third piece are first secundal, later quintal, and finally mixed. In the second part of this work *grupetti* add interest to the rhythm, which even without them is fluent and metrically varied. Again there is no clear observance of tetrachordal method, though the cadence of the first psalm is a series of skips of a fourth. A month later, Thomson completed *Three Sentences from the Song of Solomon* for tenor and piano—"Thou that Dwellest in the Gardens," "Return, O Shulamite," and "I Am My Beloved's." That the somewhat pentatonic melodies seem slightly artificial, and that the parlor seems the proper locale for the performance of these effective songs is owing to the use of outmoded harmonic devices in the piano accompaniments. The fifths that had provided the body of most of Thomson's previous work appear only in a few cadences, giving the effect of contrast that exotic objects picked up by a traveler give to his home.

A single work was written in 1925—the *Synthetic Waltzes* for piano duet. This piece brings the dance-hall into the American parlor, but it does not roll up the carpets. The changes from one waltz to another would surely embarrass the feet, but they delight one's feelings. Thomson was encouraged in his interest in waltzes (and tangos) by Satie's not having disdained to write them. But he does not present them here "straight" as Satie did in *Je te veux* and *Tendrement,* nor even much transformed, as they are in *Mercure* and *Relâche.* He highlights aspects of them and brings about juxtapositions that describe his feelings about them, exactly as the neo-romantic painters work. In one waltz two regular eight-measure phrases are pushed and pulled in the melody into a 7:9 relationship while the accompaniment is kept regular, exaggerating the distortion. Another waltz, made more difficult by *grupetti* of 4 and 2 against 3, and of 3 against 2 together with a meter of 2 against a meter of 3, is followed by an extremely simple and innocent one, the picture presented being that of a teacher playing *secundo* and a hard-working pupil playing the advanced *primo.* In still another waltz, canonic means are used first to collapse and then to spread out the melody beyond the bounds of expectation. Toward the end, the whole picture is wittily enlarged by showing the introduction and interlude material upon which the waltzes are strung to be not only a waltz in its own right, but the finest of them all, worthy of being carried step by step up a chromatic stairway, at the top of which it receives the applause of the final cadence. In this work Thomson initiated his life-long friendship with the waltz (and with the key of A Major). Two years previously, he had made advances to the tango. In his opinion, these two dances alone, in our century, are capable of a rich and varied musical expression. In this writer's opinion the waltz for Thomson is of good character, full of fun and high spirits, whereas the tango, dark, sinuous, and no stranger to evil, takes from his hands confidential messages of a more somber nature.

His next work, the *Sonata da chiesa,* is altogether extraordinary. Finished in Saint-Cloud, February, 1926, it was the fruit of several months' hard labor supplemented by advice from Nadia Boulanger. Because it was the last to benefit by such supplementary treatment, Thomson refers to it as his "graduation piece" in the dissonant style of the time. (In the days of music-guilds it would have been termed his "master-piece.") He had posed himself the problem of writing expressively and compactly for five disparate instruments, E flat clarinet, D trumpet, viola, F horn, and trombone. This was not a haphazard choice: it gave him two sopranos, two altos, and two tenor-bass instruments (the horn being alto, tenor, or bass, the trombone tenor or bass) so disparate that achieving a blending of them would indicate his acquired ingenuity. He also set himself the task of writing a sizable work that would receive favorable criticism from Nadia Boulanger. (He needed her praise, which alone could free him from her, for he was still smarting from her reaction to his *Missa Brevis* No. 1, a work in which he had not been reticent in expressing feelings he had believed to be profound.) Thus, there is in the *Sonata da chiesa* both an element of sureness and an element of caution. Every note can be explained, but not explained away, for in writing this advanced student work Thomson was faithful to his feelings but careful to objectify them in both musical and extra-musical terms.

The first of its three movements is a Chorale. Its program, unstated, reports a Negro church service that Thomson had attended in Kansas City. Three distinct parts in the exposition are followed first by the development (elaboration and extension) of the first two and then by a larger similar development of them plus a repetition (with added weight) of the third part. This third part is the chorale from which the movement derives its title; it represents a congregation breaking into song after their Amen-like responses to the sermon. The musical language in which this report is written has overtones of Mediterranean, even North African, melisma superimposed on informal two-part counterpoint in which the lines are often drawn in parallel fifths and ninths. The second movement is a Tango in which a plucked string-like accompaniment is given to the wind instru-

SONATA DÀ CHIESA TANGO

ments, while a melody that would become any of them is assigned to the viola. The perversity of this treatment is pointed up
in the B section of the ABA piece by scoring that allows the
instruments to do what is natural to them, producing by this
momentary turn toward propriety a fascinating intensity. The
whole movement is cast in a low tessitura, with the horn relegated
mostly to the bass and the upper register of the E flat clarinet not
employed. What with this somber range and the presence of
both ecclestiastical fifths and minor seconds in dissonant relation to one another and to the melody, one is confronted with
a work in which the question is no longer of gargoyles but of
the celebration of a Black Mass in the very House of the Lord.
That House, known in the Orient to be a duplex lodging good
and evil in equal portions, has not often in the Occident been
hospitable to his Satanic Majesty. For us, accustomed to pursuing
material matters and to ignoring states of spiritual awareness, a
work like this church sonata brings to the surface of our consciousness the deep memory within us of something not expres-
sible in words, something we have known in darker ages but
have, since the advent of Reason, chosen to forget. The result, to
say the least, is disturbing.

The third movement of the *Sonata da chiesa* is a Fugue
to end fugues. It is double (the second subject derived from the
Tango) and has inversions, retrogrades, retrograde-inversions,
augmentations, counter-subjects, and modal alterations of the
themes. In the peroration it makes use of all these plus the
chorale from the first movement, which itself concludes in canon.
Its *grupetti* and the final appearance on the trombone of the
first subject (a widening to the extent of an octave and a fourth

SONATA DA CHIESA FUGUE

· 1926 (February)
Copyright 1945 by Virgil Thomson. Published by New Music Edition.

of Bach's E Minor "Wedge" theme) provide the finishing touches. This Fugue is a field day for the procedure studied in the *Fanfare,* that of following the letter of rules but not their spirit. But here, because of the detailed workmanship, the result is hilarious. One sympathizes with this bright student who knew the rules so well that he could use them to turn out an unruly result and think, in handing the finished work to his teacher, "That'll show you!" Nadia Boulanger's only comment was: "It is not the kind of music I would write, but it is entirely successful. I have no criticism." Though not pleased, Thomson was satisfied. His subsequent works clearly demonstrate the freedom he had won, at no little labor, for himself and for his music.

The most salient characteristic of his early works is their emphasis on spontaneity of feeling. They reflect a refusal to use rules or an insistence on misusing them, perhaps because at first he had taken them too seriously. Without *a priori* structure or consistent method, his music up to this point is a direct expression of his attitude toward life, of his perception of truth being beyond good and evil alike. The material is varied, but when it loses its novelty for him, he becomes bored with it and treats it impatiently. His refusal to put into action his personal sense of order and discipline deprives his youthful effusions of a place in the intellectual world despite the fact that the *Sonata da chiesa* and the *Pastorale on a Christmas Plainsong* remain explosive in effect. His position in relation to the art of music is that of an independent mystic in relation to established religion. As the visions of Blake leave the Catholic Church unmoved, so modern music is not likely to change its course because of Virgil Thomson's power to express his feelings.

2

IN 1926 THOMSON SKETCHED THE FIRST TWO MOVEMENTS OF THE *Symphony on a Hymn Tune* and wrote *Susie Asado,* his first work with a text by Gertrude Stein. Both the words and the music of this song with piano accompaniment are extremely funny. Its humor is the kind known as "dead-pan." The minimal musical events employed in the piano part are preceded and followed by silences. Stripped of context, they resemble the sounds that issue from single percussion instruments. Though fresh in effect, they are in themselves as commonplace as the is's and the and's of Miss Stein's prose. Elements of C Minor are present, its tonic triad and its straight scale (distorted by being stated in parallel sevenths and once parallel ninths that turn back into parallel sevenths); but these elements are so isolated that the key itself

SYMPHONY ON A HYMN TUNE

is not established. "Casey Jones" puts in a brief appearance, and one cadence suggests a hymn tune. A triad on the tonic built up of fifths instead of thirds is used as an ostinato in a 3/4 meter. Another ostinato employs a single B flat grace—noted C. The tonic triad is outlined once more, and the word *unison* provokes a new triad of fifths based on the dominant. The song ends here, and one finds oneself a little more innocent and a little more idiotic for having enjoyed it.

Perceiving that he was within a stone's throw of the mysterious

138

land of drums and cymbals, Thomson decided to explore it. To this end he revised and added to his earlier *Three Sentences from the Song of Solomon*. These songs, which already diverged from straight diatonic scales in the direction of the pentatonic, were sufficiently exotic to suggest scrapping their original piano accompaniments and substituting one for percussion instruments.

Gertrude Stein

SUSIE ASADO

Sweet, sweet, sweet, sweet, sweet,   tea.—   Su - sie A - sa - do.

1926 (April)

The result was *Five Phrases from the Song of Solomon* for soprano and percussion (tomtom, cymbals, gong, and woodblock). The melodies of the first, second, and fourth songs are those of the earlier work with few changes. The third, "O, My Dove," is more modal in character than the others; the fifth, "By Night," is by reason of its crescendos and repeated notes more dramatic and insistent. "Return, O Shulamite," the second song, is unaccompanied. The first, "Thou That Dwellest in the Gardens," and the third, "O, My Dove," flow above a tomtom ostinato (quarternote sound, quarter-note silence). The sole appearance of the gong is at the end of "O, My Dove," where a single stroke is sounded. In the fourth song, "I Am My Beloved's," there is more rhythmic interest in the cymbal accompaniment owing to the variation of the ostinato employed (♩ ♪ ♩ ♪) by means of permutation (♩ ♪ ♩ ♩ ♪ and ♩ ♩ ♪ ♩ ♪) and the use of contracted rhythmic patterns. The woodblock accompaniment of the last song, "By Night," is the most elaborately developed: five static motives, really four, since B and D, framing central C, are identical (♫♫, ♪♩ ♪, ♫, ♪♩ ♪, ♫♫) are used in serial or "circular" method (*e.g.*, ABCDCDCDEDEDDCDCDEDED). That this method was followed freely rather than rigorously is shown by a passage in which it is not observed (CEDCDE).

As might be expected, Thomson's next work, *Five Two-Part Inventions,* for piano, is not exotic at all. It lies at the halfway house established by Bach to provide refreshment for climbers from the valley of canon to the peak of fugue. But on noticing that a theme in the first Invention has the same wedge-shape as the first subject of the Fugue of the *Sonata da chiesa,* and that the fourth and fifth Inventions closely follow the Bach double counterpoint models, one perceives that Thomson had reached the top in the *Sonata da chiesa* and was here on his downward way. Wit appears, but as he drew on previous works to pay his compliments to baroque structure, it is not clear whether that wit is directed against Bach or against himself. The imitations are secundal and sometimes quintal in the first, whereas in the second, fourth, and fifth Inventions they are all at the octave. Some loss of interest overcame Thomson in the course of putting these pieces together, for the imaginative workmanship of the *Sonata da chiesa* is absent. A somewhat fresher feeling enters in the third Invention, a piece that simply flows, as a stream flows through a landscape. Unhampered by the presence of canon, this centrally placed Invention shows Thomson unconcerned with the façades of broken rules that he had been so busy erecting.

THE TIGER
William Blake

Ti - ger! ti - ger! burn ing bright

mf martellato ma sostenuto possibile. senza pedale

1926

His next work, *The Tiger,* for soprano and piano, with text by William Blake, suggests a music of which the rules have not yet been formulated. It carries repetition to a point unfamiliar to those restrained by the bonds of the European Renaissance. The

accompaniment of the modal and freely declamatory melody is a
5/4 ostinato passage (repeated 28 times) followed by another 5/4
ostinato passage (repeated 18 times) followed by still another 5/4
ostinato passage (repeated 8 times). The last, totally different
from the others, which are arbitrarily percussive in character,
outlines the C Major triad beneath a tetrachordal ostinato, B, A,
G sharp, F sharp. The voice is for an alarming moment left unaccompanied, after which the first ostinato recommences and is
ruthlessly repeated 14 times. In this work, more than in any previous one, Thomson walks arm in arm with Satie, who had written his *Vexations,* a piece lasting 52 seconds to be played 840
times in a row, and his interminable *Musique d'ameublement.*
In his own way he also keeps faith with Debussy, who had asserted that any sounds in any context were henceforth to be used
for musical purposes. *The Tiger* recalls the works of Edgar
Varèse, too, not by any specific detail, but by their highly imaginative use of unconventional sound. Had the two not crossed
the Atlantic in opposite directions in the twenties, Thomson's
subsequent development might have followed a different course.
Encouraged by Varèse in those lively days before the League of
Composers took over musical New York, as he had been encouraged by Sauguet in Paris, he might have continued in the direction indicated by *Susie Asado* and *Five Phrases* or developed the
facet that *The Tiger* indicates. It was, of course, the word *anvil*
and Blake's question about "fearful symmetry" that propelled him
into the unknown.[7]

In his next work, *Ten Easy Pieces and a Coda,* for piano,
Thomson indulges his sense of humor—in this instance quite
amiably, for he was writing for a friend more familiar with contemporary art than skilled in piano playing. He calls these his
"baby pieces," though they were not composed for children. The
first, "A Plain Song (and its accompaniment)," which is *slow and
soft,* and quite beautiful, consists of two Gregorian-style melodies,
one for each hand, which always move by parallel motion in
thirds, fourths, and fifths except in the cadence, which introduces
a seventh. The second, "Light Fingers," marked *some faster and
louder,* is more odd than pleasing. The left hand, no longer

copying the right, is less melodic. The third, "Pathos," marked *strong and not too slow, dignified,* has an oom-pah-pah Alberti bass that refuses to fit the scalewise melody. The fourth, "Counting," marked *fairly loud but not fast,* has a tonic-dominant melody suggestive of *Chopsticks,* the left hand playing scales and an Alberti bass. The fifth, "Marching," marked *not too fast, but punch it,* contains some chords in the right hand, first in inversion, then in root position. The sixth, "Two-Part Invention," *medium slow,* ends with a bugle call. The seventh, "Two People," *medium fast,* contains only black notes in the right hand. The first phrase sounds therefore Chinese, though the second resembles more an out-of-tune hymn. The eighth, "Improvising," begins black and white, moves on to tone-clusters, and is full of surprising shifts of register. The ninth, "The Night Before Christmas," *quite slow and soft,* is written in what Thomson calls his "imbecile style" and suggests a barcarolle by its meter and slow-rolling bass. The tenth, "Assembly," marked *military style,* is right hand black, left hand white, but not at all Chinese. Its fourths and fifths show that it is a hunting song. The coda has concealed canons—concealed because the imitating part, before providing the required imitation, busies itself otherwise.

Delighted with his seemingly aimless travels in these lowlands of humor, and not too sure whether he was moving about or standing still, letting ideas come to him, Thomson next wrote four sets of *Variations on Sunday School Tunes,* for organ: *Come, Ye Disconsolate; There's Not a Friend Like the Lowly Jesus (No, Not One); Will There Be Any Stars in My Crown?* and *Shall We Gather at the River?* Taking the form of a gadfly, he proceeds to torment the noble and heroic pipe-organ. The word variations here has no other meaning than varieties: anything that would make the largest musical instrument in the world sound ridiculous. The result is a series of miniature crimes impossible to commit because no God-fearing or even music-respecting church would permit the performance of these works as part of a service. In *Come, Ye Disconsolate* the theme goes along incorrectly both rhythmically and harmonically until a simple octave passage tosses aside the whole problem. The first variation is a plainsong

for the organist's feet, three measures of it in octaves. The second
provides him with five-finger exercises in a series of keys that is
utterly non-sequitur. In the third, a twice-repeated phrase with
carefully prepared false relations brings about an ostinato of
flat-hand tone-clusters and trills and an ornamented brief restatement of the whole. The tone-clusters idea continues in the fourth,
with one manual playing in D flat Major, the other in D Major.
In the fifth, major chords are piled up to create by their parallel
motion in two-parts contradictions that any child could understand. The sixth is a barcarolle for merry-go-round. The seventh consists of scales in various keys, and has a Bach-like
pedal interlude with trills and octaves. The last is a fugue, but
in name only, a house of fun in which standard fugal practices
are reduced to absurdities that include a pompous restatement
of the original hymn.

The concluding fugue in *There's Not a Friend Like the Lowly
Jesus* is even more absurd. This set also has a barcarolle (Variation No. 6) and a strict canon (No. 7)—strict because it was more
comical to write it that way. *Will There Be Any Stars in My
Crown?* is memorable for the frequent appearance of the casual
direction to the organist: "Add something"; also for the raucous
and highly danceable fugue. *Shall We Gather at the River?* points
to surfeit with the whole idea, for Variations 2, 3, and 4 are
nearly identical. Possibly Thomson had come to suspect that in
thus spending his time he was not only getting even with the
organ, but also letting the organ get even with him. In another
sense, these Variations were not a waste of time. They provided
an escape valve for that resentment toward Protestant Church
music that Thomson knew he felt but did not wish to express
in his *Symphony on a Hymn Tune,* of which the first three movements were being completed in sketch at the time, late in 1926,
when the first three of these *Variations and Fugues* were thrown
off. The Symphony, too, was to include high spirits, but, in contrast to the Variations, it was to be an ambitious and noble work.
After bidding a derisive farewell to the pipe-organ, Thomson
turned to the orchestra in his most pleasing and punctilious
manner.

He divided his attention at this time between his Symphony and setting texts by Gertrude Stein. In putting *Susie Asado* to music he had, so to speak, held a microscope over the text, emphasizing by parallel musical means the discontinuity of the words. After completing three movements of the Symphony, he wrote *Preciosilla,* for voice and piano, and *Capital, Capitals,* "for 4 men and a piano." In *Preciosilla,* rather than examining under a microscope the details of Gertrude Stein's methods, he made use, so to speak, of a telescope, for viewing the intellectual significance of those methods. Recognizing the "modernity" of her texts, he chose to set off *Preciosilla* with an accompaniment clearly not modern. Its division into a recitative and an aria transports the hearer back to the eighteenth century, somewhere south of the Alps or east of the Rhine. The words remind us that we are living in the twentieth century; the music convinces us that we are listening to a baroque cantata.

In earlier works like the *Synthetic Waltzes,* Thomson had experienced the pleasures of time-travel, and he was not by nature afraid of being reactionary. But he had an itch to appear before the world as an up-to-the-minute composer or at least as a member of the avant-garde. In *Susie Asado* he had shared with Gertrude Stein the burden of being "modern." With *Preciosilla* he chose to appear outlandishly behind the times because the words he was setting were outlandishly ahead of them. In this song Miss Stein shoulders the whole burden, and Thomson's embarrassment over the situation is evident in his music. In the thirtieth and thirty-first measures, the false relation D flat-D natural stands out in a cadence in which the voice-leading is forced. Some of the extended sequential passages verge on parody. *Jingle Bells* is suggested through such an impressive harmonic setting that it might easily escape notice. On the other hand, genuine emotional intensity is achieved in the cadences of both the recitative and the aria—in the former with the words "Go, go, (*p: con intensità*) go go go. Go go. Not guessed. (*dim.*) Go go (*espressivo*). Toasted Susie (*ff: maestoso*) is my (*poco rall.*) ice cream." Throughout both songs, particularly at the cadential points, Thomson makes clear that by simply borrowing an earlier musical manner one may compensate for the absence of familiarity and sentimentality in an ultra-modern text.

In *Capital, Capitals,* his third setting of a Stein text, he assumed the attitude of a manufacturer who, in possession of the necessary patents, decides to go into production. He did not limit himself to the means employed in *Susie Asado,* a three-page work, and in *Preciosilla,* a nine-page work, but in this thirty-four-page work made full use of chant means, which he owned by right of so many of his early works. Thus, in one instance, seventy-one words of text roll by on one tone, though out of the total of fifty-five such chant-like passages in this song, the average number of words appearing on a repeated tone without any given rhythmic pattern is a more modest seventeen and a half. We have noticed in Thomson's earliest works the fluent character of his rhythm, derived from the natural rhythms of speech. In his Stein settings he retains this rhythmic fluency, at the same time bringing to a point of high refinement a knack for setting words so that they are not only singable, but also understandable. This ability had been of special advantage to him in framing Stein texts with old-fashioned accompaniment. Had the words not been made intelligible, an entire piece might have risked slipping anywhere from fifty to eight hundred years backward in time.

Capital, Capitals is not a contrapuntal work. The text represents "a conversation among the four capitals of Provence—Aix, Arles, Avignon, and Les Baux," no two voices singing at the same time. Its static nature, which seems never to be getting anywhere, is given an accompaniment that from the opening trumpet-like octaves on C to the closing percussively repeated middle C seems to be announcing that something is about to happen. The fact that the piece takes a long time to accomplish nothing is the secret of its strength and its effectiveness. Thomson had again observed Gertrude Stein's work from a distance, but instead of concerning himself with its intellectual characteristics, he had observed its form—the expressiveness of its continuity, which is static rather than progressive. There are no climaxes; now and then it becomes luminous, but it is never excited. Just as he had opposed old to new in *Preciosilla,* he here opposes the form-feeling in the music (something is about to happen) to the form-feeling in the text (nothing is ever going to happen). Besides the imitation of trumpets, there are left-hand tremolandos suggesting tympani, treble tremolandos suggesting xylophones, high major chords suggesting church bells, ornaments and scale passages suggesting Czerny exercises, step-by-step enlargement of intervals suggesting vocalises, a Spanish passage suggesting the Mediterranean, and a Protestant hymn tune suggesting Thomson himself. It is significant that this hymn tune passage accompanies the phrase "as they say in the way they say they can express in this way tenderness." The text is so crowded with words that some means of setting them smoothly was imperative. For this reason *Capital, Capitals* is largely in the key of C without any chromaticism. To avoid monotony, black notes are introduced diatonically in the Spanish section. Thereafter there are superimpositions in different keys, the most painful being a reiterated C natural in the voice over an A major triad in the accompaniment (the words here are "very happily properly placed as a castle"). This dissonant relation is repeated just before the final cadence (under the words "of precaution, of accentuation and of attraction"). Thomson also develops here a mannerism in the use of diatonic scale passages: two or more scales beginning together and ending quite surprisingly apart, or the reverse. Both these usages had appeared casually in earlier works. Here they are an integral element in the continuity.[8]

While setting *Susie Asado, Preciosilla,* and *Capital, Capitals,* Thomson did not have in mind the writing of an opera with text by Gertrude Stein, but to all who heard these songs it was evident that such an opera would "work." Thomson and Miss Stein were both convinced that it would, so at Thomson's invitation she began in the spring of 1927 the libretto of *Four Saints in Three Acts.* Thomson sketched Act I of his setting the same year and then wrote *Une Mélodie dite "La Valse grégorienne"* [9] for voice and piano, a continuous setting of four poems by Georges Hugnet: *Les Ecrevisses, Grenadine, La Rosée,* and *Le Wagon immobile.* This was Thomson's first encounter, as a composer, with the French language, his first gesture in music of friendship

FOUR SAINTS IN THREE ACTS

for the people among whom he had chosen to live and work. These short lyrical poems are strung together in the necklace arrangement used in the *Synthetic Waltzes*. But the waltzes of *La Valse grégorienne* have a French folksong flavor, lightly spiced

LA VALSE GRÉGORIENNE
Georges Hugnet

1927 (November)

for the most part, but heavily in the last song, by the admixture of ingredients that give a declamatory or ecclesiastical taste. *Les Ecrevisses* (in C Major moving to A Minor) is an ingratiatingly innocent waltz with a scalewise melody and an "oompah" accompaniment. Twelve measures of 3/8 are preceded by two measures of the trumpet-like octaves employed in *Capital, Capitals* and followed by three vamp-like measures in B flat Major (a key out of relation to both the section it ends and the one it announces, both of which are in C Major).

In *Grenadine,* Thomson plays a trick that was to become one of his favorites. A 3/8 accompaniment goes on in blissful ignorance of the fact that the melody is in 2/4. Confident that by putting metrical matters out of kilter he had provided sufficient complexity to maintain interest, he limited the harmonic accompaniment to a see-sawing between tonic and dominant. The four-measure vamp on F Major overlapping the end of the melody similarly ignores the fact that it concludes a piece in C Major and introduces one in A Major, growing louder with repetition. *La Rosée* (in A Major) begins *p subito* and in an innocent mood. Though it employs seventh chords and passing dissonances in the melody, the waltz rhythm is undisturbed. A reminder of Satie occurs at one point, the first to appear in Thomson's music: the sequential passage, F sharp Minor, C sharp Minor, D Major, B Minor, F sharp Minor, G Major triads in succession. The song moves without transition into the final waltz, but not without introducing a ninth chord on the dominant that seems slightly out of place. *Le Wagon immobile* (in G Major) achieves dramatic expressivity as a result of the voice remaining almost throughout on the dominant, declamatory fashion, while the accompaniment, no longer that of a waltz, moves from one triad to another in liturgical progressions. The dissonance so highly prized in *Capital, Capitals,* is again brought about here, for at the most poignant moment, where the voice moves to E flat, the accompaniment states a major triad on C. "Avez-vous pleuré ce soir comme moi," following a brief return to the waltz, is declaimed on D and leads to the dominant cadence on this note ("devant un wagon immobile?") dramatically intoned *ff* and an octave lower. There is a fastidious elegance about *La Valse grégorienne.* Simple as was Thomson's choice of materials, his handling of subtle variations of scalewise melodies in *Grenadine* and of displacements of conventional phraseology in *La Rosée* reflects the influence of Paris.

After working again for a few months on *Four Saints,* Thomson relaxed by writing two more pieces for voice and piano, both with French texts: *Trois Poèmes de la Duchesse de Rohan* and *Le Berceau de Gertrude Stein* (Georges Hugnet). The *Trois Poèmes* are three separate songs: *A son Altesse la Princesse Antoinette Murat* (the history, told with both wit and respect, of a Russian princess turned vegetarian who tended her own garden in the south of France); *Jour de chaleur aux bains de mer* (a

LA SEINE
Duchesse de Rohan

Est - il rien de plus beau que la Sein - e la nuit lors - que, Noble.

tous feux é - teint, l'astr - e blanc re - splen - dit sur Pa - ris qui s'en - dort? É - tan -

dant sa grande ai - le, la lune tu - té - lai - re - lors vei - lle sur el - le.

1928 (May)

beach picture); and *La Seine* (a description of Paris by night).
A new kind of humor and a new musical means are evident in
A son Altesse. The means are those of narrative French folksong.
The harmonization, by using the subdominant region, modulatory sequences, seventh and altered chords, gives to the simplicity
of the over-all musical picture the character of the development
section of a sonata. In form, the piece resembles a story that begins and ends pleasantly, but goes dramatic in its central section.
Here appears for the first time that special brand of humor
which, characteristic of Thomson the music critic, may be called
"Herald Tribune"; a humor distinguished by clarity of observa-

tion (high-fidelity reporting), elegance of manner (not without dashes of vulgarity, partly put in for shock purposes, partly for drawing attention to its own elegance), and an almost surgical removal of the fatter kinds of human feeling.[10]

The 3/8-2/4 opposition of *Grenadine* is again employed in *Jour de chaleur aux bains de mer*, and the waltz accompaniment is likewise a tonic-dominant oompah in C Major. The melody, however, is not based on the major and minor seconds of the diatonic scale, but rather on that scale's tonic triad, expressed over the range of a twelfth. Halfway through the song, the harmony is sent on an errand to other tonal regions from which it does not return, but where it settles down in B Major to its original chordal melody. In the final measure, B Major turns out to have been a dominant mistaken all the time for a tonic. *La Seine*, barcarolle-like in feeling and characterized by economy of means, exhibits the next step in melody-writing, composing a melody not on chords in root position, but on chords in first inversion, and not only on triads, but on seventh chords as well. It is two-part writing. When the melody outlines a harmony, only a bass is added. When it moves stepwise, the accompaniment fills in a complete harmony. The cadences of this song all contain the false relation E flat-E natural (the E flat moving through D to C, the E natural to F), the same one Thomson had used in *Preciosilla*. On its second appearance it is repeated, heard again two measures later, and at the end a last time, leaving the listener suspended on the dominant F rather than at rest a fifth lower. One part of this song exploits the stuck-record idea, this time expressively rather than impatiently. Grandiose melodic heights and far-reaching harmonic implications convey Thomson's reaction to a text stating that whereas bourgeois beings are "dans leurs maisons clôses, les artistes sont seuls à pénétrer ces choses." The unconsciously comical lines were the more choice to him for their naïveté.

His next work bears the elaborate title page: *"Le Berceau de Gertrude Stein" ou "Le Mystère de la rue de Fleurus," Huit poèmes de Georges Hugnet to which have been added a Musical Composition by Virgil Thomson entitled "Lady Godiva's Waltzes."*

This is the string-of-waltzes type of piece with which we are by now well acquainted. The usual tonic or dominant call to attention is here a trill on the submediant. This may be construed as balancing a surprise cadence at the very end. The 3/8-2/4 opposition, already familiar, is here varied so that the voice sings the French-style melody (based this time on both scales and first inversion triads) in 3/4, while the accompaniment, a tonic-dominant oompah, remains in 2/4. The subdominant is substituted for the dominant once. The melody ends with the stuck-record idea employed in *La Seine*. The second poem has a more elaborate accompaniment, a series of four ostinati in 6/4, except one (the third) in 8/4, and tonic-dominant oompahs in different keys (C Major, A Minor, D Major) excepting the third, which introduces the subdominant. These ostinati are repeated the following number of times: 5, 3⅔, 5½, and 4⅓. The melody continues that of the first poem, introducing *grupetti* and concluding with an ostinato of its own, in 6/4, based on the first inversion of the tonic triad of D Major. The third poem continues the 6/4 ostinato idea in the accompaniment, but has only two ostinati. The first is in C Major, the second in A Minor. Both are tonic-dominant. The first is repeated nine times, the second four times. And a cadence is provided (IV, V, I), the tonic being treated to a trip through a little more than three octaves. For a change, the melody (E, D, C, E, D, C, E, D, C, etc.) begins rather than ends with the stuck-record idea.

The fourth poem has no ostinati in either melody or accompaniment, and thus gives an effect of aimless wandering from one note and chord to the next. The text offers an explanation: "Nous ne savons plus danser, Gertrude, Gertrude. Nous avons perdu l'habitude. Gertrude, Gertrude, Gertrude, apprenez-nous à danser." The fifth is written in both 3/4 and 4/4, the melody being irregularly in 4/4, whereas the oompah accompaniment is consistently that of a waltz. At the point where Miss Stein's manner of wearing her hair, "coupés à la Titus," is described, the modal harmony is reminiscent of Satie's *Gymnopédies*, though rhythm and tempo are quite different. The sixth reverts to the idea of accompaniment 2/4, melody 3/4, but the accompaniment modulates a great deal, whereas the melody insists on staying in C Major until the end, where it adopts A Major and shifts to a 4/4 meter. The seventh is in E Major. The previous double rhythm continues. The last poem is simply an extended cadence in E Major, with special emphasis given the subdominant. All waltz movement has vanished, just as it had in "Le Wagon immobile," also the last in a chain of Hugnet settings. Nine words are chanted after the fashion of *Capital, Capitals,* with E Major made clear again in the voice alone. And while the pianist unexpectedly plays the C Major scale cut into halves (one given to the right hand, the other to the left, in contrary motion), *Lady Godiva's Waltzes* ends on the open octave C-C, proving that the composer, unlike some listeners, had not forgotten that the piece began in that key. The frequent appearance of the word ostinato in the descriptions of both *The Tiger* and *Le Berceau de Gertrude Stein* does not indicate that technical relation exists between the two, for the ostinati in *The Tiger* were discovered sounds, their meaning unmodified by any context, while those in *Le Berceau* are made of commonplaces that from an ultra-sophisticated point of view might be considered as novelties. But to be seen in this light they would have to be treated as novelties, that is, freed from their usual modifying conventions, which, in *Le Berceau,* they are not.

After his victory in the "battle of Boulanger"—the *Sonata da chiesa* marked both the end of a campaign and the signing of a truce—Thomson began his *Symphony on a Hymn Tune.* As might be expected, he exhibits in this work a happy-go-lucky frame of mind. In a sense, he sets out to do for the symphony what he had done for the fugue in the third movement of the *Sonata da chiesa,* and for double counterpoint in the *Five Two-Part Inventions:* to take it for a spin, so that he would never afterward have to concern himself with it as a problem. He analyzes the *Symphony on a Hymn Tune* thus: "It is a set of variations on the hymn 'How Firm a Foundation'; each movement consists of a further set of variations tightened-up in various ways, the first in the manner of a sonata, the second as a Bach chorale-prelude, the third as a passacaglia. The fourth is twice tightened-up, once as a fugato, once as a rondo." However, one may observe the appearance not only of "How Firm a Foundation," but also of "Yes, Jesus Loves Me," "For He's a Jolly Good Fellow" (a secular "hymn" on male fellowship), and passages suggesting both Roman Catholic and Anglican Church music. All of these themes have musical aspects that distinguish them from one another. "How Firm a Foundation" is a melody based on the second inversion of a tonic major triad. "Yes, Jesus Loves Me" is based on the second inversion of a seventh chord on the submediant. "For He's a Jolly Good Fellow" is a diatonic scalewise tune. The injections of Roman Church music are modal and generally heard as parallel open fifths. And relationships among all these themes permit pun-like uses of them. The upbeat of "How Firm a Foundation" (from the dominant through the submediant to the tonic) suggests the minor third characteristic of the seventh chord of "Jesus Loves Me," and the seconds in both tunes suggest those of "For He's a Jolly Good Fellow" and of the Gregorianisms.

While working on the *Symphony on a Hymn Tune,* Thomson hit upon a device of harmonization which becomes so frequent in his later work that it amounts to his personal signature. Here, it is a means of referring simultaneously to sacred and secular life, Protestant and Roman Catholic. He harmonizes a descending scale (secular) in such a way that the lower voices move in parallel fifths (Roman), while the upper voices move in parallel thirds (Protestant). This device begets still another Thomsonism: the expression of ornaments (secular) usually found only in a solo line through four-part root-position harmony, with all parts moving simultaneously in trills or turns. Extended passages that parody Beethoven's scalewise sequences, a cowboy tune, a toy piano waltz, a march, a fugato, an unadorned descending scale four octaves long all serve to oppose aspects of secular life to each other and to the two churches. The title of the work might be *Musique concrète; Four Adventures in Collage Twenty Years Ahead of Their Time.* (Pierre Schaeffer first experimented with magnetic tape in 1946.) Its continuity is not that of narrative. It is related rather to painting, and to painting that substitutes for brush and pigment scissors, paste, and various ready-made materials. These materials retain their original colors, which are enhanced by juxtapositions and superimpositions, and the fact that their number is limited to four—lavish for symphony, economical for collage—excludes (if one excepts the irritating *cadenza obbligata* for trombone, piccolo, cello, and violin with which the first movement ends) the sense of bewilderment that so often accompanies collage, leaving the Symphony as transparent as it is brilliant.

The first two movements have a centrifugal energy. They move, like so many contemporary American works, outside their frame. One must rely on the keenness of one's listening powers to discover a center of interest. However, the following movements draw the attention first back to the work (the cadence of the third movement is a quotation from the first), then to the frame itself, a resounding reiteration of the tonic, A Major, thus diminishing the feeling of collage and asserting that of classical architecture. The work is clearly in A Major. Even the second movement, which is in D (a plagal relation), ends on its dominant A. This A is given a bell-like character suitable to the introspective mood into which the whistle of a distant passing train (a fragmentation of the first three notes of "How Firm a Foundation") seems to intrude itself. Both the first and third movements appear to end on B flat. Actually, in the third movement this lone note follows an utterly A Major composition. In the first, the situation is more serious: after devious wanderings, rest is taken on E flat Major, the tonic high in the sky of the piccolo, the dominant (B flat) deep in a pedal note of the trombone, and the violin and cello left trembling on the D and E of what must be a dominant seventh chord that leads to the annihilation of all tonality in a burst of pure percussion. The Devil, who, in the form of his tango, is conspicuously absent, must have guided Thomson's hand in writing this cadence that is so deceptively an assertion of the Evil One's tritone.

No tone among the twelve is left without emphasis in some part of the work, though at times, as in the case of F sharp or G flat, the emphasis is slight. Most of these emphases on distantly related tones occur in the first movement. This section gives initially the feeling of being in A flat and in G as strongly as in A Major. In its fourth part other tones are stressed. The fifth part is a recapitulation in A Major (expressed as a mode on D) of the Introduction. This is followed in the cadenza by tonal wanderings. The second movement offers only the subdominant and the minor of the tonic. The former is presented in certain places as simultaneously minor and major, producing an unforgettable octave passage that goes major seventh on one's ears in the most surprising way. The third movement (not a passacaglia) is based on an ostinato that never leaves A Major at all, being not only its "firm," but also its unswerving "foundation." The fourth has something of the divergent tonal references characteristic of the first, but the energy necessary for travel seems to have been spent. One wonders, considering the revisions of the fourth movement, particularly of its coda, whether the *Symphony on a Hymn Tune* has ever been properly concluded. The emphatic ending in the published version suggests the substitution of strength and loudness for conviction. The final pages are introduced in the same manner as the astounding cadenza of the first movement, but the expected passage revealing new elements does not occur. Still, one cannot complain,[11] for one has been lavishly entertained. Not even Thomson, whose habit as music critic it was to doze, could sleep during a performance of this work, which so touchingly recalls the Sunday services and Wednesday prayer meetings of provincial America. The orchestration is light, in every way French. The instruments have been treated like a highly flexible organ, able to move about without pause from one complex combination of stops to another. And the music has an extraordinary range of amplitudes, from the intimate "loudness" of the cadenza's quartet to the martial swing of the final tutti.

The success of Thomson's next work, the opera *Four Saints in Three Acts,* arises, like that of the *Symphony on a Hymn Tune,* from his affection for the elements employed. To this affection add that of his collaborators—Gertrude Stein, Florine Stettheimer, Maurice Grosser, John Houseman, and Frederick Ashton—for their respective materials. Multiply this by the sympathetic understanding mutually entertained, and the total is a quantity of quality. For the composition of *Four Saints,* Thomson applied a new creative method: seated at his piano, text before him, and singing, he improvised an entire act at a time until it became clear to him that the vocal line and the harmony had taken stable form. This procedure placed faith in what he terms the "well-springs of the unconscious," and does not view as a pollution the intrusion of individual taste and memory into those universal waters. One may question the purity of such a modus, however, for the thematic relationships in his score are very knowing, and few of them differ from his earlier practices. This score stands apart from his previous Stein settings in that it defies analysis. Scholarly study of it yields nothing but statistics. These give the impression that the materials of music, in contrast to those of poetry, are becoming impoverished. There are 111 tonic-dominants, 178 scale passages, 632 sequences, 38 references to nursery tunes, and one to "My Country, 'Tis of Thee." Where the text darts about in unpredictable directions, the accompaniment is merely repetitive, rarely more than linear, monophonic, and harmonic. The appearances of counterpoint are not only rare but also brief, and they occur for structural rather than textural or expressive effect. No attempt to grasp *Four Saints* will take hold of it. To enjoy it, one must leap into that irrational world from which it sprang, the world in which the matter-of-fact and the irrational are one, where mirth and metaphysics marry to beget comedy. And like any other work of high comedy, it leaves few traces. It does not clutter up the memory, but it elevates the spirit.

Some find the opera too long, though its playing time is only ninety minutes. Actually, it is as long as might have been mathematically expected. *Susie Asado* is 3 pages; *Preciosilla,* 9; *Capital, Capitals,* 34; *Four Saints* (in piano score) takes up 144. The implication is a continuation of a series of works, respectively, 648, 3,240, and 17,826 pages long. Short as it thus relatively appears to be, *Four Saints* is nonetheless a whole lifetime of time: a marriage. And as with successfully married couples, one wonders what either partner would be like without the other. The text, of course, may be read alone, for it is available separately. Divorced from it, the music would surely lose something of its strength. Its thematic relationships, though structural in effect, function insufficiently as architecture to produce an independent work. Going along with the text, its effect is additive, and this quality makes the ambiguity of the text less baffling, more immediately enjoyable. In fact, some academic institutions, bent upon gilding the pill of modern music, dispense *Four Saints* in the form of RCA-Victor's Thomson LP.

Four Saints started life in 1928 as a vocal line with figured bass. Midway in 1929 a piano score with all the harmonic filling was completed. Maurice Grosser worked out the scenario that year, and Gertrude Stein approved it. When the Hartford Atheneum production was arranged in 1933, Thomson decided to make deletions. In some instances the words alone were omitted, their original melody and accompaniment remaining. The cutting and the orchestral scoring were completed late in 1933. In actual performance a few more minor cuts were made in order to tighten-up the continuity. The published version observes all cuts. For other musical occasions samplings of *Four Saints* were made. These include *Pigeons on the Grass, Alas,* Recitation and Air for baritone solo with piano accompaniment, and *Saints' Procession,* in two versions, one for full chorus, one for men's chorus, both with piano accompaniment.

3

THOUGH THE FIRST PORTRAITS (SEÑORITA JUANITA DE MEDINA AC-
compagnée de sa mère and *Madame Marthe-Marthine,* composed
in 1928) were written between periods of intensive work on the
Hymn Tune Symphony and just after the completion of *Four
Saints,* they show no signs of being *oeuvres de repos.* Modest in
length and in instrumentation (both are for unaccompanied violin), they are concentrated movements in a new direction.[12] Their
point of departure is the Symphony and the opera. The line is
diatonic and triadic except when dissimilar musical objects are
presented in collage, but these pieces arrive at a degree of
atonality definitely twelve-tone in character, though not serial.
Whereas in Act I of *Four Saints* Thomson allows one hundred
and forty-six measures to pass before he introduces a C sharp
or D flat, and nearly another one hundred measures before introducing the twelfth tone (F sharp), all twelve tones appear in
Juanita de Medina four times (with the exception of C sharp
and F sharp the last time) in the course of the work's sixty measures. In *Madame Marthe-Marthine* they appear five times (with
the exception, again, of F sharp the last time) in the course of fifty-
nine measures. More Portraits for unaccompanied violin fol-

PORTRAIT de Mme. Marthe-Marthine

lowed: *Miss Gertrude Stein; Cliquet-Pleyel en fa; Georges Hugnet, poète et homme de lettres; Mrs. C. W. L.;* and *Sauguet,
d'après nature.* With the last, Thomson adopted the practice of a
painter who works in the same room with his sitter.

He did not always manage to catch in these Portraits a likeness
recognizable to persons acquainted with the sitter, many of them

159

having more to do with their composer than with their titles. In the present group this seems evident. The first two are adventurously chromatic and lacking key signatures. The next, *Gertrude Stein* and *Cliquet-Pleyel,* are tonal, the first entirely in

CLIQUET-PLEYEL en fa, son portrait pour un violon

1928 (October)

B flat Major, the second in F. The latter, however, includes passages both chromatic and atonal in character and so placed as to give a feeling of flying off the handle. Only thirty-five measures long, the *Hugnet* portrait nevertheless sets forth all twelve tones five times (if one grants the practice of overlaps, as Anton Webern did). *Mrs. C. W. L.* starts gaily in E flat Major, encounters familiar wedge and hunting-horn ideas, and survives only to be engulfed by the composer's interest in chromaticism and atonality. *Sauguet, d'après nature,* presents the twelve tones six times, only a G sharp being omitted the last time. Like *Señorita Juanita,* it opens with runs of stacked-up thirds. These pieces may be considered a portfolio of spontaneous, hastily dashed off sketches. Modest in length, they may be disregarded if found eventually to be lacking in interest; or they may serve for the germination of later works, or themselves be amplified through orchestration and grouped into suites.[13]

In December, 1928, Thomson left Paris for a four-months' trip to the United States, where he gave a one-man performance in New York of his *Four Saints* (at the house of Carl Van Vechten), directed from the piano a performance of *Capital, Capitals* at a Copland-Sessions concert, and conducted in Boston his *Sonata da chiesa.* Mabel Dodge Luhan, hearing *Four Saints,* predicted that it would "do to opera in America what Picasso did to Kenyon Cox." A more professional expression of admiration for Thomson's music came from Gaston Hamelin, first clarinetist of the Boston Symphony, who after playing in the *Sonata da chiesa* requested a work for clarinet ensemble. *Five Portraits for Four Clarinets* followed, scored for two clarinets in B flat or A, basset

PORTRAIT OF LADIES
for Four Clarinets

1929 (January)

horn, and bass clarinet. The first is a *Portrait of Ladies,* the second a *Portrait of Christian Bérard, prisonnier,* the third a *Portrait of a Young Man in Good Health.* The two others are both of Bérard, *Bébé Soldat* and *En personne* (*chair et os*). The Ladies were four direct descendants of Peter Stuyvesant whom Thomson had known and visited in various places. He observed that they produced in conversation—sometimes speaking all at once, sometimes singly or in twos and threes—a "lovely shape suggestive of a string quartet." The observation may account for the novel departures in this piece. Opening on a unison D with ascending scales of varying speeds (9 against 8 against 6 against 4, followed by 10 against 9 against 6 against 4), it reaches a major triad on E flat. Developments of this procedure take place later in the score. For example, the four start out from an octave D that ascends in the ratio 1:2:3:4, arriving at a complex of fifths (B flat, F, C, G). Though tonally asymmetrical scale devices appear in some of Thomson's earlier works, the extension of asymmetry to durations is fresh.

That he was not entirely at home with his thought in the *Portrait of Ladies* is shown by an error in the original notation, sixteenths being written where eighths would be correct. The scale ideas, however, are developed with virtuosity, these appearing in superimpositions of lines composed diatonically, tertially, and with fourths. The presence of all twelve tones, as in the Portraits for unaccompanied violin, occurs also, the major triad in E flat being followed by an atonal progression, and the last four measures of the piece presenting the full chromatic scale in the form of two complexes and two major triads (one on E flat, the other on E natural). The high spirits of this piece are probably the result of all the inventiveness called into play, but they are reinforced by the presence of waltz tunes, sudden flurries of scales, and a wholly unpredictable continuity.

The portrait of *Christian Bérard, prisonnier* was doubly drawn from life. While Thomson composed the music, Bérard was painting his portrait. Though less dodecaphonic than its predecessor, the piece contains the same ideas enhanced by more ornaments and a tendency to introduce canon and contrary motion into the scale passages. The *Young Man in Good Health* was Maurice Grosser, actually ill. But to Thomson his way of having a very bad cold, without loss of energy, only proved the more firmly his good health. This portrait is not an atonal experiment. It is in A Major, and is distinguished by further development of scale ideas, two lines starting from the extreme high and low points of the pieces's compass, approaching, crossing, and thus exchanging places. *Bébé Soldat* is also less twelve-tonish. Ornaments harmonized note by note (as in the *Hymn Tune Symphony*) and tango and waltz evocations are followed by references to the military life. With *En personne (chair et os)*, wrong-note diatonicism replaces the previous interest in atonality. However, with a Spanish touch, triads galore, and a carrying of conventional procedures to outlandish lengths, the piece is one of wit. These works for a clarinet ensemble carry forward Thomson's interest in athematic (non-repeating) continuity, which Aaron Copland was to advance some twenty years later as an urgent contemporary concern.

Le Bains-Bar is a *valse* (actually a necklace of waltzes, many of them "hesitation"), of which several arrangements exist. The earlier versions are for violin and piano and for an ensemble of two violins, cello, bass, and piano. The later are for trumpet and piano and for trumpet and band. This work is Thomson's Continental answer to his more American *Synthetic Waltzes*. Rhythmically it is more symmetrical, and the presence of modulatory progressions causes it to seem less youthful tonally. It continues the athematic procedure on a larger canvas than the Portraits and without reliance on structural uses of tonality. Beginning in E flat Major, it moves through some five keys to its ending in F Major, substituting grandeur of manner for any reference to E flat.

Portrait of F. B., for voice and piano, has a text by Gertrude Stein. The fact that Thomson had just finished the piano score of *Four Saints* explains why this song continues the octave-scale melody of the opera's first-act finale, accompanying it in true *Four Saints* style with a tonic dominant oompah in three, the melody's meter being in four. Other *Four Saints* characteristics—length and children's tunes—are also present. Through the introduction of too much variety, the piece borders on the tedious, in contrast to its more static source.

Two piano solos followed: *Portrait of Alice Branlière,* now subtitled *Travelling in Spain,* and *Portrait of Maurice Grosser,* entitled also *Alternations.* Full of deliberate non-sequitur, *Alice Branlière* is likewise twelve-tonal; the first two measures and following quarter note present all the tones, as do the next three progressions. Scales, waltz evocations, and the musico-technical clichés, however, are not absent; and the practice, noticeable in many subsequent Portraits, of writing outrageously dull endings is here established. *Alternations,* following Thomson's tendency to shift from one technical stance to another, coming to rest on the more conservative one, is not twelve-tone at all. It may, however, be regarded as an addition to the literature of athematic continuity, for after opening in étude style it moves to the church and into scales, on to the waltz and to "Jolly Good Fellow," from there to counterpoint of a purposely inept nature, settling finally through irreducible musical elements (here trills), to an ending of the nature noted above. *Portrait of Ramon Senabre (Catalan Waltz),* from the same year, also for piano solo, is in Thomson's out-of-focus harmonic style, and, like the preceding piece, a mixture of athematic concerns, strings of waltzes, and collage-like juxtapositions.

Thomson next wrote his Sonata for Piano No. 1. Two years later this work was translated into orchestral terms. Today it is known as Symphony No. 2, in C Major. Two *allegro* movements, the first *con brio,* both in C Major, frame an *andante* in A flat.

No concern with chromaticism or atonality is evident. The musical world is seen here as pan-diatonic. The progress is not one of opposition of themes or of development through variation of a single theme. It is rather the presentation of three separate pieces, the first characterized by the interval of a fourth, the second by that of a third, the last by that of a second. Each movement being essentially a linear invention, it is the melodic line of the Sonata No. 1 to which the Symphony is for the most part faithful, other elements often not being kept (*e.g.,* silences which often become percussion solos, and dispositions of accompaniment, the latter moving from thinness in the Sonata to density in the Symphony, and from a closed position of the harmonies in the Sonata to a more open one in the Symphony). Still other elements are freshly introduced (*e.g.,* transitions, additional lines, the latter even sometimes melodic). The octave in which a tune appears is often changed, and there is a tendency toward higher rather than lower acoustical frequencies. Nearly sixty measures near the end of the Sonata do not appear in the Symphony at all, being replaced by nine new ones.

The Sonata is generally cheerful, but it moves from the "dancing and jollity" noted by the composer in his preface to the published work toward strategically placed passages evoking states of musical and social ease. The latter include the American parlor and Sunday church service; the former, Brahms (opening of the *andante*) and Thomson himself (his signature in the form of "Jolly Good Fellow," harmonized). These evocations are made more touching in the final cadence by emphasis on the dominant. The military element present in the Symphony is specific to its orchestration. It is less apparent in the original piano work. Though not a hymn tune symphony, this is a tune symphony, differing from the earlier piece in an ideological rather than technical or expressive way. The opposition of sacred and secular no longer obtains. What is under examination is the diatonic world itself; though multiple and different, activities within it are seen in a state of unanimity. An arrangement of this Symphony for piano, for four hands, was made by the author in 1932. It opens with a twenty-eight-measure Introduction (*lento*) in E Major, not found in the published score of the Symphony or in its parent Sonata, though it exists in the first orchestration.

The Piano Sonata No. 2 has three movements: *cantabile, sostenuto,* and *leggiero e brillante,* each in its own key: E flat Major, G Major, and C Major respectively. Conventional diatonic procedures are superimposed to produce a situation in and out of consonance. Fragmented references to the Brahmsian moments of the first Sonata, the hymnal aspects of the first Symphony, and the general world of musical cliché emerge with some clarity. These references, together with the involvement of the procedures of consonance in dissonantal results, make these pieces highly amusing. It is curious that the "wrong-note" technique as practiced in music's vertical aspects by Bartók should yield an effect of power, whereas here, applied horizontally, the effect is side-splitting.

The year 1930 brought forth more Portraits. *Clair Leonard's Profile,* for piano, is more a mask than a likeness, for fragmented musical ideas in juxtaposition remove any aspect of mobility. *Madame Dubost chez elle,* also for piano, includes one atonal passage and several evocations of the waltz; also, in measures 17–20, an allusion to the neo-classical piano works of Stravinsky. *Jean Ozenne,* or *Pastorale,* also for piano, is more out of focus than the others. All three pieces end by continuing movement above and below a held tone, letting the latter's resonance conclude them without a further stroke. *Alice Toklas* is for violin and piano, and though clearly in F Major, it is at times both chromatic and dissonant. Beginning tunefully, the piece becomes more and more an exploitation of musical devices: wedges, sequences, scales at various intervals, etc. The two instruments are treated as independent musical entities. *Anne Miracle* and *Mary Reynolds,* also for violin and piano, are less tuneful, continuing the emphasis on musical devices and adding larger linear leaps and double stops in the violin part.

Le Singe et le léopard (fable de La Fontaine), for voice and piano, opens with the voice in a meter of four accompanied by a waltzing piano. Greater diversity in the relation of accompaniment to song than Thomson has employed in earlier situations of this kind is introduced—the influence, no doubt, of the text, which also brings about an early departure from, but rapid return to, G Major for the Leopard's discourse.

Oraison funèbre d'Henriette-Marie de France, Reine de la Grande-Brétagne, a setting of Bossuet, exists in two versions: one for tenor voice and piano, one for baritone and orchestra, the scoring of which was never completed. Both are declamatory in style and evince no interest on Thomson's part in collage, fragmentation, or atonality. Dissonance enters, but it arises from relations (*i.e.,* seventh chords) within the expressed tonality. The text brings to mind Satie's *La Mort de Socrate,* but Thomson's work is less static in character, more flowing and intentionally majestic. There is also a phraseological parallelism between the declamation and its accompaniment that makes Thomson's piece less interesting rhythmically. The revision includes several cuts (*circa* thirty-five measures), some metrical and melodic alteration, and toward the end a thickened accompaniment.

Russell Hitchcock, reading, for piano solo, returns to the familiar wedges, parallel sixths, etc. This Portrait was followed by Piano Sonata No. 3, "for Gertrude Stein to improvise at the pianoforte," and the Sonata for Violin and Piano No. 1. Unlike his other piano sonatas, the third is in four movements and uses only the white keys. The absence of black notes was a blessing to Miss Stein, whose ability as pianist was limited. Indeed, on account of their absence, the athematic continuity proceeds very smoothly, each new dissimilarity being a refreshment. This is not a children's piece, of course. It was written by a sophisticated young musician for an extremely knowing, though not gifted, pianist. The Sonata for Violin and Piano No. 1 is in four movements. The first two, *allegro* and *andante nobile,* are in F Major, the third, *tempo di valzer,* in D Major. The last opens *andante* in D Minor, passing soon *doppio movimento* to F Major, in which key the work ends insistently and nobly on the dominant. The continuity is entirely athematic. The dissonances enter integrally, like those of the *Oraison funèbre.* There is much crossing of the instrumental parts, providing depth and seriousness. All the movements are expressive in character, with lines continued to lengths unusual for Thomson and genuine climaxes prepared, presented, and resolved. The third movement resists any temptation to become a simple string of waltzes. Though no text is present, emotion is. With this work we are in the presence of what Thomson has termed neo-romanticism.[14] Politically, this is a powerful term, for it brings to mind neo-classicism and the name of Stravinsky, receiving from both some reflected brilliance. In the context of Thomson's own work, however, it is less an ism than a serious attempt to write his own music, to free one whole piece from the hymns and popular tunes that had so insistently permeated his previous work. He had tried with the Portraits for Unaccompanied Violin to bring this freedom about through the use of atonality, but obviously with no sense of satisfaction, as with the Sonata for Violin and Piano No. 1 he moved toward the same freedom in a more conservative manner.

The *Air de Phèdre* (Racine), for soprano and piano, is a song in narrative style. Here and there the line and accompaniment bring to mind again Satie's *La Mort de Socrate.* There followed *Film: Deux soeurs qui sont pas soeurs,* a song with piano accompaniment to a text by Gertrude Stein. Played by itself, the accompaniment is a portrait of Miss Stein's dog Basket (the First). The song is in G Major, and both tonality shifts and final cadence are reminiscent of the *Hymn Tune Symphony.* The text, written for a projected film that was never made, recounts the circumstances in which Miss Stein acquired the famous poodle.

SONATA FOR VIOLIN AND PIANO, NO. 1

Thomson's String Quartet No. 1 has four movements (*allegro moderato, adagio, tempo di valzer,* and *lento,* introducing the final *presto*). These are respectively in G Major with a final cadence on the dominant, G Minor with a final cadence on the relative Major (B flat), E flat Major ending on a B flat (now the dominant), and G Major (the *lento* is in G Minor, as is the opening of the last section of this movement), ending with an entire page of the tonic in G Major. This tonality scheme, more rationally interesting than that of the Sonata for Violin and Piano, shows a more thorough return to past models and gives technical inflection to the term neo-romanticism. Though much that de-

STRING QUARTET NO. 1

scribes the Sonata for Violin and Piano No. 1 applies to the String Quartet No. 1 (it is athematic, enjoys climaxes), the Quartet is more dialectic. The opposites presented are harmonic, pure and simple triadic harmony on the one hand, harmonizing involving seventh chords on the other. Brief flashes of the former relieve the overstuffed effect of the latter, and the entire work is illuminated by the body of the *presto* (two hundred measures of unusually simple harmony and a transparent structure involving undisguised repetitions). Full use, linearly, is made of the scales, chromatic and diatonic (the fourth-octave one of the first Symphony appears twice in the *presto*). The stacked-up thirds of *Juanita de Medina* also occur, most emphatically at the end of the first movement and at the climax of the third.

In *Stabat Mater* (text by Max Jacob) [15] for soprano and string quartet, there are few signs of thematic procedure. The entrance of the first violin is an imitation at the seventh (with rhythmic variation) of the opening second violin motive (F, E flat, D, G in continuous descent). The cello's earlier entrance could be similarly construed (the third tone is omitted, the fourth transposed an octave). This motive is found again in the viola part shortly before the end of the piece. However, stacked-up thirds appear here even more thematically, discernible variations occurring nine times in the course of the soprano line. With them, the use of seventh-chord harmonies continues, but their earlier over-stuffed effect is modified by the occasional omission of one of the notes of the chord. The *Stabat Mater* thus achieves a quality of directness and simplicity.

La Belle en dormant, of 1931, is a group of songs for mezzo-soprano or baritone with piano accompaniment, all on texts by Georges Hugnet. Thomson's ability to write ostinati not having been recently exercised, these have here a semblance of fresh-ness. The first and fourth songs are accompanied by harp imita-tions, the third *alla ghitarra.* The last ostinato, for *Partis les vaisseaux,* not being tonic-dominant, recalls *The Tiger* of 1926. Fourteen measures of F Major and B flat Minor triads accompany a largely D Minor scale melody (which includes a descending series of thirds); three measures of A Minor and B Major under-score a melody based on the thirds of a seventh chord on F Major. Rising stacked-up thirds conclude the song with the cry "L'Enfance au gouvernail!"

Following the Symphony No. 2, Thomson wrote his Serenade for Flute and Violin. The five movements proper for a sere-nade are present. The March, though *allegro militare,* proceeds either on the off-beat or by dotted quarters. Via an ascent of nearly two chromatic octaves of thirds in the flute, harmonics in the violin, the Aria dissolves in trills and tremolos, an essay in *le style oiseau.* The Fanfare, Flourish, and Hymn are, no doubt, likewise jokes, though to what point is not clear. This work was written for a Paris concert series called La Sérénade. The violin-ist who was to perform it asked for "something bigger."

Thomson filled the order by writing his String Quartet No. 2, but the absence of technical experimentation in this work—it marks a total, if temporary, divorce from official modernism—ex-cluded it from the programs of the Concerts de la Sérénade. Thomson tells that its initial measures (stacked-up thirds, as-cending and descending through a two-octave range and incorpo-rating both syncopation and a minor-major tonality shift[16]) oc-curred to him while he was napping before dinner, in a state between sleep and the "well-springs of spontaneity." He dined before writing them down, certain he would not forget

STRING QUARTET NO. 2

1932

them. The actual work of composition was conducted with a view toward flowing continuity. Yet though written by means of what he calls "the discipline of spontaneity," the Quartet is not an example of automatic writing. Thematic relations abound: *e.g.*, following a repeated exposition in the first movement (*allegro moderato*) a theme appears which by means of rhythmic variation initiates both the second and fourth movements. Nothing in the entire work occurs out of context or in collage; all is well-knit. Thus, the greatest difficulty this work presents to the understanding is that it presents none. The paths by which a die-hard modernist may enter into it lie outside the domain of music. The events of its conventionlized continuity are based on an equilibrated and static, if dualistic, view of humane and (since it

is a composer speaking) musical matters. Significant in this respect are the time-lengths of the four movements, the first and
last of which are each about six minutes long, the second and
third each three and a half. Also notable is the fact that both
interior movements involve the dance, one being a *tempo di
valzer*, the other (*adagio sostenuto*) containing as its middle section a tango. This placement of the tango (concealed as the B of
an ABA) suggests that the element of evil, which it always seems
to represent in Thomson's work, is not alien to our deepest
cries of spirit (the subject of the third movement). It appears
again, though surreptitiously, just before the end of the last
movement, embedded, as it were, in a passage expressing utter
peace of mind. Though this Quartet does not proceed by climaxes
of feeling, it is clearly an affirmation of life. Within the body of
contemporary music it stands as independent and counter-revolu-
tionary. Within Thomson's own work it marks the end of a series
of pieces for strings. Familiar with the organ and the voice, and
with a view to writing idiomatically for the orchestra, in which
strings play a part *sine qua non,* he had with good professional
sense imposed on himself this concentration.

Twenty months passed without the appearance of a new work
from his pencil.[17] During this period *Four Saints* came to complete realization—its orchestration, casting, rehearsal, the Hartford and New York runs—and music for *A Bride for the Unicorn,*
by Dennis Johnson, staged as the 1934 spring production of the
Harvard Dramatic Club, was written. This score calls for male
chorus and three percussion players. The latter, on cue, perform
simple ostinati, a metronome-like pianissimo beating of bass
drum under a particular speech, and at one point a version of
Mendelssohn's *Wedding March* on the glockenspiel. The chorus
provides an intoned recitation above percussion ostinati, several
old tunes ("For He's a Jolly Good Fellow," "Summer Is Icumen
In," "The Sweet By and By," and "Ben Bolt"), and an original
two-part song in the Lydian mode, "Sing, O Children of Trium-
phant Zeus." The melodies of this song move both scale- and
clock-wise, and the counterpoint is triadic. On its first appearance, the accompaniment is a bass drum and chime on every thir-

teenth beat. At the end of the play, cymbals are added, their
sounds issuing independently every fourth beat.

On returning to Paris, Thomson composed *Seven Choruses
from the "Medea" of Euripides* in Countee Cullen's English translation and a Mass for Two-Part Chorus.[18] Both works are provided with percussion accompaniment *ad libitum.* The melodic
material of the *Medea Choruses* is derived from scales and tertial
chords, the intervallic relations being also tertial. The cadences,
however, are all surprising, owing partly to an ambiguity of the
scales, which, in *O, Gentle Heart,* for example, shift from the
mode on E to suggestions of E Major, and partly to a readiness
on the part of the music to stop (as the text does) in the middle
of a movement, the ending of the chorus cited being on the dominant seventh of E in its second inversion. Though in E Minor,
Go Down, O Sun concludes on an A flat triad; and though in D
Minor, *Weep for the Little Lambs* ends on B flat. One is here in
a world of extraordinary tonal flexibility, though its musical objects are common. Stylistically, too, there is ambiguity. At moments a Negro spiritual atmosphere settles over an otherwise
Caucasian landscape (at the mention of "little lambs"). *Behold,*

"MEDEA" CHORUSES
IMMORTAL ZEUS CONTROLS THE FATE OF MAN
·Euripides, Countee Cullen, trans.

1934 (August)·

O Earth and *Immortal Zeus Controls the Fate of Man,* the final
choruses, share an opening mannerism, repeating, for melodic
purposes, tones distant from one another: with Zeus, the octaves
of E and F. This brings about in the scalewise context an expression of grandeur and extreme tension.

The counterpoint of the Mass for Two-Part Chorus is not tertial at all, but quintal and secundal. Thus, between these two choral works a dialectic obtains similar to that expressed within the String Quartet No. 1. In the Quartet, however, the concern had been harmonic; here it is contrapuntal. Though not rhythmic or tonal in structure, the Mass makes use with structural effect of movement toward atonality. The central *Credo*, the exterior movements (*Kyrie* and *Agnus Dei*), and the *Benedictus qui venit* are in the ambiguous tonal-modal world already referred to, whereas the second movement (*Gloria in excelsis*) and the *Sanctus* employ atonality. In the *Gloria* the twelve tones are expressed twice; in the *Sanctus* all the tones are present except B flat, which is reserved for the written key signature. The structure of the entire work is one of simple symmetry befitting the quasi-archaic character of the counterpoint. The interest in thematic relations evinced in the String Quartet No. 2 is apparent also in the Mass. The opening of the *Credo* is imitated three times in its course. The *Benedictus* and *Agnus Dei* resemble the *Kyrie* thematically (an intervallic movement that suggests the "harmonized ornaments" of the *Hymn Tune Symphony*, but, in being expressed contrapuntally, also suggests an ostinato). The resemblance emphasizes the frame-like structure that encloses the central movement. In general, however, there is a tendency to conceal contrapuntal imitations rather than to proceed by evident canonic or thematic devices. Thus, in the *Gloria* the final cadence, though a canon at the octave, emphasizes cross-relations, an F natural becoming an F sharp, a B flat becoming a B natural. The *ad libitum* percussion parts of both choral works are mostly simple ostinati and, occasionally, acoustical reinforcements for climactical effect. The New York music critics failed to hear this work on its own terms: an evocation of ancient times, rich in poetic ambiguity, architectural symmetry, and rugged strength. They had expected, apparently, something more like *Four Saints*.

The year 1935 saw the composition of more Portraits for piano solo: *Constance Askew* (also entitled *Sea Coast*); *R. Kirk Askew, Jr.; Paul Bowles* (*Souvenir*); *Carrie Stettheimer* (*An Old Song*); *Ettie Stettheimer; Henry McBride* (*Tennis*); *A. E. Austin, Jr.*

(*The Hunt*); *Josiah Marvel* (*Hymn*); and *The John Mosher Waltzes.* Neo-romanticism is conspicuous by its absence from these problematic pieces, which continue the atonal search, but in the terms of harmony (*i.e.*, bitonality). Unrelated triads and seventh chords are superimposed, often in inversion and with some tones omitted. The effect in *Constance Askew* is atmospheric, and though four measures waltz straightforwardly, this quality no doubt suggested the alternate title. Superimposed tonalities as expressed in these Portraits recall Milhaud's *Saudades do Brasil,* though they have little sweetness of either feeling or sound. The fragmented character of some of the earlier Portraits gives way in *R. Kirk Askew, Jr.* to more extended passages, used to express more unequivocally the disjunction of the elements combined. The stacked-up thirds reappear toward the end of *Ettie Stettheimer,* outlining a ninth-chord in the base of an oom-pah pattern. The seventh above each of these notes is taken as the root of a triad for the weak beats, thus creating a dissonant situation, as no melody is there to relieve it. The piece is in *tempo di polka,* starts and ends squarely on A flat, and includes unabashed scale passages. *Henry McBride* expresses the bitonal ideas with baroque canonic figures. *The Hunt* and *Hymn* are more faithful to their titles than are the others, though the former has its share of waltzes. *The John Mosher Waltzes* resembles these last two Portraits in its fluency, but it greets one with a more immediately perceptible musical gesture.

Thomson's next group of Portraits, also for piano solo, are entitled *Miss Agnes Rindge* (*Prelude and Fugue*), *Helen Austin, Jere Abbott* (*Meditation*), *Harold Lewis Cook,* and *Herbert Whiting* (*A Day Dream*). *A Lullaby* (*Go to Sleep, Alexander Smallens, Jr.*) also suggested itself at this time. The Prelude of *Miss Agnes Rindge* opens with a phrase of seven beats (G Major characterized by the interval of a fourth and the presence of the whole-tone scale). This phrase, extended to include an eighth beat, is the subject of the Fugue, which presents a fully developed exposition in four voices, but an underdeveloped consequence. The piece includes canons, "harmonized ornaments," and melodies bitonally accompanied. *Helen Austin* and *Jere Abbott* are contrapuntal studies in superimposed parallel intervals. In *Helen Austin,* following an introduction in informal counterpoint, and the appearance of fourths against single tones in parallel, oblique, and contrary motion, thirds are played against thirds, fourths against fourths, seconds against fourths, thirds against fourths, and finally, fourths are waltzed against fourths to end in a fourth on F. In *Jere Abbott,* sixths and fifths are included, and the Portrait resolves to simple octaves on F. In *Harold Lewis Cook,* Thomson left superimposed intervals behind him and returned to the key of A Major, with triadic relations modified by the bitonality of the Portraits of the previous spring. In *Herbert Whiting,* phrases of relatively triadic character have whole-tone cadences. *A Lullaby,* for voice without accompaniment, pursues the interest in equal intervals (major thirds, minor thirds) with an unusual degree of purity. "For the personal use of Alexander Smallens, Jr. and his parents" appears on the manuscript. Young Smallens's parents being experienced musicians, the absence of tonic-dominant relationships provided a song suitably difficult of execution. A second lullaby, *Go to Sleep, Pare McTaggett Lorentz,* written a little later and also for unaccompanied voice, might induce somewhat fitful slumbers, disturbed by frequent appearances of the augmented triad.

Works for film and theater followed. *The Plow That Broke the Plains,* music for a United States Government film written and directed by Pare Lorentz, was composed in 1936. A Suite for Orchestra arranged from it in 1942 preserves and clarifies the architecture of the original, which is identical with that of the Mass for Two-Part Chorus. The central section is occupied by two contrasted popular movements: *Cowboy Songs* ("Houlihan," "Laredo," "Git Along Little Dogies") in B flat Major; and *Blues,* in D Minor. These are preceded and followed by a series of incomplete canons, orchestrated antiphonally, given an ABA structure by the presence of an interlude and return. The *Pastorale* (*Grass*), which precedes the *Cowboy Songs,* is in E Major, whereas *Drought,* which follows the *Blues,* is in E Minor. The opening and concluding pieces (*Prelude* and *Devastation*) are likewise related—to the earlier *Hymn Tune Symphony* as well as to each

THE PLOW THAT BROKE THE PLAINS

other. The total plan of these exterior sections involves a prelude, fugue, and final tango. The tango in both versions appears only in the Finale, leaving the door of this house wide open. (The film having been propaganda for Franklin Roosevelt's Resettlement Project, this open structure served to emphasize the need for action.) The prelude and fugue occur at the beginning and end of the film, whereas in the Suite the *Prelude* omits the fugue. Other omissions in the Suite are the *Homesteader* and *War and Tractor* sections, both of which quote colloquial tunes, in the case of the latter, one associated with participation in World War I, "Mademoiselle from Armentières." The orchestration of this music adds saxophones, banjo, guitar, and, in the film, a harmonium to the usual complement. It is clear, colorful, and varied, though the clarity is somewhat obscured in its film use by the narration, which is heard at times several decibels above. Unless Muzak-inclined, one would do better to hear *The Plow* accompanied by pictures of one's own invention, which, thanks to the composer's faithfulness to those of Lorentz, may well resemble them.

This was the period of WPA. With Orson Welles, John House-man, and others, Thomson became part of the non-relief 10 per cent professional assistance quota permitted. The group achieved a notable production of *Macbeth,* staged by Welles at the Lafa-yette Theater in Harlem with Negro actors and with voodoo chants and dances directed by Asadata Dafora Horton. Musical arrangements were assigned to Thomson, who orchestrated Lan-ner waltzes and worked out with Welles weather effects calcu-lated to build up the sound of the actors' voices. His original contributions were trumpet fanfares, one of which involved three players in the production of a tone-cluster. Then, as now, he was generally unenthusiastic about the musical possibilities of a Shakespearean script. "One can get in a little weather music," he says, "and, once the characters are dead, sometimes a funeral. Otherwise it is mostly fanfares to get the actors on and off the stage." He points out further that Shakespeare, initiating a the-atrical movement in an England that had a strong and established musical life, had arranged matters so that his speeches and scenes would be forever free of competition from musical quarters.

Orchestrating music by Paul Bowles for Labiche's *Le Chapeau de paille d'Italie,* produced by WPA and translated by Edwin Denby as *Horse Eats Hat,* offered more scope. Virtually every production facility known to man being available for its presen-tation at the Maxine Elliott Theater, Thomson decided to do a very fancy job on the music. There were thirty-two men in the pit, three dance orchestras of varying style spaced about, two grand pianos in the lower boxes, and a trumpet soloist, all pro-grammed in such a way that almost no moment, not even during the intermissions, was without sonority. Music that he prepared for the Federal Theater's *Injunction Granted* was scored for pic-colo, fife, trumpet, and the following battery (used to create noise rather than rhythmic lines): thunder drum, rattle machine gun, railroad train effect, ratchet machine effect, rumble cart, thunder sheet box, trainbell, fire department bell, electric bell, factory whistle, locomotive whistle, ocean steamboat whistle, wind whistle, washtub for glass, and cuckoo call; also sixteen snare drums, sixteen bass drums, and sixteen Bronx Cheers. For Leslie Howard's 1936 production of *Hamlet* he provided, in addition to a military intermezzo, a funeral march, the usual fanfares, four scalewise songs for Ophelia (two minor, one major, one modal, all in E), and a "Gravedigger's Song" in B Minor of which the melody is triadic; also music for recorder and horn to be played in unison with the intonations of the Player King and Queen. Other instruments required in this score are two natural trumpets (in A and D), extra low chimes, thunder sheet, thunder drum, outsize cymbals, small kettledrums, two bagpipes, and a small snare drum manufactured for the production.

SUITE FROM "THE RIVER"
II. INDUSTRIAL EXPANSION IN THE MISSISSIPPI VALLEY

Used by permission of Southern Music Publishing Company, Inc.

In 1937 Thomson extracted an orchestral suite from his music for *The River*, a United States Government film written and directed by Pare Lorentz. His program note explains:

The music of *The River* is partly original, but mostly it is just the music of the Mississippi Valley.

It is hymn music of the sort known as white spirituals; which is to say, the ancient Scottish and Irish tunes that our Southern and Western forefathers learned in the rural districts of the British Isles and brought with them to this continent as their musical heritage. Although their association with sacred words dates mostly from the 17th and 18th centuries, the greater antiquity of these melodies is proved by their largely pentatonic character. An exception is the

tune known to hymn books as *Mississippi* and commonly sung to
the words "When Gabriel's Awful Trump Shall Sound."

This tune is written in the full Aeolian mode and is probably, according to Dr. George Pullen Jackson of Vanderbilt University, an
Irish sea-chanty of great antiquity. It is used in this film in the form
of canon, fugue, and finally its own full harmonization (that rich
and strong medieval descant harmonization, which, though first published in William Walker's *Southern Harmony* in the 1830's, is
probably as old as the tune) to accompany the rising waters of the
Mississippi, its namesake, and the awful terrors of their overflowing.

These white spirituals are not a rare or antiquarian music. They
are normal and ordinary music in the rural South. The so-called
Negro spirituals are their offshoots, as are the cowboy songs of the
West. Their chief repository, *The Sacred Harp,* sells a half million
copies per annum, year in, year out.

The complete list of all the tunes other than original musical material used in this film is as follows:

> *How Firm a Foundation,* or *Convention* (Introduction, also
> Finale, view of TVA dams).
> *My Shepherd Will Supply My Need,* or *Resignation* (Scenes of the
> big river; also interior scene of sharecroppers' house).
> *Rose of Alabama,* or *Carry Me Back to Old Virginny*—original,
> though not the best-known, version (cotton picking and steam-
> boats).
> *What Solemn Sound the Ear Invades,* or *Death of Washington*
> (Civil War aftermath).
> *Hot Time in the Old Town Tonight* and *The Eagles They Fly
> High in Mobile,* or *Captain Kyd* (logging and industrial se-
> quences).
> *When Gabriel's Awful Trump Shall Sound,* or *Mississippi* (flood).
> *Go Tell Aunt Rhody the Old Gray Goose Is Dead,* or *Saviour,
> Visit Thy Plantation* (eroded land).
> *Yes, Jesus Loves Me* and *There's Not a Friend Like the Lowly
> Jesus* (poor white cotton picking).

The ironical appropriateness of these titles need not be taken to
mean that they have been chosen for their topical references. Quite
the contrary. It is simply that tunes which have an expressive or

characteristic quality usually end by getting themselves words of the
same character.

Rose of Alabama, Old Virginny, and *Hot Time* are, of course, not
folksongs at all but extremely successful popular ditties whose words
and music happen to be well married.

One need only add that "The Old South," the first movement
of the Suite, opens with material from the third and fourth movements of the *Hymn Tune Symphony;* that the finale is that of
this Symphony, with the end reworked and the orchestration
changed; that the most distinguished new material in *The River*
is a "Forest Theme" that both acts expressively and integrates the
composition. In a distorted variation it opens the movements
"Soil Erosion" and "Floods." In the film, the music once deliberately "jumps the gun" on the picture it accompanies, "A Hot
Time" regularly eliciting laughter before its witty scalewise sequence extensions, Thomson-introduced, are heard. The organization of this Suite is less structural than that of *The Plow.* On
the other hand, more interesting and more detailed relations
exist between the sound-track and the film than in the earlier
Lorentz-Thomson collaboration.

A number of smaller works date from this year (1937). These
include Thomson's arrangement for *My Shepherd Will Supply
My Need* (Isaac Watts's paraphrase on Psalm XXIII) in the form
of an unaccompanied hymn. (The original appears in *Southern
Harmony* under the title "Resignation." It is entirely pentatonic,
both in the tenor melody and in the soprano and bass quintal-
tertial "counterpoints." No dynamics or changes of tempo are
given, and the A's of its AABA structure are harmonized identi-
cally.) Though the melody in Thomson's arrangement is still
pentatonic, the tertial "counterpoints" are not, making full use
of the key of D Major. (A subsequent arrangement made for
women's chorus is in G Major, another, for male chorus, in F
Major.) The three stanzas are given three tempos: *allegro ma
sostenuto, meno mosso,* and *maestoso.* Though each stanza remains a melodic repetition, the A sections within them all are

varied in harmonization. Except for one case of parallel fifths
between the outer voices, the arrangement schools this song for
taking its place in a musical society far removed from its back-
hills American associations. During the same year Thomson completed his *Scenes from the Holy Infancy,* for mixed chorus.
Joseph and the Angel, in F Major, has intoned solo passages.
Triads and seventh and ninth chords are employed in its harmonization, and it ends, as he so often arranges, on the dominant.
The Wise Men and *The Flight into Egypt,* though not Southern
hymn tunes and not pentatonic, show a tendency toward less
than seven notes, no F sharp occurring in either, though it is the
second tone of E Minor (in *The Wise Men*) and the leading tone
of G Major-Minor (in *The Flight into Egypt.*) These melodies
are therefore hexatonic. *The Wise Men* is provided with a largely
ostinato humming accompaniment made up of "weak" progressions (I-VI-III) against which the tenor melody evolves independently. Seventh chords, but not ninth, reappear in *The Flight,* and
a scale passage (from which the *Scenes from the Holy Infancy* is
otherwise free) is introduced.

Thomson also wrote at this time incidental music for a production of *Antony and Cleopatra.* Needing something oriental in
flavor for a "Sailor's Song," he made a variation of his "Thou
That Dwellest in the Gardens" (*Five Phrases from the Song of
Solomon*), keeping the original accompaniment. For Cleopatra
(Tallulah Bankhead), he wrote a modal dance-like tune for oboe
and tomtom. The usual Shakespeare fanfares and drum rolls were
also supplied. *Filling Station,* still another work of this active

FILLING STATION Ballet-Document in One Act

year, was composed for Lincoln Kirstein's Ballet Caravan, and
with divers omissions has often been played as a Suite for
Orchestra. The *John Mosher Waltzes* became the sixth of its
twelve numbers, a variation of them No. 3. The re-orchestrated
Tango of the *Sonata da chiesa* became No. 7, an excerpt from it
No. 10. "For He's a Jolly Good Fellow" (*i.e.*, "harmonized ornaments") was made into a whole piece, No. 2, and it appears in the
conclusion as Nos. 2 and 12. Thomson's intention in writing this
"signature" once again and in developing it here at some length
was finally to be done with it. Hymns, Americana, fugatos, the
stacked-up thirds, a Streets-of-New York type of waltz, a "Big
Apple," and a piece involving two-handed repeating-note tremolos on the piano complete the work.

Filling Station was the first ballet on an American subject using
American musical material, a *ballet réaliste* in the tradition of
Satie's *Parade, Relâche,* and *Mercure*. It further resembles *Relâche*
(with which Thomson was not then acquainted) in that it is a
simple set of "numbers," their characteristics established in direct
relation to the persons of the ballet and derived from patriotic
musical sources. And though, like the films *The River* and *The
Plow*, it follows from the *Hymn Tune Symphony* rather than
from the intervening string works, the techniques of collage characteristic of the Symphony are evident only where sections of that
work are actually employed. Cutting and piecing are present in
Filling Station and in both film works, but the materials are
longer. The composer's eye for detail has moved over to orchestration. The freedom from popular tunes that marked Thomson's string works of 1930–1932 is renounced in these pieces of
1936–1937. In the First String Quartet there were indications of
giving up the athematic continuity of the early Portraits and the
Violin Sonata. With the ballet and film works, this renunciation
is fully realized, not in favor of thematic development through
variation, but in the acceptance of literal repetition and reprise.
The study of Southern hymns involving only five tones is in opposition to the atonal search initiated in the Portraits for Unaccompanied Violin, which involve twelve. Thus, Thomson can

be seen to be as unbiased as he is active in his quest for useful means. Dedicated to no technique, he continually observes his surroundings; and when his eye lights on something he deems of use to his purposes, nothing in him restrains his taking it. Even his purposes move about, sometimes toward the expression of his sentiments, sometimes toward the acceptable-to-him expression of everyone's sentiments. The opportunity offered, and made sufficiently attractive, he will leave neo-romanticism, social realism, or any other ism and energetically take up abstraction, Dada, or whatever. But he is never aimless.

The following year (1938) brought another commission from WPA, for music for Shaw's *Androcles and the Lion*. Complying in absentia (he had left New York for a visit to Kansas City), Thomson mailed in his score, never rehearsing it or even knowing if the performance came about. The music includes choral arrangements of Southern hymns, excerpts from *Le Bains-Bar,* and one new waltz, simpler and more American in flavor than those with which it is here associated. This year also saw Thomson's return to Paris and to Portrait-"painting," again for piano solo. *Claude Biais,* for white notes only, avoids scalewise motion, leaping about in an unanalyzable way. *Louis Lange,* also for white notes, exploits scales, ostinati, sequences, etc., becoming through the absence of melody somewhat abstract. He laid down his brush and palette to write *Dirge* (from John Webster's *The White Devil*), for voice and piano, a song in D Minor with a syncopated scalewise melody, a rolled-chord accompaniment, and passing dissonance, only to resume portraiture with a new vigor. *Sherry Mangan* (*The Bard*) opens with a hexatonic tune (lacking the D of E flat Major). Its harmony is made to slide in and out of focus by its chord-outlining and scale-defining accompaniment. A loud dissonant passage, partly whole-tone in make-up, ends with parallel minor ninths performing a baroque pattern conventionally associated with more consonant intervals. The opening tune, more out of focus, then "introduces" a passage totally consonant.

Lise Deharme (In a Bird Cage) is in *le style oiseau.* Four opening measures, quite atonal though whole- rather than twelve-

IN A BIRD CAGE: A Portrait of Lise Deharme

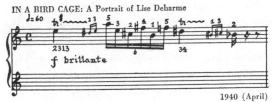

1940 (April)

tonal, are repeated note for note halfway through the piece. In between, at the lowest point of a scale of unequal intervals (a minor third in a diatonic setting), the lowest note of the piano is struck for the first time in Thomson's music. The minor thirds are exhibited also in whole-tone settings that consist of groups of three, four, or six such intervals linked by half-tones. The piece trills, leaps, shakes, trembles, and, though coming to rest on A Minor, manages, via an ascent involving tritones, to float on the dominant. Repetitions begin and close *Louise Ardant (En cors et trompettes)*. At the opening, the tonic and dominant octaves of A flat Major are the simple fare; at the end these are again presented, thickened with root-position triads. Hunting motives and fanfares, served up realistically askew, provide the *pièce de resistance* in B flat and C Major.

The explanation of *Hans Arp (Poltergeist)* lies in its not having any repetitions of parts, only of figures (superimposed fifths in secundal or tritonal relation) and chords, sixteen soundings of the same one providing a passage equal to one-fourth of the entire piece and immediately preceding the final tone-cluster, from which a fourth ultimately resounds. *Max Kahn (Fanfare for France)* is an ABA piece (with a literal *da capo*). The G Major trumpetings of the A section are pentatonic, but the five tones used are the first diatonic five together with the octaves, fourths, and fifths consequent from them. These tones are presented straightforwardly and, what with the inventiveness lavished upon them, give a lively military effect. The B section, though opening as a continuation, goes on to some out-of-focus images and pertinent tunes ("Yankee Doodle" enters Thomson's music here for the first time), of which one is presented as a double canon (the tune in fourths imitated by the same in fifths). *Georges Hugnet (Barcarolle)* opens antiphonally with a canon at the seventh. A new statement gets the previous reply. A crescendo-ing newer statement evinces something irrelevant. The fourth attempt indicates conclusively that the dialogue is hopeless. A boat trip ensues, but only the non-melodic essentials of a barcarolle are given, secundally in two keys, so that the effect verges on that of seasickness, though the waters are clearly calm. The piece closes with a reference to the earlier conversation. This time both voices speak at once, one saying twice what the other requires twice the time to say. The end brings a major seventh, both voices continuing to talk at once but in blissful ignorance of each other.

Sophie Tauber-Arp (Swiss Waltz) is an alternation of canons and waltzes in E flat Major. The first canon is tertial and at the octave. The first waltz is in E flat, but its tonic-dominant accompaniment is in D flat. The following canon is at the major seventh, and the following waltz is an abstract of the waltz, as the *Hugnet* barcarolle was an abstract of the barcarolle. A repetition of the opening with a reversal of the voices (the high is low; the low is high) is followed by an extended coda which, starting with canons, turns into dominant and tonic ostinati in figurations and finally becomes a simple E flat Major line with eight measures of the tonic, repeating itself utterly alone, discovered, as it were, *en deshabillé. Madame Kristians Tonny (Eccentric Dance)* is in the style of a habanera, and its harmonic make-up (abrupt changes of key in a see-saw order) threatens, after the manner of a chaconne, to be treated thematically, each appearance of it prompting variety in the melody. A wealth of other ideas removes any possible academic interpretation. There are whole-tones, bitonality, stacked-up thirds, the abstraction treatment previously given the waltz and the barcarolle, and an ending on the tonic seventh.

With *Flavie Alvarez de Toledo (Tango Lullaby)* there appears an original Thomson melody that is as persistent in the memory as the popular tunes he so often quotes. This piece appears to have a lovely simplicity, but analysis reveals an underlying balanced complexity: the whole is in an ABA, of which the first A is

TANGO LULLABY: A Portrait of Mademoiselle Alvarez de Toledo

also an ABA, the last A being a variation melodically of the opening eight measures, and the accompaniment a variation of that of
the end of the first section. This accompaniment is a tango
ostinato shifting from A to B flat Minor, the melody remaining
in the former key. A held tone of the accompaniment in the first
return of the A section is a later addition, suggested by the orchestration given this piece in 1944. The B section, only eight measures long, is bitonal (F Minor and F Major) and serves for a
momentary contrast. The haunting opening melody returns, and
the curious scalewise descent of the accompaniment to F (melody
remaining in E) at the end balances the earlier scalewise ascent
introducing the B section. The wit absent from this Portrait
returns in *Theodate Johnson (Invention)*. This results from a
canonic treatment of scalewise and chord-outlining material, an
exchanging of the leading and following functions between the
two voices, and the abrupt introduction of totally non-canonic
treatment of similar material.

Pablo Picasso (Bugles and Birds) refers equally to brass instruments and to our feathered friends, who are presented in all
sizes and dispositions. Beginning in A flat Major, the piece is in
many keys, of which the last two, E flat Major and E Major, are
heard at the same time. There are waltzes, ostinati, trills, outlined and interior repetitions, presenting a wide variety of events
with a tendency toward shortness of phrase. This kaleidoscopic
effect is probably a reference to cubism. *Guggenheim Jeune
(Peggy Guggenheim)*, a piano piece in three movements, is pub-

lished as Piano Sonata No. 4. The first movement, *allegro* (G Major), is largely made up of canons utilizing nearly intractable material: the effect is one of stick-to-it-iveness. The final cadence, though sweetly dominant, is one of fatigue. The second movement is an *adagio* (C Minor with references to E flat Major) introducing some Sunday service feeling. The *vivace* (F Major) is a short finale that takes time out, without loss of spirit, for an eight-measure canon. *Howard Putzel* (*Lullaby Which is Also a Spinning Song*) manages likewise to become a canon. Canons appear also in *Léon Kochnitzky* (*Five-Finger Exercises*), presented first in E Major, then with humorous effect in F and E Major at the same time. A passage ensues in which the two hands play repeated single tones, intervals, and seventh chords in unpredictable sequence. A short canon brings about an immediate return to this xylophonism, and the piece concludes somewhat cacaphonously, a scalewise canon at the minor second producing, in turn, parallel tritones and reiterated minor seconds in a crescendo to *fortissimo*. The closing chord, marked piano, is only dynamically apologetic, sticking to its guns intervalically.

The Dream World of Peter Rose-Pulham is free from canons. Having three distinct sections, it might have been called Piano Sonata No. 5. The first section is concerned with the opposition between D flat and D Major, expressed sequentially in the first four measures and thereafter by superimposition. The second is a waltz, *un poco più mosso,* short and to the point: E flat versus D Major. The D flat-D Major opposition is the subject of the last part, which employs a change of meter but not of tempo. The final tone-cluster pays equal attention to D flat, D, and E flat. The whole is in what Thomson calls his "imbecile style." *Dora Maar* is also in three parts, all in the key of G Major, though at first no feeling of this key is communicated. It is as if F sharp were a wrong note and the piece actually in C Major. The counterpoint is informal, but its curious cadences are repeated every two measures, so that any doubt about its correctness of printing or of performance is dispelled. The second part opens with a canon imitating the opening of the first part. This is followed by a mosaic canon: two voices begin together and continue by imitating one another. An interlude introduces all the tones foreign to G Major and to Part III. The latter also imitates Part I, but in augmentation. The ending on G is made to sound like the dominant of C Major, all F sharps being canceled in the last eight measures.

Tristan Tzara (Pastorale) is a string of abrupt shifts of tonality expressed in terms of 6/8 pastoral banalities. The opening twenty-four measures (8 plus 8 plus 8) are innocently in F Major. Without transition, as though one were at a motion picture, the worlds of D flat Major, A Major, A Minor, and A flat Major are exposed. A mosaic canon and some dissonant counterpoint in the last key precede a shift to F Minor/C Major, the tonality being blurred. Back in F Major, the meter shifts to one of two in the time of three. Ultimately this shift is canceled out, and all becomes as it was in the beginning. *Germaine Hugnet (Aria)*, like the earlier *La Seine*, is a florid composition in two voices without further expressed harmonization. The lines sometimes suggest the clichés of Italian opera, but the shifts in tonality (G Minor, C Major, A flat Major, B flat Major) are by no means commonplace. Thomson's ability to write bitonally is fully displayed in *Mary Widney, Toccata*, and with a certain ruthlessness about the acoustic consequences. F Major and Minor are first heard in concert, each expressed through its more unusual aspects, such as the tonic seventh chord. The meter changes, and a canon that crosses itself shifts from imitation at the minor third to that at the tritone five-eighths of the way through its course. The piece concludes with a measure-by-measure shift of two-tonality superimpositions, but its climax is a major-minor situation so shifting both vertically and in continuity that it is difficult to decide which way is up and whether one is coming or going.

Like much of Thomson's music, *Pierre Mabille* consists of eight-measure phrase lengths. The first five of these phrases are a single line (F Major), the next three informal two-part counterpoint. There follows one of chords against a bass line. The next five are two-part counterpoint. A simple interval of the ninth is then repeated for eight measures. An imitative passage, in first-species informal counterpoint, and then a single line conclude the piece. *Nicolas de Chatelain (Cantabile)*, like *Mabille*, is without wit. It is a piece of tertial counterpoint with that amount of chromatic spice acceptable to baroque taste. It opens in E Major with two voices active (eighteen measures). A third enters for seventeen measures, leading to C sharp Minor, in which key the composition continues its flowing existence, only one phrase being eight measures in length. Permeated with motivic feeling, this Portrait alternates two- and three-part counterpoint, resorting only once—and most expressively—to a passage in octaves. Nor are *Clarita, Comtesse de Forceville, Jamie Campbell,* and *André Ostier (Canons with Cadenza)* characterized by mirth. The first, though largely for white notes, begins in A Minor, has only two "wrong" F sharps, and is somber in mood. Though it opens with a single voice, it is mostly in two voices, employing a kind of second and third species counterpoint dominated by octaves, fourths, and sevenths. There are two-measure repeats that have more the mystery of echos than the monotony of ostinati. The *Campbell* Portrait is a club sandwich of marches of the "circumstance" type and passages of imitative counterpoint. The concluding octaves are played sometimes parallel, sometimes tremolando. The cadence of the *Canons with Cadenza* recalls the pomp of the previous Portrait, but by and large it reflects the interest Thomson took in counterpoint, which is here tertial and canonic. The canons are at various distances and intervals, and at cadential points politely non-canonic. The piece is in A flat Major, but ends over an *fff* G with a trill (C, D flat, and finally struck C).

Shortly before he became critic of the New York *Herald Tribune,* in 1940, Thomson composed *Alexander Smallens (Fugue),* for piano solo, and *Ruth Smallens,* for unaccompanied violin. The piano piece is a further continuation of his interest in counterpoint. The exposition starts fugally (four voices, one countersubject); the following interlude presents material from the subject; a passage suggests the presence of still another exposition (thus a double fugue). But the piece ends without becoming, academically, what its title announces. Part of its subject appears in diminished and augmented variations and in stretto, and through chromatic entrances of these frag-

ments it becomes a sturdy exercise in twelve tones, even though
it is in C Major. The violin piece opens with a hexatonic tune in
E Major. Complete scales lead to C sharp Minor. Abrupt changes
of key, church cadences, and violinistic treatment (double stops,
melody with pizzicato accompaniment) characterize this Portrait.
Church Organ Wedding Music, written for the marriage of the
poet John Latouche, consists of two parts: *To Come In,* in A
Minor, *To Go Out* (once-and-a-half as fast), in C Major. Both are
in secundal imitative counterpoint, and their cadences are on the
dominant.

Thomson's next work, a "music and sound score" for *The
Trojan Women* of Euripides (in Edith Hamilton's English translation), was his first for radio (CBS Workshop, 1940). He had in
earlier incidental music matched percussion instruments with
human voices, with an ear for acoustical support. Through trial
and error he had found precisely which cymbal, for instance,
suited a given actor's voice. With this radio work he employed
woodwinds, not only for the same function, but also to help a
listener identify the unseen female characters. A flute always
sounded with a particular woman's voice, a clarinet with another,
an English horn with a third. Percussion instruments and sound
effects of wind and marching provided the architectural aspects
of the program. *The Sound-Track of the Life of a Careful Man*
(CBS, 1941) employs a short theme given repetition, variation,
and canonic treatment. Whenever more music than written is
required, the direction, already given in earlier incidental music,
is: "Repeat one tone higher." For the *Oidipous Tyrannos* of
Sophocles, produced at Fordham University in 1941, Thomson,
not knowing Greek, received from Father William Lynch, of
that university, a complete lay-out of the choruses: the meaning
(syllable by syllable), the tonic accents, the quantities, and the
cadences (rises and falls). The strophes and antistrophes of his
score are straightforwardly in D Major over percussion ostinati.
Between verses, a flute in melodic imitation of the preceding
vocal cadence or a cymbal in punctuation gives structural definition. At the end, a flute concludes with the simple elegance of an
ascending two-octave scale.

More Portraits ensued. In *Mina Curtiss (With Fife and Drum)*, for piano solo, the first sixteen measures, through melodic triplets and adherence to D Major, swing along beautifully. A short canon becomes non-canonic. Though the melody remains in D, the accompanying full tonic chords present the whole-tone scale. Distorted tunes and parallel sevenths follow. The piece includes a passage of five metrical changes that on analysis add up to eight measures of 4/4. A coda refers to the opening triplets and D Major, but the situation is dissonant. The opening of *Insistences (A Portrait of Louise Crane)*, also for piano solo, is not immediately apparent as canon. Four parallel octaves are, however, followed by a seventh, which on scrutiny is seen to be the result of strict imitation. Bitonality, sequential enlargement of intervals, and cross relations enter to make this piece amusing. Its slow, "idiotic" conclusion, being intended, is stylish. *Jessie K. Lasell,* also for piano solo, and three school choral works —*Welcome to the New Year* (Eleanor Farjeon), *The Bugle Song* (Tennyson), for voice and piano, and *Surrey Apple-Howler's Song,* a round, all concentrate on fewer tones than seven. *Jessie K. Lasell* is mostly a single pentatonic line, though chords built of fifths and the whole-tone scale come in. The *Welcome* is in horn style, and though in B flat Major it uses neither G's nor E flats. The only E's that appear are in the soprano, and all are natural. The *Bugle Song* is a four-tone work in G Major. Its ABA structure is given rhythmic articulation by balanced alternations of 4/4 and 3/4 meters. The round is hexatonic (D Major without any B's). All of the tones are called back into service for *Florine Stettheimer (Parades),* a piano solo. The opening eight measures (bitonal, D/E flat Major) are elegantly, though dissonantly, composed in two-part counterpoint, perfect fifths being reserved for cadential points. The expressivity continues, the tonalities not only shifting but also changing obliquely within a single voice. The feeling follows suit: an ABA parade ensues, with G Major appearing, bugle-like, in the A's above four and then seven tonic chords. The B of this ABA is in E moving to D Major above six different tonalities. There is a return to the beginning, but parades (one simply in C Major), strains of "Yankee

PORTRAIT OF FLORINE STETTHEIMER

1941 (October)

Doodle" in imitative counterpoint, and bitonal flourishes end the piece. With its complexity, variety, and finish, this short work suggests a finely painted minature.[19]

In 1942 André Kostelanetz, having heard about the Portraits, proposed to Thomson that he and a few other composers write portraits to be premièred during the Kostelanetz guest engagements as conductor of various symphony orchestras. Aaron Copland, Jerome Kern, and Thomson accepted the project, Copland supplying his *Lincoln Portrait*, Kern his *Mark Twain* Portrait. Because Thomson would compose portraits only from life (*d'après nature*), he fell in with Kostelanetz's suggestion that his subject be Mrs. Franklin Roosevelt. The First Lady, however, was not available, so The Little Flower sat for Thomson's *The Mayor La Guardia Waltzes*, for full orchestra. Ensconced in a corner of the Mayor's office, while people entered and left and the Mayor made decisions and gave orders, Thomson spun waltzes that are as bumptious, lively, and American as the earlier *Synthetic* ones, and that conclude with equal brilliance: a fluttering of trumpets on high B flat. This Portrait being not very long, *Canons for Dorothy Thompson*, also for full orchestra, was composed to partner it. Some of Thomson's pieces that are not called canons are more faithfully canons than others so-named. The *Dorothy Thompson* canons include a non-canonic introduction and non-canonic interludes, and the canons themselves are unruly at points. Sometimes the rhythm is imitated while the tones, though almost, are not accurately repeated. At other times the interval of imitation is changed midstream. Several appearances of the whole-tone scale emphasize the inclination of these *Canons* toward another region than the simple major-minor one employed for the Mayor.

The next Portrait is likewise of a political figure, James Patrick Cannon, then head of the Workers Socialist (or "Trotskyist") Party of the United States of America. A piano solo, it opens in D Major with a single voice bringing about not only bi- and whole-tonality but also a generous sprinkling of "wrong" notes. Eight measures suggest that the difference between *Pierre Mabille* and *James Patrick Cannon* is that between a ninth and a seventh, the latter interval being here given the reiteration accorded the former in the earlier piece. *Scottish Memories (A Portrait of Peter Monro Jack),* also a piano solo, opens in E Major with a strong tendency toward six rather than seven tones. It superimposes, in turn, fifths and thirds and includes a waltz in A Major and a total restatement of its opening measures in minor rather than major, and in two-part canon rather than melody without accompaniment. *Schuyler Watts,* also a piano solo, is completely canonic, variety being the result of alternations of A Major and A Minor. A concluding passage opens very consonantly to become dissonant, less cheery, resting finally on an empty octave. *Jean Watts (Wedding Music),* still another piano solo, is a happy, churchy, straight 6/8 A flat Major piece. It has triads, thirds, tenths, and a climax.

Aaron Copland was a piano solo in its original version. It is in G Major and opens with gracefully flowing fourth species counterpoint in which thirds, vertical and horizontal, play a characterizing part. Canons follow, and a melodic line traced in parallel thirds introduces chords and a reiterative passage. The melody returns, calling forth the four-octave descending scale passage of the *Hymn Tune Symphony* and further reiterations. No sharps or flats foreign to G Major are to be found in this piece, just as none separate from A flat Major was required for the depiction of *Jean Watts.* There are two orchestrations of *Max Kahn (Fanfare for France).* One made in 1942 uses six horns (eight, if available), four trumpets (one in D), and field drums. A later version employs four horns, three trumpets, three trombones, side and field drums. In this scoring, tutti are used sparingly, and all the pairings of two among the three available instruments are employed for variety and color.

Thomson's Etudes for Piano, begun in 1943, are published as a set of ten with technical notes by the pianist E. Robert Schmitz. The one first composed is not alarmingly difficult to play. Entitled *Tenor Lead (Madrigal)*, it is thirty-two measures in G Major and their repetitions, which, by a shift of emphasis from the soprano to the tenor line, reveal the piece to be an arrangement, with a deft modal touch given by a progression from dominant to subdominant, of "Drink to Me Only With Thine Eyes." *Double Glissando (Waltz)*, marked *brillante* and in C Major, presents a multiplicity of glissandi: for two hands, for one hand, on white keys, on black, using besides single notes parallel thirds, fourths, fifths, sixths, sevenths, and octaves, alone and in combination, and a whole-tone glissando that is found more satisfactory to the ear when fingered rather than sinusoidally swept. The piece also includes bitonal passages (C above or below C sharp Major). More thorough-going use of bitonality is present in *Repeating Tremolo (Fanfare)*. The result is a trumpet imitation as, according to the composer, *Mary Widney* is a balalaika imitation, but the concentration of expressed tonalities within a single measure here reaches a higher point than in Thomson's earlier works, threatening to rise to the saturation level of the tone-cluster.

In *Fingered Fifths (Canon)*, in G Major, fifths imitate fifths,

FINGERED FIFTHS (Canon)

IHR

1943 (July)

with perfection of interval maintained at the expense of tonality, and cross relations (C sharp, C natural, F natural, F sharp) develop. Shifts of the interval of imitation and of the leader function between the parts take place. And as both hands keep playing, filling in the gaps between strict imitation, a certain obscuration of canonic procedure results. A repetition of the opening is preceded by a short passage of superimposed fifths, which is striking both for its sound, fresh in this context of works, and for the reason that it defies analysis. Questioned about the passage, Thomson held that it was canonic, perhaps with some tonal alterations. When it was demonstrated that this view was untenable, he offered seventh chords as an explanation. This being shown to be equally untenable, he stated that he had learned from Gertrude Stein, as he had learned from the painters among his friends, that a successful technique of composition lies in "keeping one's attention on the object." Asked what constituted the object in this case, he referred to the benefits derived by a baseball player from keeping his eye on the ball and by a singer from listening to the sounds he produces. These remarks were summed up under the heading "Physiology of Action." No doubt, in writing a passage such as this one of superimposed fifths, one's mind would be on fifths; the mystery lies in the fact that this particular passage—there are many superimposed fifths in Thomson's earlier works—sounds fresh, as though something new had been discovered. But the discovery was achieved unconsciously. An objective explanation of the passage could be arrived at by removing one's attention from it in isolation, and viewing it in context as a "variation" of the preceding and following canons: it then sheds the characteristic of imitation, keeping that of the interval of the fifth only.

The next Piano Etudes were *For the Weaker Fingers (Music-Box Lullaby)* and *Ragtime Bass (Tempo di Two-Step)*. The *Lullaby*, set in a high register, has an ostinato accompaniment and a superimposed melody mostly in thirds with chordal figurations. It is an expression of childhood in an atmosphere of charm and gentility. The *Ragtime* is in C sharp Major and whirls Turkey-in-the-strawish material through part of the circle of fifths. An amusing fanfarish episode in E Major is followed by a recapitulation with added intervals in A Major, and this time by a true repeat in the original key sparkling with octaves. *Five-Finger Exercise (A Portrait of Briggs Buchanan)* is another addition to the literature for white notes alone. A fanciful ascending and descending scalewise accompaniment begins as an ostinato, later diatonically investigating the keyboard in an unpredictable fashion. The whole, through use of the deeper pedal, is intended to produce the effect of "a faint blur." Eight concluding measures superimpose intervals most curiously, descending thirds outlined by the lower line being the only familiar device discernible. *Parallel Chords (Tango)* has the sound of an out-of-tune player-piano. This is the result not only of superimposed tonalities and constant shifts of major and minor in both melody and accompaniment, but also of the use, melodically, of two tetrachords: the lower, minor diatonic, the upper composed of a minor second, minor third, and minor second.

Invited by the flutist René Le Roy, Thomson interrupted the Etudes to compose a Sonata for Flute Alone. The first movement, in C Major, is an *allegro* with an *adagio* introduction. Its structure resembles that of an academic sonata. Though in C Major, this short linear piece shifts its tonal emphasis frequently, includes chromatic and whole-tone scales, and gives interiorly an atonal feeling. The second movement, *adagio,* is in A Minor, and the third, *vivace,* in G Major (recalling the introduction to the first movement). The upper tetrachord of the *Tango Etude* enters into the familiar Thomson bouquet of all the various scales, stacked-up thirds, etc. The phraseology of the Flute Sonata is, however, of other measure lengths than eight. In the first movement, for example, the slow introduction is twenty-seven measures long, the faster exposition eleven plus nine; the development and recapitulation are twenty each.

Another Piano Etude, *Oscillating Arm (Spinning Song),* was then composed. A suggestion by E. Robert Schmitz brought a counter-rhythmic emphasis of three against four in this piece. In view of Thomson's long experience with two against three, it

was natural for him to accept the idea. *Fingered Glissando (Aeolian Harp)* completes the Ten Etudes for Piano. It also establishes a new musical idea, that of the total independence of simultaneous parts. The first eight measures are all white notes, but the tone of the melody is never present in the accompanying hexatonic fingered glissando. As the melodic line moves, the accompanying glissandi change according to this principle of total independence. In the subsequent eight measures, the same procedure is followed, but in terms of the whole-tone scale. The continuation inverts the parts, placing the melody above and the glissandi below. Another eight measures, instead of being entirely whole-tone in make-up, open with a mixed black and white note situation brought about through use of the "tango tetrachord," A, G sharp, F, E. The piece concludes with a five-octave whole-tone glissando, fingered. The total independence of parts, or "mutual exclusiveness," is analogous to bitonality. Collage as a working method is basic to both, but the strict separation between elements superimposed insures a state of "purity." No "wrong" notes or "out-of-focus" situations can arise. The rigorous control of this method suggests the equally rigorous ones dodecaphonically used by other twentieth-century composers. But where the latter often ignore the fact that the instruments for which they write were invented in the seventeenth and eighteenth centuries, before the tempered scale was established, Thomson does not. Instead of exploring the unknown in a way that frequently remains visible only to the eye and theoretical to the mind, Thomson, by composing for the actual sounds of instruments, revitalizes the familiar scales and writes a music that "works" acoustically.

Meanwhile he had embarked upon the orchestration of a selection of his Portraits: *Nicolas de Chatelain (Cantabile for Strings)*, *Georges Hugnet (Barcarolle for Woodwinds)*, and *Flavie Alvarez de Toledo (Tango Lullaby)* were scored for woodwinds, bells, and strings; *Jere Abbott (Meditation)*, *Picasso (Bugles and Birds)*, *Alexander Smallens (Fugue)*, and *Jessie K. Lasell (Percussive Piece)* for full orchestra. Originally he thought of grouping these works in Suites for Orchestra, No. 1 and No. 2, but dropped the idea in favor of greater flexibility of programming. Orchestration has been estimated as amounting to 50 per cent of composition, an original sketch being the other fifty. In the *Percussion Piece*, the scoring is more nearly 99 per cent of the finished product. The original Portrait is merely a straight line, very slight, and would not have suggested to any other than its composer its suitability for orchestra. Nevertheless, a brilliant work has resulted, and its colors are those of the Far East. Doublings occur at intervals pentatonically appropriate, the perfect ones. The simpler Portraits are all orchestrated in a way that maintains their transparencies, while the complexities of the *Fugue* and the *Picasso* are all clarified by their instrumentation.

In 1945 Thomson provided music for a documentary film directed by John Houseman, *Tuesday in November*. An explanation of how America elects a president, the film has chiefly been seen publicly in foreign territories, though it was made with all the professional facilities of Hollywood. The score is in two large parts: *Prelude, Pastorale* and *Cartoon; Voters, Election, and Finale*. It is heard continuously with the film, the pauses between movements being no longer than those that would take place at a concert. There is also abundant narration, beneath which the music frequently all but disappears. The *Prelude*, in G Major, is ten measures long and serves to establish "Yankee Doodle" in chorale form. This tune will later permeate the third part, *Car-*

toon. The *Pastorale,* also in G Major, is the *Portrait of Aaron Copland,* composed in 1942. The *Cartoon* is an alternation of fugal expositions on a "Yankee Doodle" subject and of hymnal episodes. Seventh chords color the triadic counterpoint. Variety is obtained through shifts from major sections to repetitions of them in minor, through alterations of the "Yankee Doodle" subject, through introduction of episodic material (sometimes tuneful, once signature-like but with a use of contrary motion not found in the original *Hymn Tune Symphony* form) and through movement to various keys. The chorale of the *Prelude* enters here in a new harmonization, and is completed by eight new measures. The *Cartoon* ends with a *da capo,* of which the hymnal episode is extended, given full chords and the D Major scale in an ascending and descending ostinato, and followed by a simple repeat of the *Prelude* and its completion. *Voters (Walking Song)* is a charming piece with an "out-West" flavor, banjo-like accompaniment, and ABA structure. *Election* is a waltz in F Major, parts of which are taken from No. 8 ("Valse à trois") of *Filling Station.* While both are "Streets of New York" waltzes, the latter is the type associated with vaudeville acrobats, whereas the *Election* waltz is more out-of-doors and arm-in-arm in character. The finale is a sequence of excerpts from the "Yankee Doodle" *Cartoon,* ending with the hymnal episode and D Major scales, a "credo" that is, or affirmation, which ends the whole work in the dominant of its opening key. Also dating from 1945 is *A Portrait of Lou Harrison (Solitude),* for piano solo. The piece opens with a single line reminiscent of the Copland portrait and introduces a second line at first in dissonant relation and then imitative in character. Parallel fourths, the whole-tone scale above consecutive thirds, reiterated sevenths like those of *Mabille* and *Cannon,* and a conclusion on the dominant enter into a work that threatens to sag part way through but somehow regains vitality.

Early in 1946 Thomson wrote and orchestrated two movements of his Cello Concerto. Dissatisfied with the third movement, he laid the work aside, returning to it intermittently until its completion in 1950. In October, 1946, he began music for Gertrude

THE MOTHER OF US ALL   ACT I, Scene 4   Prelude
("Snow Music")

Copyright 1947 by Virgil Thomson. Used by permission of Mercury Music Corporation.

Stein's libretto *The Mother of Us All,* completing all but the
last scene in December. The scoring was finished in March, 1947.
Neither the music nor the text of this opera is "abstract," as
Four Saints may be considered to be. Thomson's primary con-

THE MOTHER OF US ALL   Act I, Scene 5
("Wedding Hymn")

Copyright 1947 by Virgil Thomson. Used by permission of Mercury Music Corporation.

cern here is communication. The rigors of wintry weather
prompted the superimposition of independent parts in the Prelude to Act I, Scene 4.[20] Bitonality occurs chiefly at troublesome
episodes in the drama, such as the forbidding of a marriage or an
outburst of temper on the part of Ulysses S. Grant. Other passages
of memorable expressiveness, such as the "Wedding Hymn" that
opens Act 1, Scene 5, the "carpet sweeper music" that ushers in
Act II, and Susan B. Anthony's declamatory funeral oration, are
straightforwardly tonal. Thomson waited a month before he let
himself write the final scene: he wanted the opera to settle in
his mind so that its summation could be essential. But this is

THE MOTHER OF US ALL   Act II, Scene 3
("Funeral Hymn")

no conventional finale with everyone romping about. At the last curtain Susan B. Anthony, in the form of her own statue, occupies the stage alone, singing of her "long life of effort and strife (dear life)," as the music diminishes to a vanishing point. The orchestra, though it is complete, plus piano, harp, celesta, xylophone, and percussion, never acts as a screen through which one barely hears the singers. It makes them all the more audible, supports them in the true meaning of the term, and without losing its own luminosity adds richly to theirs.

Much of the music in the opera has a familiar ring because it evokes familiar things; everyone thinks he remembers the tunes, but no one knows what they are. Actually, except for "London Bridge Is Falling Down" (Act I, Scene 2), they are all original. The swinging one that begins in Act I, Scene 5 is the "Election Waltz" from *Tuesday in November*. Expressed first objectively, it later is planted like a seed in the orchestra, and each repetition of it there brings forth new melodies from the singers. The lovely "Wedding Hymn" is equally fertile. This development of melodies by means of a procedure analogous to passacaglia or chaconne creates an atmosphere of celebration and generosity which Thomson's abrupt shifting of tonalities—no key in the twelve-tone gamut is left out—keeps fresh and clear. And this effect is preserved by the melodic lines, which in large part are those proper to bugles. One could submit that *The Mother of Us All* is in F Major, that it begins there and ends on its dominant, that the tonality structure of the entire work is classic in architecture. (These remarks apply also to *Four Saints.*) But this argument would not report the listener's actual experience: he hears at a given point a particular tonality of which the statement is entirely transparent; from such a position in tonal space he may be transported to any other position—an experience that is anything but classic; it is proper to a period of aviation and space travel. No underlying tonality scheme is made apparent by devices of repetition and variation. One cannot even discover a Thomson-flavored progression, though the composer himself finds that he frequently moves to the dominant minor. The situation might be described in Susan B. Anthony's words (in the libretto) as "Where is where." The question really is, to paraphrase Miss Stein, "Is there any there there?" To Thomson, this "there" is "the degree of immediately discernible difference and the consideration as to whether or not this degree corresponds to that of the desired change in expressivity."

In *The Mother of Us All* everything Americans feel about life and death, male and female, poverty and riches, war and peace, blacks and whites, activity and loitering, is shown to be real and true. It is everything an American remembers, if he remembers how it was at home of an evening when friends and relatives played and sang, how it was to hear a band playing in the park, a Salvation Army band on a corner, a soldiers' band going down Main Street, an organ when somebody was married or had died. To quote Susan B. again (on having forced the word male to be written into the Constitution of the United States concerning suffrage), "Yes, it is wonderful" that this music, though everyone remembers it, is original.

4

THE SEINE AT NIGHT, THE FIRST OF A GROUP OF LANDSCAPE PIECES, was composed in 1947. Thomson's program note outlines his nature-painting technique:

The Seine at Night . . . is a memory of Paris and its river, as viewed nocturnally from one of the bridges to the Louvre—the Pont des Saint-Pères, the Pont des Arts, or the Pont Royal. The stream is so deep and its face so quiet that it scarcely seems to flow. Unexpectedly, inexplicably, a ripple will lap the masonry of its banks. In the distance, over Notre Dame or from the top of faraway Montmartre, fireworks, casual rockets, flare and expire. Later in the night, between a furry sky and the Seine's watery surface, fine rain hangs in the air. . . .

The form of the piece is simple AABA. The melody that represents the river is heard in three differing orchestral colorations. Between the second and third hearings there are surface ripples and distant fireworks. At the very end there is a beginning of quiet rain. The technical means by which these effects are, if not achieved, essayed are of interest chiefly to persons capable of recognizing them without analytic aids. If my picture is resembling, it will need no explanation; if it is not, no amount of harmonic or other analysis will make it so. Let us admit, however, for the sake of the record, that the melodic contours are deliberately archaic, with memories of Gregorian chant in them; that the harmony, for purposes of perspective, is bitonal and by moments polytonal, that the rocket effects involve invented scales and several different sets of four mutually exclusive triads, as well as four sets of three mutually exclusive four-note chords, and that there are several references to organ sonorities. The orchestra consists of three flutes (one doubling piccolo), three oboes (one doubling English horn), three clarinets (one doubling bass clarinet), three bassoons (one doubling contrabassoon), four horns, three trumpets, three trombones, bass tuba, triangle, cymbals, tamtam, two harps, and the usual strings.

Some find *The Seine at Night* disappointing as landscape
simply because the rocket-depictions lack brilliant bursts of color.
These listeners would do well to ignore the program note and
open their ears rather than their mind's eye. For Thomson's
technique, which in his verbal outline of it appears somewhat
forbidding, is actually productive of a charming piece of music,
exceedingly easy to take and to understand. Total independence
of parts, as studied above, is here contrasted with its opposite,
the latter's judicious placement at phrase beginnings and endings
removing any sense of tension or conflict. The effect is one of
artistry, and this effect is enhanced by subtle changes in the
second and third A's of this AABA piece. Thus a C Minor triad
in the twenty-first measure becomes C Major on its first repetition,
C Minor again on its second; and in the twenty-seventh measure
a triad is that of E Minor on the first and second hearings, E
flat Major on the final one. These, and other such changes, do
not seem like compositional oversights; they suggest a special regard for each situation, letting it be, as is a leaf of a given tree,
at one and the same time very much like all the others and yet
different, uniquely itself. The result is music that is genuine as
an object, never setting out, as that of others sometimes does, to
interrupt one's activity of listening in order to establish the brilliance of the composer's mind or the depth of his emotional perceptions. The end of each of the A sections is a magnificant polytonal complex, each voice moving, generally by scalewise descent,
though sometimes plagally or upward, to its own independent
conclusion. C sharp, E and G sharp Minor, F and C Major, movements from A Minor to A Major, from C Major to C Minor, from
E Major to C Major, others purely whole-tone in character, are
all heard at once in a rich cadence.

The B section of *The Seine at Night* is especially interesting.
It contains what may be, previous remarks notwithstanding,[21]
Thomson's first deliberate presentation of all the twelve tones.
This occurs in a situation so quiet and so gently prepared as to
suggest a reverential attitude. He begins with the familiar scales,
major diatonic and chromatic, goes on to those that change in their
course, from major to minor to chromatic or whole-tone, or

THE SEINE AT NIGHT

1947 (December)

from whole-tone to chromatic. He then introduces a half-dozen new ones, some of which yield to analysis more readily than others: three ascending tetrachords (minor second, major third, minor second) connected by minor thirds, continued chromatically; four tetrachords (minor second, minor third, minor second) connected by major seconds with whole-tone extensions. Others become logical only by being given "proof by repetition," each time up a half-step. Still others, unique ascents, are not scales at all, but gamuts covering more than two octaves. What precedes, follows, or is sustained above this lively linear assortment is, first, root-position triads, then two mutually exclusive such triads (yielding six tones), and finally four such triads (yielding all twelve). An entire passage is developed from this procedure, involving all twelve tones arranged in three mutually exclusive four-note aggregates. Four different sets of three such aggregates are introduced in varied and delicate orchestral dress. As the twelve tones are not arranged in a row, none of the intellectual problems associated with their use arises. If one has a distaste for conventional dodecaphony, here there is nothing about its sound to dislike. The flavor of the twelve tones is, in this otherwise triadic menu, appetizing.

It was also in 1947 that Robert Flaherty asked Thomson to write music for his film *Louisiana Story*. Nature herself has the principal role in this film. Opposite her are members of an Acadian family into whose life an oil company intrudes. Flaherty, like the Acadian family, viewed the circumstance for what it was: a marsh-buggy, a motor-boat, a derrick, a rough-and-ready crew, drilling operations, and finally a newly established oil well that increases the family revenue. Where another composer might have been tempted to add a note of *Weltschmerz*, Thomson was not. He determined which scenes were primarily humane and gave them the tunes belonging to the people of the land.[22] Where landscape dominates he has provided original music. For the machinery, with the exception of the derrick's arrival, for which he reserved an ecclesiastical touch, he did nothing, letting it make its own sound.[23] He even for moments employed total silence. Everything made to be heard is heard: the narration, the conversations, the music. In this clear atmosphere the music assumes its full role. This is by no means either that of background music or of a coincidental symphonic concert,[24] but that of an informed chorus, announcing events to come, commenting on action in progress (with remarkable wit in such passages as the dances associated with the swimming raccoon and the Passacaglia that evokes old-fashioned "scarey" movie-music). Near the beginning, for instance, a change in musical expressivity coincides with a smile on the Acadian boy's part, the two together introducing the pet raccoon. Later, with terrorizing effect, the hiss of the attacking alligator follows a lengthy chromatic preparation (the final variation of the Passacaglia). The end of the film is also announced by the music, which quotes bits and pieces from its entirety in the finale fashion of *The Mother of Us All*. This quasi-architectural action of the music is its least happy function in *Louisiana Story*. It attempts to seal a package that remains more usefully open; for the contrast between the diatonic folk-settings and the chromatic landscape, derrick, and alligator movements is always maintained, never giving rise to drama or any attempt at integration. This separation of expressive function, never treated by Thomson as a problem requiring dialectic solution, provided him with the good fortune of being able to extract not only one but two Suites for Orchestra out of the Flaherty film.

The first Suite, *Louisiana Story,* has four movements: Pastoral, Chorale, Passacaglia, and Fugue. The Pastoral moves from an archaic opening (pre-diatonic octaves and fifths) to a relatively modern coda involving the definition of both major and minor. The simplicity of its over-all structure (ABCBACA and coda) is balanced not only by a wealth of variation of orchestration and figuration, but also by a play of musical invention within the sections themselves. The A sections, four eight-measure lengths, are rhythmically (by opposing syncopation to movement on the beat) ABAB, melodically AABB. The second melody, B, begins in imitation of the first, continues differently, and on its repetition receives a slightly varied bass. When this whole section is heard again, it is entirely different in orchestration, figuration, and expressivity; also, an alternation of soft and loud underlines the ABAB. The final hearing of the section is like the first, but a minor third higher, bringing about for the A sections an ABA layout. The hexatonic melody constituting the B sections of the Pastoral is heard first once and twice later, the tonality and the phraseology being different each time. The C's, thirteen and twelve measures long, functioning as interludes, are intervalically more informal and varied than the rest of this piece. Including stepwise progressions that add up to no known scales, they tend toward the Thomson impenetrability elsewhere remarked.

The Chorale opens deceptively with a hexatonic Walking Song in F Major (no B flat). Its accompaniment is in D Minor, which resolves to F Major on its repetition. The chorale itself is the composer's second intentionally dodecaphonic work. In *The Seine at Night,* counting up to twelve had produced harmonies of chords. Here it is employed for leading of the outer voices in a four-part harmony of root-position triads. The plagal cadence preceding the whole-tone codetta brings about a repetition in the bass of the second tone of the row before the appearance of the twelfth. An ABA follows, the A's being the opening folk tune, the B's a new, dancier one. A return to the chorale is followed by two variations of it, the first primarily rhythmic, the second primarily tonal, new twelve-tone rows being thus arrived at in both bass and soprano. The original phrase of the chorale, orchestrated as a tutti and complete with whole-tone codetta, concludes the movement. The final isolated E Major chord has no tonality significance: it is simply the next step, previously not taken, of the six-tone scale.

LOUISIANA STORY CHORALE

The subject of the Passacaglia, though chromatic, is not twelve-tone, there being no A flat in it. Heard first as octaves with a pedal point on F above, it moves by a series of scalewise descents from F Minor to a chord of minor thirds having a tendency toward E Major. Its second appearance is as root-position triads accompanied by an ascending melody in contrary motion which, finally falling, is bitonal in feeling toward its conclusion. The third appearance keeps this melody and adds another in A flat Major. With orchestral variations, the next three appearances are a repeat of the above. Following a twelve-tone interlude based on the four mutually exclusive triads, there is a further departure from strict passacaglia, what happens being, in Thomson's words, "in the shape of an inversion of the subject," and yet not demonstrable as such. Subsequently, the events, though witty, as previously remarked, are so removed from the opening of the piece that they refer, as variations, more convincingly to the *Cold Weather Prelude* from *The Mother of Us All* than to the subject of this movement. Calling a halt to digression, Thomson picks up the original thread (the orchestration alone changed), follows with variations of the first variations (turning the piece into an AABA), and concludes with a new one (coda): the subject and its inversion heard simultaneously.

The Fugue has four two-measure subjects, highly differentiated, both intervalically and rhythmically. The first emphasizes the interval of the tritone, expressing in this way the alligator's terrifying presence. The second, which appears as its countersubject, rises diatonically to descend chromatically to a leap of the major third, describing the physical effort of the Acadian boy as he attempts to capture the beast. The third involves eleven tones, and is chromatic in character, jerky in rhythm, and wedge-like in shape, remarkably like the movements of the alligator struggling to free itself from the boy's hook. The last, expressive of the father's anxiety at not immediately finding his son, falls minor-diatonically and, following a descent of the perfect fourth, rises chromatically. After the first sixteen measures, the second and fourth subjects, father and son, producing together all twelve tones, appear in a counterpoint characterized by contrary motion.

All the subjects are composed in such a way that any one may appear above or below any other, so that, in this respect, the work is a double chromatic fugue. The continuity is largely one of expositions sixteen and eight measures long made up of subjects, countersubjects, and derived material, giving an effect of building blocks related, as in pre-fabricated architecture, to an established module of proportion. There are no episodes, and had the conventional fugal tendency of referring all events to unity been observed, this piece would lack vitality. But the counterpoints, maintaining the high differentiation of the subjects from which they are derived, flash back and forth, giving a sense of event and also of unpredictability. The eight-measure blocks, changing the distance of entrance from two measures to ½ and then ¼, suggest stretti. But they precede a reprise that suggests a song form. The coda is collage: a passage in C Major, a fragment of the third (eleven-tone) subject, and a quick cadence in A Major. This is the logical key for conclusion: the third subject begins and ends on E flat, which being the tritone, is at the central point of a chromatic scale based on A; further, this interval of the tritone is the opening and repeated one of the first subject (expressed, however, by B and F). The choice of major rather than minor, conventionally known as the Picardy third, and simply acoustical in its early European usages, is here made in reference to the happy ending of the battle with the alligator, the boy being at the last moment rescued by his father.

The second Suite for Orchestra from *Louisiana Story* is entitled *Acadian Songs and Dances.* The first movement, *Sadness,* employs two four-note (I, II, III, and V), four-measure Acadian tunes. Their accompaniments, though fifths or root-position triads, are in and out of focus, sometimes through bitonality, at other times through faithfulness to the whole-tone scale. *Papa's Tune* opens with a tonic vamp in F Major preceding a sixteen-measure hexatonic tune with a I-IV-V accompaniment (a rare acceptance of the subdominant convention, Thomson's oompahs being generally just tonic-dominant). Eight measures of the vamp (still in F) make the repetition of the tune in G Major surprising. The piece then fades away, the vamp remaining alone on D, then G, finally F. *A Narrative* is distinguished by the contrast of its two syncopated dance tunes, one emphasizing G sharp, the other G natural. *The Alligator and the Coon* shifts abruptly every eight measures from one key to another, and though made up largely of three four- and five-note tunes it introduces a twelvetone interlude (four mutually exclusive triads) and repeats it. *Super-Sadness,* in minor, is a hexatonic tune heard three times, each statement being in a new key, always in horn-like two-part counterpoint. *Walking Song* also opens hexatonically, but includes what Maurice Grosser refers to as the "Standard Oil" chorale of the other Suite and quotes now and then from *A Narrative* of this one. The *Squeeze-Box,* a waltz with a skipped beat, frames a two-step in Thomson's *Ragtime Bass* piano étude style, involving alternations of diatonic and pentatonic tunes, the latter employing the wa-wa-muted trumpet. *Papa's Tune* is quoted; an accordion is used; the piece concludes, after a *da capo,* on the dominant seventh.[25]

The quality of mastery moves through the music of *Louisiana Story.* All the notes perform the composer's commands, never once seeming to be useless or engaged on their own independent projects. Collage, here not present, frequently gives the reverse impression—that is, that the events themselves are in the driver's seat. This score is a string of accomplishments, one after another, of straightforward sixteen-measure (or less) intentions. Equally true of folklore settings and of the original music, it is at this structural point (closer to Debussy than to Satie) that the stylistic differences are made compatible. Neither a paste-up job nor a neo-romantic expression of personal feelings, *Louisiana Story* is a public project. The musics that go in and out of it are not all as "socially realistic" as those of *Filling Station,* but they have all accepted convention and, without hiding their idiosyncrasies, make no display of them, appearing well behaved, well spoken, well dressed.

The year 1948 brought a Louisville commission, not of the Rockefeller kind (the establishment of which owed much to Thomson's influence), but of the older form founded by America's No. 1 music-lover, Louisville's former Mayor Charles Farnesley, which brings into being a new work for each pair of the Louisville Orchestra's concerts. The *Louisiana Story* practice of building a score out of an assemblage of independent blocks is continued in this work, entitled *Wheat Field at Noon,* though Thomson's orchestral invention is continuous here, giving the actual sound of the work the form of an open curve. Including repetitions, there are twelve of these blocks, eight of them distinct from one another. The first, ten measures of 2/2, is a melody accompanied by parallel fifths in strict counterpoint (octaves and fifths). The melody is initially twelve-tone (though the fifth note repeats the second), but its continuation is not; and though it starts in quintal counterpoint, it renounces this method also, introducing one interval of the third. The second block (seven times four measures) is a whole-tone four-note sixteen-measure melody in four-part canon at the octave, each part accompanied in parallel motion by voices of identical timbre arranged in major and minor root-position triads. The latter being mutually exclusive, all twelve tones occur both sequentially in each part (excepting measures 5 through 12, where an overlap appears) and simultaneously when all four parts are in motion. This amounts to an intensification of the similarly schematic make-up of the *Louisiana Story* Fugue. The third block, sixteen measures long, has been termed by Thomson in program notes "second twelve-tone theme." Melodically, however, two tones (B flat and E flat) are missing, though the line somewhat resembles the original row. And the parallel triads this time are not strictly mutually exclusive (excepting in measures 9-12), doubling reducing to eleven in some measures the number of sounds simultaneously heard. The fourth block is a repeat of the second, the fifth of the third. The sixth is the second treated—without canon but with rhythmic variation—in the quintal counterpoint manner of the first. The middle section (*Wheat Field at Noon,* like *The Seine at Night,* being essentially AABA) is a two-part informal counterpoint of mutually exclusive triads. It contains three blocks, the lower line of each becoming the upper of the next. Thomson calls this device (which is, of course, simply canon at some distance) "the rising bass." The tenth block is again strictly and closely canonic, but transitional, leading by descent to the eleventh block, twenty-four measures, which is the third (the ten-tone "twelve-tone" theme) treated canonically in the manner of the second. A coda brings the piece via a sequence of whole tones to an E Major conclusion.

WHEAT FIELD AT NOON

1948

The relative strictness of this music corresponds, according to Thomson, to the geometrical lay-out of wheatfields. On the basis of his *Louisiana Story* Fugue, an alligator could argue the matter. Nevertheless, in this piece the momentary presence of all twelve tones produces an auditory sensation remarkably like that of a hot day when the air itself visibly vibrates. Its expressivity is its outstanding characteristic. Though for Thomson technically adventurous, its purely musical aspects do not contribute to the "advance" of contemporary music, since problems embodying them were customarily submitted by Henry Cowell in the thirties to his students at the New School for Social Research.[26]

After refurbishing his twenty-year-old *Le Bains-Bar* (by making the accompaniment more elaborate, the ending fast and brilliant, and the title *At the Beach (concert waltz for trumpet and piano)*, Thomson was commissioned in 1949 by the League of Composers to write a birthday-celebration piece for the Goldman Band of New York City. He consulted Richard Franko Goldman about the instruments, many of which are specific to bands and little

used in the field of serious music. He also suggested writing a
march. But Goldman reminded him that through the senior
Goldman's efforts the literature was in this respect over-stocked.
So Thomson decided to write a funeral piece that would express
his feelings about the recent deaths of Gertrude Stein and Christian Bérard. *A Solemn Music,* scored for full band, is an ABA
with coda. The structure of this Apollonian lament is established
both rhythmically (five times eight measures, three times eight,
five times eight, plus another eight) and tonally (the ten divisions
of the A section all begin, and the coda both begins and ends,
with a C Minor root-position triad; the three divisions of the B
section begin, in order, on E flat, G, and F, the last leading to a
return to C by means of the dominant, G, making the situation
unequivocal). The method employed is twelve-tone, Row I [27] being, in all eight measures of the A's, the bass of a progression of
root-position major and minor triads. Row II,[28] on the second
appearance of I, enters above it, remaining with it throughout
the A's, and in the transpositions noted (E flat, G, and F) takes its
place as the bass of the three divisions of the B section. Its partner
there is first Row III,[29] then Row IV,[30] and, finally, somewhat
impaired (see below), it carries the dodecaphonic responsibility
alone, returning it to the recapitulation (orchestration and sometimes the figuration changed). Rows V [31] and VI [32] (bass and soprano respectively of the coda's major and minor progressions)
conclude the piece.

In addition to placing one row on top of another, the third
eight-measure block adds a third, more flowing and dodecaphonically freer, line. This is kept, and a fourth, a chromatic and repetitive two-tone line, added. The fifth eight-measure block adds
its melody (in C Minor) to the total conglomerate. Dynamics are
arranged so that in each case the basic twelve-tone rows, rather
than being *Hauptstimme,* are simply underpinning for the new
and initially emphasized additions. For those from Vienna let it
be noted that an F sharp (in order to make a fifth with the bass)
is added to Row II in measure 24; that this row is reinstated in its
original form in measure 32; that on its fifth appearance Row I
allows the position of its last two notes to be reversed; that Row

A SOLEMN MUSIC

II, in its first appearance as the bass line, adds a B flat to itself; that it manages to do without this addition immediately thereafter; that, owing to the exigencies of the strong tonality feelings superimposed in imitative counterpoint above it, it thereupon gives up an E flat and accepts as partner a soprano melody lacking two tones (B flat and F). It is noteworthy that the A's (five times eight measures) build up to a simultaneous movement of five parts, while the B section (three times eight measures) is consistently movement on the part of three. It is also interesting that of the six rows employed, I is characterized by the interval of the minor third, II by that of the major second, III by that of the minor second, IV by equal use of major seconds and thirds and minor seconds. These lend variety to the course of events; Rows V and VI, both emphasizing the minor second, bring all action to a concerted close.

A Solemn Music, objectively viewed, is a masterpiece. It indicates graduation, not from the school of another, but from those dodecaphonic studies that Thomson had been pursuing independently.[33] One might wager that just as he never wrote another strict fugue after that of the *Sonata da chiesa,* so he will never again write as thoroughly twelve-tone composed, though also heterodoxical, a work as this. However, one might lose the bet.

By now it had been borne in upon Thomson that of all his published music *My Shepherd Will Supply My Need* was the bestseller. It had risen over a fifteen-year period from an annual sale of some ten thousand copies to one in 1955 of some twenty-six thousand copies. (This and similar statistics enabled him to state in a radio interview about 1954: "How do I make my living? By my music.") So he arranged three more *Hymns from the Old South* as choruses for mixed voices: "The Morning Star" (author unknown), "Green Fields" (John Newton), and "Death, 'Tis a Melancholy Day" (Isaac Watts). But none of these sells more than one or two thousand copies a year. Thomson suggests that though "Death" is listed in William Walker's *Southern Harmony* as the first of "the more lengthy and elegant pieces commonly used at concerts," some of its words, such as "Awake and mourn, ye heirs of hell," are not attractive to twentieth-century church groups, fire and brimstone as focal points of worship having given way to peace of mind. One may also adduce that these pieces are not so polished as the earlier arrangement that inspired Thomson to write them. Idiosyncratic preferences show through the Handelian surface. "The Morning Star" and "Death" have many more fourths and fifths between their outer voices than they should; and "Green Fields" is too plagally orthodox. On the other hand, changing phraseology that is in the old hymns interestingly asymmetrical, so that it conforms with the usual eight-measure lengths, is sound business. These changes, it must be admitted, are in accord with the usage given the hymns in the South, holds and final cadences of phrases three and seven measures long extending them to four and eight. That Thomson observed these conventions distinguishes him from other composers, who would have been pleased by the written asymmetries to copy and even exaggerate them. He not only "squared them up," as in practice they often are, but searched his own response to musical history, attempting in his harmonization to place each hymn as accurately as possible at that point in European time most becoming to it.

In 1949 Thomson was asked for a piece for the Knoxville Symphony Orchestra, and "ran up" a Suite for Orchestra from *The Mother of Us All.* In four movements, it is a kind of potpourri from the opera. With the exception of its second movement, *Cold Weather* (a new piece, developed from Act I, Scene 3, and intended to add emphasis to the work's "modern" aspects), it constitutes a thorough-going use of the "bits-and-pieces" composing means of the opera's final scene. Events take place in quite another order than that observed in the parent work. The third movement, *Hymns,* is an orchestral transcription of the wedding hymn, funeral music, and final aria of the opera. The last movement, *A Political Meeting,* includes material from Act I, Scene 2. The first movement, *Prelude,* is an overture presenting material from both acts, such as the wintry prelude to Act I, Scene 4, and the carpet-sweeper music. The augmented triad plays a large part in the new *Cold Weather.* This is the only chord made up solely of thirds that the whole-tone scale makes possible. Play against it, as in the passage from which the movement is developed, is provided by 6/4 chords. With this Suite, Thomson somewhat imprudently answers the question many incline to ask: "What would a Thomson setting of a Stein text amount to if heard apart from the words?" The answer, as far

as *The Mother* is concerned, is "Not much." The music of the
Suite is at all times mono-referential. The sameness of its objects
produces a monotony increased by all attempts (except a brief
passage for piccolo written in étude style) to relieve it; and the
latter (changes of melody, rhythm, harmony, and tonality), being
an emphasis of only one immediately perceptible aspect of the
text, communicate an atmosphere of desperation that fails to
arouse one's sympathies. The strength that is missing is that of
poetic ambiguity. The only way the music could have had this
strength, which the text has, would have been by being itself:
paying no attention to the words. The two arts might then have
performed in a theater of equals, and through mutual independence have become inseparable.

The Concerto for Violincello and Orchestra was completed in
1950. The last movement was the cause of the delay—a circumstance recalling the trouble Thomson had with the last movement of the *Hymn Tune Symphony*. He was determined to arrive at a last movement for the Concerto that would preclude
any suggestion that it be revised. This work graphs the physical
state of a healthy human being, a type well exemplified by
Thomson himself. Sickness on his part, never serious, is simply
"a good chance to get a rest." And it is thus that the Concerto
appears. The middle movement, *Variations on a Southern Hymn
Tune,* is a meditation placed between spirited pieces, *Rider on
the Plains,* which opens the work, and *Children's Games,* which
closes it. The first is descriptive of energy; the last, despite its
title, infects even adults with a compelling desire to play. Yet
this work is no description of a manic-depressive state. Each
movement is whole in expression. The sharp contrast between
the *Variations* and the other two movements is as normal as
that between night and day; the contrast between soloist and
orchestra is that between the individual and the society of which
he is a member. The opening *allegretto* (D Major, 6/8 time) has
been termed by Thomson a "classical sonata" form. The opening
theme, ranging through three and one half octaves (thus being
suitable to the cello that announces it),[34] employs nine tones
(opening "pentatonically" on D Major), juxtapositions of F sharp

Major, F sharp Minor, and G Minor, and a return to D Major giving rise to a repeat in the orchestra and a melodically derived section tending toward D Minor. A "second" theme, *meno mosso*, numerically the third, is in A Major (actually D harmonized as A). It increases the chromaticism, using all twelve tones, and moves to E, the dominant of A Minor. Because all the foregoing, plus cadenza and appropriate emphasis on D Major, appear in variation in the recapitulation, and because it all conveys the character of a development more than that of an exposition, the actual development section, thirty-eight measures beginning in C Major, that precedes the first cadenza[35] could escape notice. The recapitulation and the interior repetitions are characterized by a device of "exchange." Whereas the cello opened the movement, the orchestra opens the recapitulation. The vice-versa procedure is in this movement broadly employed for complete statements, in detail in *Children's Games*, where the tunes (mostly folksy and original) are divided into their minimal useful parts and tossed back and forth from soloist to orchestra and from orchestra to soloist like rubber balls. *Children's Games, vivo ma non troppo* (D Major), is a rondo. Its three sections, the third a shortened repeat of the first plus cadenza and coda, all begin with the same tune. The tunes that follow receive nearly as much attention as the first, being refused entrance only to playground B. The coda includes the rhythmic pattern 3, 3, 2. This commonplace, employed by Thomson, is in context actually surprising.

The middle movement (*andante*, opening hexatonically in B Minor) is a series of short pieces, each differing in tempo and orchestration from the preceding one. The first is the Southern hymn "Death, 'Tis a Melancholy Day (Tribulation)," and the Southern phraseology (4 plus 3 plus repeat) is, as customary in performance, changed to 4 plus 4 plus repeat. The opening notes in the model, unequal in length, are here two quarters. The harmonization from *Southern Harmony* is the fundamental harmony of the first variation; major triads built on each of its tones evoke an old, out-of-tune, yet beautifully musical pipe organ. Two pentatonic variations of the hexatonic tune follow. What with the soloist playing harmonics and the accompanying orchestra being

CONCERTO FOR VIOLONCELLO AND ORCHESTRA

1950

reduced to celesta and three solo violas in the first, and with the melody given in the second to a clarinet, the accompaniment to harp plus the solo cellist's ascending and descending plucked arpeggios, the effect is delicious. The next melody, employing the sixth and seventh tones in passing, is in D Major. Its accompaniment, employing imitative but non-canonic informal counterpoint, gives the impression of a peaceful congregation, each member moved by the occasion but in his own way. The fifth melody (flute, pentatonic in B flat Major) and accompaniment (cello playing tremolando major root-position triads: D Minor, F Major, E, E flat Minor, and C Major) introduces asymmetry of phraseology, but not one germane to the original: 9 (4, 3, 2) plus 7 (2, 2, 2, 1). Whole-tone and diatonic tendencies (G Minor with both E and E flat) in the sixth variation precede a chromatic interlude. The twelve tones are in this situation the result of diatonic wanderings: shifting scales, sequences, stacked-up thirds, etc. Following a solo, *liberamente,* the cello soloist, accompanied by six other cellists, enters a dissonant situation involving mutually exclusive triads. The eighth event is the original melody (high cello harmonics) accompanied by two voices, each harmonized as root-position triads (sometimes major, sometimes minor). One of these voices (three solo woodwinds) is basically pentatonic, but sometimes diatonic. The other (a few low strings) is hexatonic. The total relationship here, to say the least, is informal. Though not what a purist would consider proper to his diet, it is nevertheless flavorful. The piece concludes, employing the original melody again, upbeat imitations, all types of scales, sequences, canons, a new phraseological symmetry (5 plus 5), and the tonality of D Major, the latter dissolving on its tonic thirteenth to the movement's original B Minor.

The open curve of Thomson's earlier athematic work is not to be found in this Concerto; and, as corollary, nothing is left floating on the dominant. Thematic repetitions and the establishing of a single tonality characterize this work. These are the most conventional aspects of Western musical structure. Their unobscured use places the Concerto right where composition is thickest and the demand greatest. But as they do not successfully engage the intellect, its structural aspects are not the secret of the Concerto's attractiveness. That quality issues not only from the fact that the work is a portrait of a mature and healthy man (a self-portrait), but also from its mobile interior (within the single tonality there is flexibility of emphasis) and its charming surface: the orchestration is varied and, in opposition to the musical structure it clothes, never repetitive, constantly exploring new possibilities.

In 1951 Thomson composed eight more piano études. These, plus his *Portrait of Louise Ardant* (re-named *With Trumpet and Horn*), make up his Nine Etudes for Piano. And for Samuel Barber, who was planning a surprise party and enlisting the help of his composer-friends, he provided *Happy Birthday for Mrs. Zimbalist,* a fanciful variation on the familiar tune. His most adventurous piano piece of this year is his *Portrait of Sylvia*

CHROMATIC DOUBLE HARMONIES   (Portrait of Sylvia Marlowe)

1951 (June)

Marlowe, included in the Nine Etudes, a two-part counterpoint of assorted three-note mutually exclusive aggregates. The movement is first, second, and third species; also three against two and four against three. The intervallic relation between the notes played *marcato* is informal. More precisely, there are on the first of the piece's three pages thirty-two secundal intervals, half that many tertial, nine quintal. There are also four tritones and one unison. The voice-leading is likewise informal, being wholetone or minor diatonic when scalewise, sometimes sequential when leaping. The aggregates are both the usual triads and all others that could be discovered following the rules for mutual exclusiveness: 1) use only three notes for each hand; 2) let these fall within a twelve-tone chromatic scale of a single octave; 3) avoid minor seconds; 4) let all voices move constantly, no suspension. Though chromatic, this Portrait is free not only of dodecaphony, but also of Thomson's previously accepted rule: in the situation of mutual exclusiveness, use only root-position triads.

Guitar and Mandolin, the first of the Nine Piano Etudes, is a pre-fabricated G Major structure with a Spanish chromatic façade, decorated inside and out, in repetition and development, with arpeggios that go up and down, or, if two appear together, as in the opening vamp-block, A, in both directions at once, *molto secco uguale.* The B and C blocks are, respectively, a melody with accompaniment and a canon; both appear in a repeat in which the melody remains as it was, the canon is abbreviated, the vamp developed once and finally extended. At the very end, the pianist is directed to reach into the piano and strike the strings with the flat of the hand, pedal down, in imitation of an old Spanish custom. The strings notated are E sharp, F sharp, A, and B flat. Four fingers can do the trick. *Chromatic Major Seconds (The Wind)* is a chorale expressed by an assortment of two-, three-, and four-note aggregates above which at first, and below which subsequently, major seconds rapidly delineate the chromatic scale, pausing only to trill, and following all leaps by stepwise movement in the opposite direction. The piece concludes without chorale, a breath of "wind" disappearing upward in the form of a fingered diatonic tone-cluster (in an inversion) glissando. The widely assorted aggregates of the chorale represent an interesting experiment: Thomson has here followed his *Sylvia Marlowe* mutual exclusiveness rule No. 2 (adding permission to double at the octave), has dropped Nos. 1 and 3, and, employing oblique as well as disjunct movement, has dropped No. 4 as well. Anything goes, including mutual non-exclusiveness. The substantial element in this chorale is its accompaniment, the "wind," of which the rational simplicity is comparable to Thomson's tonic-dominant oompahs. One may therefore recommend to those on whom Thomson's melodic altitudes have a dizzying effect simply to follow the accompaniment no matter where it is, above or below.

The Harp has no other title, nor does it require one, in spite of a few chromatic harmonic progressions. *Pivoting on the Thumb* is a white-note piece, but within this color limitation it shows a tendency toward the total independence of two parts. *Alternating Octaves,* a canon by inversion, is off-black and off-white, one hand playing in G flat Major, the other in G Major. Halfway through, the two hands exchange keys and the follower becomes the leader. At the final cadential non-canonic point, the intervallic relations are major thirds and fourths coming to rest on a major seventh. *Double Sevenths,* like *Pivoting,* is a white-note piece, and though primarily "mosaic" and only partly by inversion, also a canon, like *Alternating Octaves.* The higher note of each right-hand seventh (the soprano) is imitated at the octave by the lower (or bass) note of the left hand. Some of the lines are conventionally diatonic; others are based on sequences or stacked-up thirds. Slight relaxations of strict imitation toward the end of some of the "mosaics" (variation as to their length and the direction of imitation) are movements toward freedom. This freedom, though used to suggest canon, characterizes the final thirteen measures. *Broken Arpeggios (The Waltzing Waters)* is a beautiful work having the sound of one of Bach's "Goldberg" Variations and the vertical symmetry of structure of a piece by Satie.[36] Thus, three waltzes (D Major, twenty measures; G Major, sixteen; C Major, sixteen) appear in the sequence ABCBA. Satie would have limited the structural responsibility to the phraseology, permitting spontaneity to characterize the events within. Thomson did not so limit it. He emphasized the rhythmic structure by a tonal one identical to it. The piece is exceptional, for he rarely takes such double precautions, and frequently gets along without any at all.

The *Four Songs to Poems of Thomas Campion* also date from 1951. These settings are available in various forms, those for voice or mixed chorus being arrangements of the originals (composed for Herta Glaz), for mezzo-soprano accompanied by clarinet, viola, and harp. *Rose Cheek'd Laura, Come* is in D flat Major, its dissonances either passing or prepared, its continuity that of theme (almost stacked-up thirds and a scale) and variations. It omits the clarinet in its accompaniment. *There Is a Garden in Her Face* is in G Major, in structure ABCB (the B's varied), and includes hymnal aspects (quintal relations) and a tendency toward sharp changes of tonality not found in *Laura*. *Follow Your Saint*, in F Major, moves toward unresolved dissonances arrived at through ostinato procedures. *Follow Thy Fair Sun* is a bugle-piece in A flat Major, includes ostinati, abrupt shifts of tonality, and, in the version for chorus, becomes canonic. All these songs are pleasing, but they add nothing new to Thomson's musical language.

The *Five Songs to Poems of William Blake for Baritone and Orchestra* (composed for Mack Harrell and also dated 1951) exist as well in an arrangement for baritone and piano. *Tiger! Tiger!* alone exists in two others, one for mixed voices (SATB), another for men's voices (TTBB), both with piano. In E flat Major, motivically employing sequential thirds, *The Divine Image*, though magnificently orchestrated (in part as an organ

FIVE SONGS from WILLIAM BLAKE
II. TIGER! TIGER!

Ti - ger! Ti - ger! burn - ing bright In the for - ests of the night, What -

evocation), is essentially as simple texturally as *Rose Cheek'd Laura, Come.* But it is through-composed rather than thematically repetitive, thus emphasizing the meaning of the words rather than the structure of the poem. *The Land of Dreams,* suitably complex and bewildering musically, brings into one continuity: 1) simple tonality; 2) abrupt shifts of tonality; 3) thirds stacked up as tonalities; 4) twelve-tone transitional passages; 5) melody accompanied by assorted three-note aggregates; 6) mutually exclusive triads; 7) tertial counterpoint; 8) major-minor oppositions; 9) chromatic parallel scales in varying speeds of ascent, producing alternations of vertical relations; 10) eleven-tone thematic passages; 11) final chromatic negation of the original tonality (beginning on C, ending on B Major). This is music at the service of poetry, the former running hither and thither to satisfy the other's every whim, now and then not having time to finish one job before beginning another.

The Little Black Boy employs—very elegantly indeed—still further composing means, derived from cowboy songs of the West and from the sonorities and "isms" of musical instruments (harps and bugles). The footsteps followed are those of Stephen Foster. A dramatic part of the text is underlined by a gradual approach to the total independence of B sharp and C sharp. *And Did Those Feet* adds simulated bagpipes[37] to bugles, the latter being at one point reminiscent of *Die Walküre.* Cross-metrical relation of melody to accompaniment and the repetition and elaborate variation of pentatonic blocks tend to establish a musical structure independent of a poetic one. This tendency is fully accomplished in *Tiger! Tiger!* so that, as musical setting of poetry, the song stands opposite to *The Land of Dreams*. The text is here the vehicle, not the center, of a conventionalized piece of music, a simple ABA. Though no derivation from *The Tiger* of 1926 is discernible, the new melodic line is actually a reworking of the older one. Without referring to dance hall or church, and without composing canons and fugues (though if he had done both one would not have been surprised), Thomson nevertheless reaffirms in the *Blake Songs* his acceptance of a multiplicity of means and a variety of ends. His mind, as we have seen, tends to jump rather than to move forward by cautious steps, precisely as his tonality in a single piece often does. His compositions, in turn, stand out distinct from one another and occasionally, containing this separation interiorly, fall apart on close examination. To apprehend such typically (though not definitively) Thomsonian works as the *Blake Songs,* one must do so immediately or not at all, accepting, as Thomson does and as Blake stated, that "One law for the lion and the ox is oppression."

Meanwhile Agnes de Mille had asked Thomson to compose a ballet for her. Because he had not done this, she obtained his permission to use parts of some of his works that were available in recordings. Piecing together two movements of the *Symphony on a Hymn Tune*, parts of the Concerto for Violincello and Orchestra, and the Suite from *The Mother of Us All*, she found herself at one thirty-measure transitional point up against it. Thomson came to her aid by supplying a bridge passage. *The Harvest According,* as this medley was entitled (from a quotation from Whitman—"Life, life is the tillage / And death is the harvest according") required re-orchestration. This was completed shortly before the première of the ballet at the Metropolitan Opera House in October, 1952. But Thomson found re-re-orchestration necessary, and this time did the job himself. His music for *The Grass Harp* (play by Truman Capote), also composed in 1952, is equally eclectic. Tunes, hymns, canons, mutually exclusive root-position triads (sometimes major, sometimes major and minor) employ scales that are diatonic, chromatic, pentatonic, or whole-tone. The ensemble of instruments chosen is especially attractive: flute, harp, violin, viola, cello, and celesta.

Of his *Sea Piece with Birds,* commissioned at this time by the Dallas Symphony Orchestra, Thomson wrote as program note:

> My *Sea Piece with Birds* is an attempt to portray the undertow of the sea, the surface tension of waves, and the flight of birds as they sail back and forth above the sea. Toward the end trumpets imitate their sound, the cry of sea gulls. The musical texture is that of double and sometimes triple chromatic harmonies. The form, which is free, contains no thematic repetition.

The first twenty-four measures are a two-part counterpoint of three-note aggregates which, though mostly mutually exclusive, are not entirely so. The aggregates, more mutually consistent than those of *Sylvia Marlowe,* contain a major second above or below a tritone or major third. Horizontal movement is slightly imitative, and the intervals most employed are major and minor seconds and thirds. Each musical event is surge-like, rising and falling back in terms of both frequency and amplitude. The next ten measures serve in this respect to rise to greater heights, the next five bringing an apex containing six-note whole-tone upbeats, the twelve tones twice in a measure, a new (the augmented) triad, and a four-note aggregate (the augmented triad above the tritone). On this "wave's" retreat, two eight-measure "swells" (*crescendo, diminuendo*) appear, each a two-part counterpoint of mutually exclusive augmented triads.

The "birds" appear under the guise of flutes playing chromatic wedges and whole-tone scales with tertial and chromatic connecting links. They ascend and descend in parallel and contrary motion, sometimes in canonic imitation, sometimes not. This flight appears above a continuation of the preceding counterpoint. From measure sixty-three to measure sixty-six a repetition of the pieces's first seven notes occurs, but with a new counterpoint of a variety of aggregates and a new orchestration. The birds trill as they sail about chromatically in canon at the minor second, describing also whole-tone scales. As some of the strings move

SEA PIECE WITH BIRDS

in two-part canon, producing whole-tone scales in thirds, and others trill against the florid counterpoint, the situation becomes one of intense activity (mixed scales and aggregates with some doublings), in the midst of which gulls (short descending high trumpet glissandi in chromatic chord formations) scream. The *Sea Piece* concludes at this, its most brilliant point: a type of cadential cut-off more characteristic of the work of Alan Hovhaness than of Virgil Thomson. Long recognized as musical instruments, birds have been imitated by twentieth-century composers as widely different as Fannie Charles Dillon and Olivier Messiaen. The Messiaen situation is usually that of an assemblage, birds gathered together to hear a sermon. Miss Dillon makes field trips to the mountains and deserts of the Southwest, and documents her pieces with reports on her findings as to frequency, quantity, and accent. Thomson's ornithology is all of one kind: his birds sound like themselves rather than a reportage. The *Sea Piece* is recorded, along with *The Seine at Night* and *Wheat Field at Noon,* as the third of *Three Pictures for Orchestra,* of which it is the most naturalistic.

In 1953 Thomson sketched his Concerto for Flute, Strings, Harp, and Percussion, composed his *Kyrie Eleison* (the first and as yet only movement of a new and chromatic Mass), and began a Serenade for Violin and Viola, also chromatic. The *Kyrie Eleison* was dedicated to Dr. Archibald T. Davison, whose seventieth birthday was to be celebrated musically by his former pupils, and who received tape recordings of the pieces written for him by composers who had been his pupils, in performances given them by choral directors he had trained. Thomson's piece, which was performed by the Choir of Fisk University, is an application in an ABA (*da capo*) structure of mutually exclusive three-note aggregates to the situation of strict canon in six parts. The aggregates throughout are limited to a major second above or below a tritone or major third. The score for total independence is 68 per cent in the A's and 87 per cent in the B section. Melodically the A's are characterized by the interval of the minor third, the B by fourths and fifths and the minor second. The sections are virtually equal (sixteen measures) in length, cadences to a

CONCERTO FOR FLUTE, STRINGS, HARP AND PERCUSSION

KYRIE ELEISON

1953 (August)

strong beat producing what slight asymmetry exists. While the counterpoint filling in the cadences involves tertial relations in the A's, it involves secundal relations in the B. The middle section opens with a solo line absolutely not chromatic, its fifth and octave on C bold and striking in context. Though not twelve-tone (there is no G sharp in the soprano, no D in the bass), this *Kyrie* recalls *A Solemn Music* in that it is all of a piece. Its quality, too, is that of gravity and detachment, though it is not, like the other, a lament, but a direct statement of devotion.

October 18, 1953, was the air-date for the memorable production of *King Lear* by the TV-Radio Workshop of the Ford Foundation, with Orson Welles in the title role, direction by Peter Brook, music by Virgil Thomson. In this music, which Thomson also conducted, the whole-tone scale is heard as a six-note aggregate; and, one of the six omitted, the augmented triad allows one of its major thirds to be subdivided into major seconds. This is employed for fanfares and for coherence more or less throughout. A melody accompanied by fifths recalls *The Seine at Night,* but it is somewhat more out of focus. There are parallel seconds, fifths, and thirds, and a march in 3/4 time. The "Mad Music" takes the form of a canon, nearly twelve-tone, seven tones appearing before a repetition. The nine following are chromatically related and all comprised within King Lear's augmented triad.

During the 1953–1954 season Thomson also wrote, at the invitation of Alfred Lunt, incidental music for *Ondine,* the play by Jean Giraudoux. The instruments he chose (flute, harp, percussion, celesta, string quartet) produce an ensemble similar to that of *The Grass Harp.* There are also voices. The first "Song of Sirens" is triadic counterpoint above an eight-measure harp ostinato, the second "Song of Sirens" a variation of the first. "Opera I" is bugle music, as are "Opera II" and "Lullaby I," the latter being two bugle-like parts above an ostinato. "Opera III" starts canonically and includes major-minor oppositions. "Lullaby II" is further bugle music, but lacks an ostinato. "Death's Approach" has the flavor of the *Tango Lullaby,* but a mutual exclusiveness of two elements that recalls *The Seine at Night* (the independence is total except at the beginning and at the end). This was taken from the music for *King Lear.* The purely instrumental parts of the music for *Ondine* include rain-, sleep-, and death-music. These employ three- and four-note aggregates; the former a major second above or below a major third or tritone; the latter major seconds and thirds in various combinations, the most favored of which is two major seconds separated by a major third (they appear once separated by a tritone, and farther along this tritone appears above two major seconds). A flute passage out of the *Sea Piece with Birds* (whole-tone with leaps) is heard above four-note aggregates, strings tremolando. The sleep-music employs these aggregates in mutual exclusiveness (three producing all twelve tones), but frequent doublings relax the strictness of this situation. *Ondine* also includes material from the third movement of the Flute Concerto, which had been sketched quite fully the previous summer.

Explaining his theories about incidental music, Thomson stated that he is primarily concerned with making its function clear. To this end he asks himself first, "Who is the music?" Is it the author, requesting an emotional response to his characters or commenting on the action? Original music is then required. Is it God or fatality? If so, suspense music is indicated. Is it scenery or nature, requiring auditory décor? Something impressionistic would be best. Second, he asks himself, "What is the music?" Is it actor (a brass band going down the street), stage property (a lullaby or spinning song, for example), or the arch (the proscenium) through which the play is seen (curtain-raising drum rolls, fanfares, and finales)? Given a full-length play, Thomson may use all of the functions outlined, feeling no need for unity of view. He enjoys writing music as nature (weather music) and music as props, and he avoids whenever possible writing music as commentary. Currently he is interested in extending the function of percussion (composing sound effects so that they will be performed by members of the Musicians' Local rather than the Stage Hands' Union). He continues his concern to blend his instruments (battery and others) with the speaking voices, taking pains to avoid interferences and to bring about an acoustical build-up becoming to the actors' voices and helpful to the climactic effect.

In the late summer of 1954 Thomson scored his Concerto for Flute, Strings, Harp, and Percussion in the nick of time, since it was scheduled for performance during the Venice Biennale on September 18. His program notes explain his choice of instruments:

> The chief problem for me in writing a flute concerto was to present the flute in a musical and orchestral texture becoming to the instrument. Naturally, I had already considered the expressive character of the work to be suitable to the flute. Otherwise I should not have composed it. My omission of wind instruments from the orchestral accompaniment was determined by the desire to make the solo part sound prominent and beautiful. The expressive content of the piece is double. It is first of all a portrait, but it is also bird music. That is to say, it is a portrait conceived as a concerto for nightingale and strings.

Whose portrait the Flute Concerto is remains a secret. As a portrait, however, it is Thomson's most ambitious, for he attempts a full-length picture of a person still living, just as the *Five Songs* had attempted a complete view of Blake's philosophy. The subject is a gifted individual who, concentrating on sorrow, put his gift to no use until by sheer interior energy it found a way to be expressed. The final situation is not one of joy itself, but of excitement at the prospect of experiencing joy.

The scoring is for string orchestra, harp, celesta, and one percussion player. The work is in three movements, the first of which is an unaccompanied solo for flute, marked *rapsodico*.

Forty-one measures long, this prelude is a line-drawing using all the steps and leaps available within an octave, and adding that of the minor ninth in excess. Approximately one-third of these are the latter interval or its corresponding minor second.[38] The major third appears only half as many times, and proportionately fewer minor thirds, tritones, and major sevenths occur. The augmented fifth appears four times; the major second, fourth, fifth, and minor seventh appear only two or three times, the major sixth and octave each once. The placing of this single octave at the end of the line does two things: 1) it negates the musical texture it concludes, giving the sound of a "wrong note" and reminding one of an equally unfortunate cadence, that of the Debussy Trio for Flute, Harp, and Viola; 2) it negates the rhapsodic expressivity, for it calls attention to the frame rather than to the activity within it. The form is that of a continuous invention gradually becoming more and more florid. Whole-tone scales ascending and descending and connected chromatically, chromatic scales, and trills (appropriately whole-tone and half-tone) are its ornaments.

The second movement, marked *lento,* is a study in dual chromatic harmonies, each of which is acoustically complete and wholly independent of the other. The flute solo constitutes a third chromatic element, no tone of which is ever heard at the same time in either of the accompanying harmonies. Since each of these harmonies is in four parts, the full texture is that of nine voices, no note of which doubles any other. In the two harmonies, moreover, there are no suspensions, all the voices in each four-part chord moving simultaneously to notes not included in that chord. The purpose of the dual chromatics is to produce a mood of disembodiment, unreal, non-substantial, *insaisissable*. The purpose of the constantly simultaneous part-movement in each of the constituent harmonic elements is to enable the ear to perceive these constantly as two elements only, each one compact, complete, and entirely harmonious and containing within itself no tensions.

The first eight measures, like the first movement, are a single line, but here it is drawn as a series of four-note aggregates (for strings alone) composed of major seconds and thirds, minor thirds, and tritones. There are altogether nine different arrangements of these intervals, the one used half of the time being two major seconds a major third apart. (*Ondine* had borrowed this.) The next sixteen measures include the flute, and the situation— single flute notes against four-tone strings chords—is that of mutual exclusiveness, except, as in *The Seine at Night*, near phrase beginnings and endings, only four out of forty-five counts employing doublings, giving these measures a score of 91 per cent for total independence.[39] At this point, twenty-nine measures follow in which the flute is heard above a two-part counterpoint, each part consisting of four-note aggregates in strings, the celesta entering toward the end. "The full texture is that of nine voices," but the notes that double the others bring the score for total independence down to 48.9 per cent. During an interlude of eight measures (the flute being silent), the two four-note aggregates produce more, but not total, independence. The following thirteen measures (seven of 3/2, six of 4/2) are again in nine voices, and again the celesta comes in ultimately. But the situation is still not one of total independence, the score having climbed, however, to 72.2 per cent. New aggregates involving stacked-up minor thirds now appear. These also appear melodically on the flute. But the most striking of the fresh introductions is an aggregate composed of two tritones a minor third apart.

The third movement, marked *ritmico,* is also based on double harmonies; but in this instance the contrast is between chromatic chords and diatonic chords—or, if you prefer, between chords that contain the augmented fourth or fifth and the major second (chords classically known as "dissonant") and those containing only thirds and perfect fifths, the so-called "consonant" or "perfect" chords. As before, there is no doubling of notes between the two harmonic elements, and the flute part is generally independent of both. The character of the harmonic contrast in this movement is aimed to accentuate, to dramatize, the rhythmic animation that is characteristic of the expressive content.

Root-position triads in the strings move first chromatically, then along lines of stacked-up thirds to the whole-tone scale, producing a form of rise and fall (four measures of 3/4) characteristic of this movement, its rapidity (quarter equals 120) depicting personal energy, just as a similar rise and fall *lento molto rubato* had described the "undertow of the sea and surface tension of the waves." The flute above (eighteen measures) is concerned with trills and wedges, diatonic and whole-tone. An interlude for celesta (six measures overlapping the preceding section by two measures) is made of two mutually exclusive four-note aggregates. The following eight measures (upper strings employing four-note chromatic aggregates, the lower ones employing three-note diatonic triads, plus the flute melody above) produce a low score for mutual exclusiveness: 41 per cent. Seven more measures invert the situation, putting the triads above the aggregates (score: 58 per cent), and lead to a single measure without the triads, the lower strings playing the two four-note aggregates similar to those of the celesta interlude (score: 66 per cent). The flute melody here outlines an augmented triad. In the following four measures the aggregates return to their superior position, and the score for independence drops to 22 per cent. But the five succeeding measures (two of them two four-note aggregates; the last three, two three-note aggregates) bring back total mutual exclusiveness.

A repetition of measures 5–8 now occurs, the flute's melody being given to a solo violin, which continues, on the flute's entrance, by doubling at the octave. This reinforcement, not constant but intermittent, is finally removed, leaving the "bird" independent of assistance. A celesta-and-percussion interlude follows (six measures constituted as before). Fourteen measures add a rhythmic motive (2 against 3), the melody soaring above the aggregates, which in turn move above triads in the bass (score: 35 per cent). The harp enters, outlining augmented triads (which the strings in accompaniment also employ) interspersed with whole-tone scales, the flutes playing major thirds tremolando independently of the harp, and the situation (eight measures) being one of nine tones at once, totally independent of one another for six measures, relaxing this strictness in the seventh and eighth. This passage is repeated with the orchestration changed. The flute's line now increases in floridity, and the accompaniment shifts both orchestrally and in the composition of the aggregates, more and more emphasis being given to the augmented triad in the accompaniment and to the whole-tone scale in the melody. A forty-two-measure flute cadenza follows *lento,* balancing the opening *rapsodico.* Changes from minor to major and inversion (up rather than down) communicate here a generally bright view. On the orchestra's re-entrance, augmented triads (totally independent of one another) are superimposed, while above them the flute leaps actively (and also independently) for eight measures. In the next nine, the accompaniment (still augmented triads) contracts and expands to close position and away from it, the melody also moving in whole tones and augmented triads. The final eight measures (syncopated alternations of *pizzicati* and *arco*) begin like a repeat of the beginning. Triads are on the beat; four-note aggregates are on the off-beats; the flute, ascending and descending along whole-tone scales, concludes by going up. Percussion enters (effectively, its appearances being few and brief) and the C Major triad plus a four-note aggregate (major seconds a major third apart) agree in ostinato that the total final moment is intense, exciting. In this third movement Thomson approaches the contrast between diatonic and chromatic as a problem inviting solution, as a musical dialectic. The two had been juxtaposed in *Louisiana Story,* but attempting to resolve their opposition is a new road for him. If he continues along it, two points might be reached, which are composition-as-intellectual-exercise and music-as-struggle-and-drama (sister cities East of the Rhine possessing colonies throughout the world). It is more likely, however, that whatever he does musically, the result will finally be a statement of peaceful co-existence.

In 1955 Thomson was invited by a publisher to set some hymn-texts. He chose *A Song for the Stable* by Amanda Benjamin

Hall and *Never Another* by Mark Van Doren. Whatever his treatment of the former may seem to be, it is no diatonic arrangement of a hexatonic hymn from the Old South; it is in F Major, with a first ending on D Minor, has no E, and is hexatonic in its own right. *Never Another* (D Major with suggestions of B Minor) employs passing dissonances. Neither of these hymns is problematical. In his next three works, *Old English Songs, Hommage à Marya Freund,* and *Tres Estampas de Niñez,* Thomson again uses both diatonic and chromatic procedures, only to renounce ambivalence altogether in his orchestral transcriptions of Brahms's Eleven Chorale-Preludes for organ. Each transcription is faithful note for note to the original. Only in the last is the organ evoked. The others alleviate the contrapuntal thickness of the originals toward a straightforward effect of melody with accompaniment, presenting Brahms, insofar as a chorale-prelude permits, in the guise of a French tourist.

The *Old English Songs* are eight in number. *Look, How the Floor of Heav'n* (Shakespeare) and *The Bell Doth Toll* (Thomas Heywood) continue Thomson's adventures in chromaticism. The piano accompaniment of *Look, How the Floor of Heav'n* employs aggregates consistently made up of intervals generated by the whole-tone scale (major seconds, major thirds, the tritone in various superimpositions) or of the whole-tone scale itself with or without one of the intervals mentioned. The chromatic melody results from progressions of these aggregates, always doubling one of the tones of the accompaniment or supplying that tone of the whole-tone scale which at that point the accompaniment lacks. *The Bell Doth Toll* is also chromatic, but the intervals of the aggregates are more various: all the intervals possible within an octave occurring, including the octave itself, with the exception of the major seventh. The tritone is favored, appearing systematically between adjacent tones at least once, and often twice, somewhere in every aggregate. The melody is tertial and athematic. Its relation to the accompaniment is not so transparent as its relation to the text. The song has the sound of an old bell, is ominous in expression, suggesting darkness rather than light.

The rest of the *Old English Songs* are diatonic. The melody of *Consider, Lord* (John Donne) flows naturally though athematically, emphasizing in relation to its accompaniment the simplest intervals—thirds and fifths—and not disdaining the unison. The accompaniment begins as a line doubled two octaves above, later permitting other tones to enter or surround this tonal space, first the interior octave, then exterior major and minor thirds, then fifths, and finally lightly filled-in interior harmonies. Dissonances (seconds and fourths) are resolved either up or down. Two sevenths appear to be somewhat unprepared, but no preparation is required from the point of view of stacked-up thirds expressed at these points melodically. *Remember Adam's Fall* (Anonymous, fifteenth century) is concerned with the doctrines of original sin and of redemption. The ringing of bells that this music suggests is clear and strong. With extraordinarily few means, the major triads of D, A, and G, *John Peel* (John Woodcock Graves) achieves an effect of great variety. This athematic hunting song begins with the simplicity of two voices, going on to the relative richness and effectiveness of an ending with harmony suggestive of a large horn ensemble. *The Holly and the Ivy* (Anonymous, 1557) a carol of Nativity and Lent, is diatonic, but less restricted in means, evoking both organ and choral styles. The poem has five stanzas, and the melody is slightly adjusted each time to suit the words. The ending is on the dominant, formerly a Thomson objective, in these recent works something of a rarity. *At the Spring* (Jasper Fisher), in D Major, is charming in character, including scales, figurations, waltzes. Advance notice of harmonies to come is sometimes given in the accompaniment. In its course the character of the music changes without preparation or translation, recalling similar practices by Satie. *If Thou a Reason Dost Desire to Know* (Sir Francis Kynaston) is a love song, the text intellectually conceived, for it concludes with a statement of the ultimate separation of body and soul. Thomson's setting reflects the workings of the poet's mind, beginning in D Major, ending afield in C Major, with the voices not on the dominant, but cast down to the subdominant. En route, physical bliss is echoed as diatonic (including seventh chords), the mind with its machinations as whole-tone aggregates.

Hommage à Marya Freund was originally to have been a harp étude making use of a maximum of pedal changes for the diatonic instrument. Finished as a piano solo, it baffles the analytical mind. It is entirely composed of root-position triads, major or minor, in a sequence that is sometimes diatonic, at other times whole-tone or even suggestive of dodecaphony. The tonic, followed by the dominant, suggests a chromaticism resulting from stacked-up triads. But cross-related tones, introduced immediately, falsify such a view. Likewise, progressions following the whole-tone scale are succeeded by a chromatic step. Nevertheless, this music seems quite natural to the ear, not problematical at all.

During the summer of 1956, Thomson wrote incidental music for two Shakespeare plays produced at Stratford, Connecticut. *Measure for Measure* was presented as taking place in early nineteenth-century Vienna, which allowed Thomson to write waltzes on the Schubert and Lanner models. For these he employed two trumpets, two horns, a xylophone, and a piano with tacks placed in the hammers to alter the timbre of the strings. *King John* was given straight, with ceremonial Court Music and military Battle Music. In 1957, three more plays by Shakespeare, Connecticut-produced, were provided with incidental music, and Shakespeare was given more attention than Thomson had previously granted him. The music for *Othello* includes Street Music imitative of bagpipes, a hexatonic "Willow Song" for Desdemona, and two songs for Iago, one involving trumpet imitations. Differences of locality in *The Merchant of Venice* suggested corresponding musical differences. Bells and chimes involving seven superimpositions of rhythmic ostinati, varying in length, identify Venice. The city's Jewish section is also bells, but lower in pitch. Portia's home is melodically pentatonic, harmonically diatonic, and suitably Elizabethan in feeling. Her garden is chromatic, the music involving mutually exclusive aggregates. Diversions indoors, a Moroccan Masque, are provided with music of exotic flavor, the Moroccan one involving more secundal relations than usual in Thomson's work. Festivities in Venice bring about a diatonic Carnival Music. One song, "Was This Fair Face," is interpolated from *All's Well That Ends Well.* "Tell Me Where Is Fancy Bred" is modal music full of flexibility and interesting tonal surprises. *Much Ado About Nothing* was presented as taking place among the Spanish residents of southern California in the nineteenth century. To clarify this shift of time and place, Thomson did research in southwest coast musics as he had done research in those of the Bayou country for *Louisiana Story.* Thus he was able to provide "Sigh No More Ladies" in two versions, one Elizabethan and becoming to the text, the other "rancho" and more suitable to the production.

Later in 1957, Thomson was made musical advisor for a series of TV shows directed by John Houseman. An animated cartoon by John Hubley intended to be shown with all these telecasts required music. Thomson's *Lively Arts Fugue,* in C Major and with scales at the end reminiscent of parts of *Election Day,* was found insufficiently jazzy in character; it was not used. At the same time Thomson was invited by the director, John Cromwell, to write music for *The Goddess,* a Columbia moving-picture written by Paddy Chayevsky. The score he provided employs many techniques. Sometimes pentatonic or hexatonic, it is at other times diatonic or chromatic. When a radio is turned on, the jazz that comes forth seems reasonable from that loudspeaker at that date (1928–1958), but it is all original jazz written by Thomson. Elsewhere the music for *The Goddess* is more germane to its composer, some sections (involving "Yes, Jesus Loves Me") recalling the *Hymn Tune Symphony.* Realistic in intent, the film is depressingly concentrated on neuroses following from the absence of mother-love. The music, standing apart from this concern, is optimistic in character, springing as it does mostly from the nineteenth century, when Americans saw their future in rosy tints. The positioning of the music with respect to the film is refreshing to the movie-goer as well as to the film itself; it never comments on the plot or gives the story away, but is always an object (*e.g.,* jazz from a radio) or a structural element, opening and closing the film, underlining its architecture.

In 1957 Thomson also experimented in setting Spanish texts, choosing three poems by Reyna Rivas, *Tres Estampas de Niñez*

TODAS LAS HORAS
Reyna Rivas

To - das las ho - ras las pas - sa ⌒en la ven-ta - na.

1957

(*Three Pictures of Childhood*). Each gives an exact picture of Venezuelan childhood. *Todas las horas* concerns a child sitting by a window, the sunshine streaming through a Venetian blind. Going to sleep in the barred light, the child is seen as in a moment of eternity. A shoe nearby, however, suggests a cobbler in jail. The music moves fluently in areas that resist analysis. In two of the *Blake Songs,* childhood had inspired Thomson to use a multiplicity of relatively differentiated technical means. Here the means are so fused that technique disappears from notice, sounds moving naturally to the most unexpected points. Twenty years earlier, in many of the Portraits, the same result was obtained with a maximum of abruptness. In *Todas las horas* everything happens as in dreams. *Son amigos de todos* concerns children in the square, a policeman bringing them candy and playing with them, a rat approaching just for the pleasure of hearing them speak. The E Major music is given a certain Spanish character that in the context of Thomson's work suggests also a hunting song. *Nadie lo oye como ellos* presents children awaiting the man who sells candies. Having no money, they engage in barter, the merchant going off into the distance with a little wooden horse. Here again the music is resistant to analysis, yet simple as it falls on the ear. It involves a complexity of rhythm (4 against 3), suggested by the text and accepted by the accompaniment, that has not been found elsewhere in Thomson's recent works. Multi-directional as these works appear to be, they move to no technical points unfamiliar to one acquainted with Thomson's music.

Postscript

THOMSON ONCE INFORMED THE WRITER THAT DURING HIS HARVARD
student days, experimentally in connection with research on the
part of a Missouri minister of the Gospel who was documenting
states of ecstasy, he and others among his classmates took *peyotl,*
a Mexican cactus drug. Under its influence he had a vision of his
future life on earth. In this preview, the body of his music took
the visible form of an architecture, "a large railway station, not
particularly attractive, though details of it were interesting, but
massive and full of variety, with many people going in and out
of it." He was aware then that his output would never be considered primarily in terms of beauty or ugliness, but he trusted
that his vision would come true and that his music would be
found useful. That it has.

Answering the question raised earlier about the structure of his
music, it can be said that the division of a work into parts log-
ically related through their proportions is rarely Thomson's concern. Some of his compositions, however—*A Solemn Music, The
Waltzing Waters,* the *Sonata da chiesa,* the 1953 *Kyrie Eleison,*
and several more—are from any point of view well-structured. As
to method ("How many floors and doors and windows are there
in it?"), his musical procedures, though numerable, are seemingly
countless. As to materials, he now clearly prefers the orchestra,
though he can, of course, write for anything and would no doubt
compose for magnetic tape if a corps of workers were available
to carry out his directions. As to form (which for this writer
means expressive content as distinguished from structure), Thomson can in a great variety of ways dispose his listeners to tranquillity through outlining the tendencies there of sorrow, com-
passion, fear, love, and wonder. He says that he expresses only
those feelings he actually has; at the same time, his attention
does incline to move by means of joy and energy away from an

245

inner emphasis to the outer world of nature, events, and people. Mirth remains in his hands a physical matter; he can use ridicule, but his work contains no anger.

He is intensely concerned about both good and evil, with a stronger tendency toward the former, but his delight is to mix things up a little and to keep that situation in his music one of healthy mystery. He is inveterately preoccupied with adding expressivity to available techniques and with destroying formulas. He has no respect for any formal garden that a musicologist might tend, contributing by his work only disorder where order pretends to reign. On the other hand, when approaching a musical wilderness (the realm of noises, discontinuities, Dada), he sees everything as convention, first choosing his own, then by a series of incisive actions providing Chaos with the sense organs of civilized beings, which thereupon, as in the tale by Kwang-Tse, rob poor Chaos of his life.

We know now the great variety and all but intangible nature of Thomson's work. What position has it in the field of contemporary music? Obviously, one of popularity. In my personal panorama it has today little place. For all his heterodoxical use of the twelve tones, merely providing dodecaphony with a harmonic outlet does not seem to me to be the necessary facing of contemporary musical reality. Nor do I hold with his view of the artist's responsibility. This view, which was also Gertrude Stein's, is a heretical one that gained adherents in Europe after the Renaissance: Art is the representation of an inner and outer reality. In an older view, and my own, it is the artist's duty to imitate in his work not the appearance of nature, but her manner of operation. Thomson's music, in this respect, is therefore somewhat removed from my own preoccupations. For that matter, so is most of the rest of contemporary music. Still, however remote musically from Virgil Thomson, I keep coming back to him with gratitude, as I do to some others: to Henry Cowell, Erik Satie, Lou Harrison, Charles Ives, Edgar Varèse—all of them composers who have done what they had to do without pretense and in defiance of the general run of Teutonism and neo-classicism. Among them Thomson stands out as a master of comedy, my regard for which agrees with that of Joyce, who held it to be "the greatest of arts because the joy of comedy is freest from desire or loathing." [40]

Notes

1. A few manuscripts exist without titles, having, in the composer's opinion, "no special musical value." Two, probably written at Harvard, have asymmetrical phrase lengths: one, 5, 4, 5, 4, the other, 2, 8, 9, 4 (these series of numbers appearing where titles ordinarily would). A third, probably written for Nadia Boulanger, is in Bach chorale style and entitled simply *Chorales for Four Voices*. "O, My Deir Hert," from the Oxford Book of English Verse, is probably an attempt to write a carol in the early English manner.
2. One may contrast the experience of Yvette Grimaud, the young French atonalist, who, visiting the same monastery, was influenced to write her *Chants d'espace* in microtonal dodecaphony, through observing the monks' niceties of intonation.
3. Henry Cowell was using the tone-cluster in 1911. It had previously occurred in some of Charles Ives's work around 1907. Leo Ornstein adopted it in 1917. The first public concert in the East (Cowell's early demonstrations all occurred in California) involving its use by Cowell took place in 1921. Thomson might easily have plucked it out of the musical atmosphere, of which it was very certainly a part.
4. In this variation, "God Rest You, Merry Gentlemen" appears in one of the counterpoints.
5. *Cf.* Satie's *Ogives*, also based on plain song material, in which both the phraseology and the tetrachordal method of the original material (*i.e.*, the only musical elements present) are preserved.
6. Carl Fischer, Inc., rejected *Two Sentimental Tangos*, the reader having marked the manuscript in red pencil with the comment: "Rank! Correspondence student."
7. *The Tiger*, in this version, remains unpublished and has never been performed.
8. A performance of *Capital, Capitals* at the Paris house of the Duchess of Clermont-Tonnerre brought forth an invitation to produce another work for similar usage. The project took the form of a play by Georges Hugnet, *Le Droit de Varech*, with incidental music by Thomson, but the performance never took place. What exists musically is the manuscript of an unfinished piece for accordion solo, characterized by scales and waltzes and including two leaps of a seventh (in succession) in the same direction.
9. Published in 1940 in Paris by the magazine *L'Usage de la parole* in a cover design by Pablo Picasso.
10. Contrast, for example, a Martha Graham program note with Thomson's report on April 2, 1946, of a performance by Miss Graham.
11. Though Koussevitzky did. Reading this work in 1928 with a view to con-

ducting it, he enjoyed the first three movements, but after the fourth threw up his hands and exclaimed, "What can I do with this?"

12. *Les Soirées Bagnolaises* (Georges Hugnet), for voice and piano, written at this time, is reminiscent of the *Hymn Tune Symphony*, though more experimental. Also the *Commentaire sur Saint Jérome* (Marquis de Sade), for voice and piano, is of that year.

13. Eight of the Portraits were scored for orchestra in 1944.

14. "Neo-Romanticism involves rounded melodic material (the neo-Classicists affected angular themes) and the frank expression of personal sentiments.
    "The neo-Romantic position is an esthetic one purely, because technically we are eclectic. Our contribution to contemporary esthetics has been to pose the problem of sincerity in what is for our century a new way. We are not out to impress, and we dislike inflated emotions. The feelings we really have are the only ones we think worthy of expression. . . . Sentiment is our subject and sometimes landscape, but preferably landscape with figures."—Virgil Thomson, *Possibilities*, I, p. 1.

15. This is not the *Stabat Mater* by Saint Bernard of Clairvaux, but an original prose-poem in French.

16. This theme "later engenders still more protracted serial orders based on thirds strung together, and these give the work away as contemporary." —Arthur Berger, *Modern Music*, XXIII, No. 1, 1946, p. 61.

17. The use of pen and ink is not a part of Thomson's habit, though others, notably Stravinsky, have carried it to the point of calligraphic art. When possible, he employs someone else to do this work.

18. He had been commissioned in the spring of 1934 by the League of Composers to write a work for women's chorus, to be performed by the Adesdi Chorus of the Dessoff Choirs. Having, by the end of summer, two such works available, he chose to offer the Mass because he found its dissonance context more suitable. The *Medea Choruses* were first performed in New York the same season (1934) by the Saint Cecilia Choir.

19. A handsome copy of it reproduced on pink paper was published as a supplement to *View Magazine*, accompanying the issue dedicated to the painting of Florine Stettheimer.

20. In the *Aeolian Harp* Etude this independence was total but of single lines. In *Fingered Fifths* it was an unanalyzable chord sequence produced by the independent motion of the fifths. In this Prelude (sixteen measures of a two-part counterpoint of root-position triads, and their repetition by an inversion of the two parts with the accompaniment of an added melody) the situation also is not precisely schematic. The intention is clear (total independence of parts), but it is sacrificed 50 per cent of the time in favor of melodic movement. Some of the doublings that occur suggest that an intervallic melodic motivation was present, and the following by both parts of the ascending whole-tone scale at the end (one in augmentation, the other in diminution) supports this suggestion. But analysis shows an absence of any such correspondence between the two lines of triads. The added melody (English horn) is admittedly not well written from the point of view of total independence, but it admirably

recalls the major-minor octave passage of the *Hymn Tune Symphony,* which its opening resembles to a T.

21. See, for example, the discussion of the early Portraits for Unaccompanied Violin. Note, too, that Thomson's interest in chromaticism is each time subsequent to his having written, just before, a largely diatonic work.

22. He found in Irene Thérèse Whitfield's book *Louisiana French Folk Songs* a rich treasure of musical material. From the Library of Congress he obtained recordings of fiddle music collected by John and Alan Lomax in the 'Cajun region of Louisiana. He did not himself make a trip south.

23. This was recorded and synchronized by Flaherty himself with the assistance of Helen Van Dongen. Both are to be congratulated on its high decibel level.

24. Though this was recorded, following Thomson's stipulation, by the Philadelphia Orchestra, Eugene Ormandy conducting. Commitments on the orchestra's part brought about a few months' delay, enabling Thomson to go over his scoring (notated from his original short-hand sketch by Henry Brant) with a fine comb.

25. This Suite was used by both Georges Balanchine and Ruthanna Boris for choreographics, each entitled *Bayou.* Stravinsky advised the use of the first Suite rather than this one, on the ground that, in his opinion, there was more there to "get one's teeth into." The advice was not followed; neither version has stayed in repertory.

26. "Thomson has a style, and a very definite one, but it is almost impossible to put one's finger on any detail of harmonic, melodic, or rhythmic procedure that it entails. It is unidiosyncratic. The personal element lies where it most legitimately belongs—in the emotional content, the organic whole of the music, rather than in its terms of expression. It is at the source that his music is original."—P. Glanville-Hicks, *Musical Quarterly,* XXXV, p. 209.

27. C, E flat, G flat, G, E, D, F, A flat, A, C sharp, B flat, B.

28. E flat, G, B flat, D, E, F sharp, A, B, C, C sharp, G sharp, F.

29. G, B flat, D, F, F sharp, G sharp, A, C sharp, D sharp, E, B, C. There is a lack of correspondence between this and the notes in the printed score; the latter is incorrect.

30. G, F sharp, D, D flat, C, B flat, F, E flat, B, A flat, E, A. See note above regarding errors in the printed score.

31. C, A, B flat, G, A flat, F, F sharp, B, E, E flat, D, D flat (C).

32. D sharp, E, C sharp, D, B, C, A, B flat, F sharp, G sharp, G (G flat), F, (E). The descending chromatic cadence that brings about two tonal repetitions is integral to the composition, oblique and varied scalewise cadences (ascending or descending, chromatic, whole-tone, or minor-diatonic) appearing every eight measures.

33. Confronted with the job of reviewing for the *Herald Tribune* a work by Schoenberg or Webern, it was his custom to study the score beforehand, sometimes with the assistance of some enthusiastic atonalist.

34. Thomson acknowledges counsel from the cellist Luigi Silva in composing and editing the solo part.

35. The four-octave diatonic descending scale passage of the *Hymn Tune Symphony* is heard here as chromatic and ascending through three octaves.

36. Satie employed two types of metrical symmetry: 1) "horizontal" (*e.g.*, 5, 5, 6, 4, 5) when a phrase length, once established, is then lengthened and shortened by an equal number of measures before being restated in conclusion; 2) "vertical" (*e.g.*, 5, 6, 7, 6, 5) when the phraseology is a numerical series and its retrograde.

37. In many respects these *Blake Songs* are a Scotland Story.

38. Should one attempt to give technical coherence to the body of Thomson's work, setting out to establish, say, that *his* interval is the major second (as a count might reveal), such an attempt would be punctured by this work, as any other such trial balloon would be by another work.

39. In arriving at this score the following steps were taken: 1) the total number of events within the passage, including suspensions, was counted (45); 2) those involving doublings were likewise counted (4); 3) subtraction gives the number of mutually exclusive aggregates (41); 4) taking the last number, 41, as a divisor, the score 91 per cent is obtained.

40. Cf. *James Joyce: His Way of Interpreting the Modern World,* by William York Tindall (Scribner, 1950), p. 125.

List of Works

Year of Composition	Title	Duration	Publisher	Recording Companies
	WORKS FOR PIANO			
1921 (November 25)	Prelude for Piano	2	MS	
1923	Two Sentimental Tangos (originally three)	5	MS	
	(See also listing under Works for Orchestra)			
	1. Slow and Smooth	2		
	2. Not Fast	3		
1925	Synthetic Waltzes, for 2 pianos, 4 hands; also for 1 piano, 4 hands	6	EV	COL
1926 (June and August)	Five Inventions for Piano; also arr. for 2 pianos by Fizdale and Gold	6, 15	EV	
	1. With Marked Rhythm	1		
	2. Freely	1, 15		
	3. Flowing	2		
	4. Rhythmically	1		
	5. Firmly	1		
1926 (December)	Ten Easy Pieces and a Coda (to be played as a single work)	6	MS	
1928 (November)	Symphony on a Hymn Tune, arr. for 4 hands by John Kirkpatrick. (See also listing under Works for Orchestra)	19	MS	
1929 (October 24)	Portrait of Alice Branlière (See below, Portraits Album 5)	1, 30	MY	
(October 28)	A Portrait of Maurice Grosser (See below, Portraits Album 1)	1, 30	MY	
(November 2)	A Portrait of Ramon Senabre (See below, Portraits Album 2)	1, 30	MY	
(November)	Piano Sonata No. 1 (now Symphony No. 2)	16	MS	
	Allegro			
	Uguale			
	Finale			
(Dec. 10-16)	Piano Sonata No. 2	7	MS	
	Cantabile			
	Sostenuto			
	Leggiero e brillante			
1930 (January 22)	Clair Leonard's Profile	1	MS	

Year of Composition	Title	Duration	Publisher	Recording Companies
1930 (February 1)	Madame Dubost chez elle	1	MS	
(February 20)	Jean Ozenne (See below, Portraits Album 3)	1, 20	MY	
(May 29)	Russell Hitchcock, Reading (See below, Portraits Album 5)	1	MY	
(July 17-18)	Piano Sonata No. 3, on white keys (4 movements to be played as a single work)	5	MY	
1932	Symphony No. 2, arr. 4 hands by Virgil Thomson (See listing under Works for Orchestra)	16	MS	
1935 (April 30, May 4)	A Portrait of Constance Askew (See below, Portraits Album 2)	1	MY	
(May 1)	A Portrait of R. Kirk Askew, Jr. (See below, Portraits Album 2)	1, 30	MY	
(May 5)	A Portrait of Carrie Stettheimer (See below, Portraits Album 1)	1, 30	MY	
(May 5)	A Portrait of Ettie Stettheimer (See below, Portraits Album 5)	1	MY	
(May 9)	A Portrait of Henry McBride (See below, Portraits Album 4)	1, 20	MY	
(May 20)	A Portrait of Paul Bowles (See below, Portraits Album 3)	1	MY	
(May 21)	A Portrait of A. Everett Austin, Jr. (See below, Portraits Album 4)	1, 15	MY	
(May 22)	A Portrait of Josiah Marvel (See below, Portraits Album 4)	1, 30	MY	
(May)	The John Mosher Waltzes (Published as part of Filling Station: No. 6, Family Life; see listing under Ballets)	2, 10	ARR	
(September 2)	A Portrait of Miss Agnes Rindge (See below, Portraits Album 3)	2	MY	
(September 3)	Portrait of Helen Austin	1, 20	MS	
(September 6)	Portrait of Jere Abbott (See below, Portraits Album 2; see also listing under Works for Orchestra)	2	MY	
(September 16)	Harold Lewis Cook (See below, Portraits Album 5)	1, 15	MY	
(September 17)	A Day Dream (Portrait of Herbert Whiting)	2	CF	

Year of Composition	Title	Duration	Publisher	Recording Companies
1937 (November)	Filling Station, arr. for 2 hands by Virgil Thomson (See listing under Ballets)	21	ARR	
1938 (August 15)	Portrait of Claude Biais	1	MS	
(August 16)	Portrait of Louis Lange	1	MS	
1940 (April 1)	Portrait of Sherry Mangan (See below, Portraits Album 3)	1, 30	MY	
(April 8)	Portrait of Lise Deharme (See below, Portraits Album 2)	1, 30	MY	
(April 11)	Portrait of Louise Ardant (Published as With Trumpet and Horn in Nine Etudes for Piano)	2, 30	CF	
(April 12)	Portrait of Hans Arp (See below, Portraits Album 4)	1	MY	
(April 15)	Portrait of Max Kahn (See below, Portraits Album 2; see also listing under Works for Orchestra)	3	MY	
(April 17)	Portrait of Georges Hugnet (See below, Portraits Album 1; see also listing under Works for Orchestra)	1, 30	MY	
(April 18)	Portrait of Sophie Tauber-Arp (See below, Portraits Album 4)	2, 20	MY	
(April 20)	Eccentric Dance (Portrait of Madame Kristians Tonny)	2	CF	
(April 24)	Portrait of Flavie Alvarez de Toledo (See below, Portraits Album 1; see also listing under Works for Orchestra)	2, 25	MY	
(April 29)	Portrait of Theodate Johnson (See below, Portraits Album 5)	1, 30	MY	
(April 30)	Portrait of Pablo Picasso (See below, Portraits Album 1; see also listing under Works for Orchestra)	2, 15	MY	
(May 1)	Piano Sonata No. 4 (Guggenheim Jeune)	7	EV	NED
	Allegro	2, 30		
	Adagio	3		
	Vivace	1, 30		
	(Recorded as harpsichord solo)			
(May 3)	Portrait of Howard Putzel (See below, Portraits Album 4)	2, 50	MY	

Year of Composition	Title	Duration	Publisher	Recording Companies
1940 (May 4)	Portrait of Léon Kochnitzky (See below, Portraits Album 2)	1, 30	MY	
(May 7)	The Dream World of Peter Rose-Pulham (See below, Portraits Album 3)	2, 20	MY	
(May 8)	Portrait of Dora Maar	2	MS	
(May 9)	Portrait of Tristan Tzara (Pastorale)	2	MS	
(May 12)	Portrait of Germaine Hugnet (See below, Portraits Album 2)	2, 40	MY	
(May 13)	Portrait of Mary Widney (See below, Portraits Album 3)	1, 30	MY	
(May 15)	Portrait of Pierre Mabille	1	MS	
(May 29)	Portrait of Nicolas de Chatelain (See below, Portraits Album 3; see also listing under Works for Orchestra)	4, 30	MY	
(July 2)	Portrait of Clarita, Comtesse de Forceville (See below, Portraits Album 5)	1, 45	MY	
(July 3)	Portrait of Jamie Campbell	1, 15	MS	
(July 9)	Portrait of André Ostier (See below, Portraits Album 3)	1	MY	
(September 6)	A Portrait of Alexander Smallens (See below, Portraits Album 1; see also listing under Works for Orchestra)	2, 40	MY	
1941 (June 15)	A Portrait of Mina Curtiss (See below, Portraits Album 1)	2	MY	
(July 6)	A Portrait of Louise Crane (See below, Portraits Album 4)	1, 40	MY	
(September 27)	Portrait of Jessie K. Lasell (piano sketch; see listing under Works for Orchestra)	2, 30	MS	
(October 5)	Portrait of Florine Stettheimer (See below, Portraits Album 5)	2, 20	MY	
1942 (July 21)	Portrait of James Patrick Cannon	1, 45	MS	
(July 29)	Portrait of Peter Monro Jack (See below, Portraits Album 5)	2, 30	MY	
(September 30)	Portrait of Schuyler Watts	1, 30	MS	
(October 1)	Portrait of Jean (Mrs. Schuyler) Watts (See below, Portraits Album 4)	1, 30	MY	

Year of Composition	Title	Duration	Publisher	Recording Companies
1942 (October 16)	Portrait of Aaron Copland (See listing under Works for Orchestra)	3, 15	MS	
1943–1944	Ten Etudes for Piano	17	CF	DEC
(July 12, 1943)	Repeating Tremolo (Fanfare)	2		
(July 9, 1943)	Tenor Lead (Madrigal) (also published separately)	2		
(July 13, 1943)	Fingered Fifths (Canon)	1, 30		
(Sept. 29, 1944)	Fingered Glissando (Aeolian Harp)	1, 30		
(July 11, 1943)	Double Glissando (Waltz)	2		
(Aug. 12, 1943)	For the Weaker Fingers (Music-Box Lullaby)	1		
(Nov. 8, 1943)	Oscillating Arm (Spinning Song)	1		
(Aug. 15, 1943)	Five-Finger Exercise (Portrait of Briggs Buchanan)	2		
(Aug. 16, 1943)	Parallel Chords (Tango)	2, 30		
(Aug. 12, 1943)	Ragtime Bass (published separately in two versions, one simplified)	1, 30		
After 1945– before 1950	Walking Song, arr. for 2 pianos by Fizdale and Gold from the film Tuesday in November	2	GS	
1945 (December 5)	A Portrait of Lou Harrison (See below, Portraits Album 1)	1	MY	
1929–1945	Portraits, for piano solo (5 Albums)		MY	
	Album 1			
	Bugles and Birds (Pablo Picasso)	2, 15		
	With Fife and Drums (Mina Curtiss)	2		
	An Old Song (Carrie Stettheimer)	1, 30		
	Tango Lullaby (Flavie Alvarez de Toledo)	2, 25		
	Solitude (Lou Harrison)	1		
	Barcarolle (Georges Hugnet)	1, 30		
	Fugue (Alexander Smallens)	2, 40		
	Alternations (Maurice Grosser)	1, 30		
	Album 2			
	Aria (Germaine Hugnet)	2, 40		
	A Portrait of R. Kirk Askew, Jr.	1, 30		
	In a Bird Cage (Lise Deharme)	1, 30		
	Catalan Waltz (Ramon Senabre)	1, 30		
	Five-Finger Exercise (Léon Kochnitzky)	1, 30		
	Sea Coast (Constance Askew)	1		
	Meditation (Jere Abbott)	2		
	Fanfare for France (Max Kahn)	3		

Year of Composition	Title	Duration	Publisher	Recording Companies
1929–1945	*Album 3*			
	Cantabile (Nicolas de Chatelain)	4, 30		
	Toccata (Mary Widney)	1, 30		
	Pastoral (Jean Ozenne)	1, 20		
	Prelude and Fugue (Agnes Rindge)	2		
	The Dream World of Peter Rose-Pulham	2, 20		
	The Bard (Sherry Mangan)	1, 30		
	Souvenir (Paul Bowles)	1		
	Canons with Cadenza (André Ostier)	1		
	Album 4			
	Tennis (Henry McBride)	1, 20		
	Hymn (Josiah Marvel)	1, 30		
	Lullaby Which is Also a Spinning Song (Howard Putzel))	2, 50		
	Swiss Waltz (Sophie Tauber-Arp)	2, 20		
	Poltergeist (Hans Arp)	1		
	Insistences (Louise Crane)	1, 40		
	The Hunt (A. Everett Austin, Jr.)	1, 15		
	Wedding Music (Jean Watts)	1, 30		
	Album 5			
	Travelling in Spain (Alice Branlière)	1, 30		
	Scottish Memories (Peter Monro Jack)	2, 30		
	Duet (Clarita, Comtesse de Forceville)	1, 45		
	Russell Hitchcock, Reading	1		
	Connecticut Waltz (Harold Lewis Cook)	1, 15		
	Polka (Ettie Stettheimer)	1		
	Invention (Theodate Johnson)	1, 30		
	Parades (Florine Stettheimer)	2, 20		
1935–1939	Portraits for piano, published separately			
	Herbert Whiting (A Day Dream)	2	CF	
	Madame Kristians Tonny (Eccentric Dance)	2	CF	
	Guggenheim Jeune (Piano Sonata No. 4), recorded as harpsichord solo	7	EV	NED
1935–1951	Portraits for piano, appearing as parts of other works			
	The John Mosher Waltzes (No. 6, Family Life, in ballet Filling Station)	2, 10	ARR	NED

Year of Composition	Title	Duration	Publisher	Recording Companies
1935–1951	Louise Ardant (With Trumpet and Horn in Nine Etudes for Piano)	2, 30	CF	
	Briggs Buchanan (Five-Finger Exercise in Ten Etudes for Piano)	2	CF	DEC
	Sylvia Marlowe (Chromatic Double Harmonies in Nine Etudes for Piano)	2, 30	CF	
1940 & 1951	Nine Etudes for Piano	15	CF	
(April 11, 1940)	With Trumpet and Horn (originally Portrait of Louise Ardant)	2, 30		
(June 23, 1951)	Pivoting on the Thumb	1, 15		
(June 26, 1951)	Alternating Octaves	0, 40		
(July 7, 1951)	Double Sevenths	1		
(June 22, 1951)	The Harp	2, 20		
(June 20, 1951)	Chromatic Major Seconds (The Wind)	1		
(June 17, 1951)	Chromatic Double Harmonies (Portrait of Sylvia Marlowe)	2, 30		
(July 10, 1951)	Broken Arpeggios (The Waltzing Waters)	1, 30		
(June 18, 1951)	Guitar and Mandolin	2		
After 1948	Three Pieces from Louisiana Story, transcribed by Andor Foldes for piano, 2 hands	15	MS	
	1. Bayou Pastorale	6		
	2. Chorale	3, 15		
	3. The Squeeze-Box	5, 30		
1951 (June 23)	Happy Birthday for Mrs. Zimbalist	0, 20	MS	
	Walking Song, arr. for 2 hands by Virgil Thomson	2	MS	
1956 (July 25)	Hommage à Marya Freund	1, 00	MS	

WORKS FOR VOICE AND PIANO

Year of Composition	Title	Duration	Publisher	Recording Companies
1920 (July)	Vernal Equinox, for soprano (Amy Lowell)	1	MS	
(September)	The Sunflower, for soprano (William Blake)	1	MS	
1924 (August)	Three Sentences from The Song of Solomon, for tenor	3	MS	
	1. Thou That Dwellest in the Gardens	1		
	2. Return, O Shulamite	1		
	3. I Am My Beloved's	1		

Year of Composition	Title	Duration	Publisher	Recording Companies
1926 (April)	Susie Asado, for soprano (Gertrude Stein)	1, 30	CC	
(September)	The Tiger, for soprano (William Blake)	3	MS	
1927 (February)	Preciosilla, for soprano (Gertrude Stein)	5	GS	
(November)	Une Mélodie dite La Valse Grégorienne, for soprano (4 poems by Georges Hugnet, to be sung without pause)	4	PP	
1928 (May)	Trois Poèmes de la Duchesse de Rohan, for soprano	6, 30	MS	
	1. A son Altesse la Princesse Antoinette Murat	2		
	2. Jour de chaleur aux bains de mer	1, 30		
	3. La Seine	3		
(May)	Le Berceau de Gertrude Stein, for soprano (8 Poèmes de Georges Hugnet to which have been added a Musical Composition by Virgil Thomson entitled Lady Godiva's Waltzes), to be sung without pause	4, 15	MS	
(October)	Commentaire sur Saint Jérome, for soprano (Marquis de Sade)	1	MS	
(November)	Les Soirées Bagnolaises, for soprano (Georges Hugnet)	6	MS	
1929 (September)	Portrait of F. B., for soprano, also for mezzo-soprano (Gertrude Stein)	4, 30	MS	
1930 (April)	Le Singe et le Léopard, for soprano (La Fontaine)	4, 30	MS	
(April)	Oraison Funèbre, for tenor, also for baritone (Bossuet)	14	MS	
(August)	Air de Phèdre, for soprano, also for mezzo-soprano (Racine)	6	MS	
(September)	Film: Deux soeurs qui sont pas soeurs, for soprano (Gertrude Stein)	4, 45	MS	
1931 (Mar. 16)	Chamber Music, for soprano (Alfred Kreymborg)	2	MS	

Year of Composition	Title	Duration	Publisher	Recording Companies
1931 (Aug. 20 & Oct. 1)	La Belle en dormant, for soprano or mezzo-soprano (Georges Hugnet)	4, 30	GS	
	Pour Chercher sur la carte des mers	1		
	La Première de toutes	1, 15		
	Mon Amour est bon à dire	1, 15		
	Partis les vaisseaux	0, 45		
Arranged 1934	Pigeons on the Grass Alas (from 4 Saints in 3 Acts), for baritone, also for baritone and orchestra (Gertrude Stein)	3	MY	
1939 (July 19)	Dirge, for mezzo-soprano (John Webster)	1, 30	GS	
1941 (September)	The Bugle Song, for mezzo-soprano or baritone (Tennyson)	1, 30	MS	
1951 (July)	Four Songs to Poems of Thomas Campion, for mezzo-soprano (also published for acc. of clarinet, viola and harp; also arr. for mixed chorus)	9	RIC	
	Follow Your Saint	2		
	There Is a Garden in Her Face	2		
	Rose-Cheek'd Laura, Come	2		
	Follow Thy Fair Sun	3		
(August & October)	Five Songs from William Blake, for baritone (also with orchestra)	18	RIC	
	The Divine Image	3		
	Tiger! Tiger!	4		
	The Land of Dreams	3		
	The Little Black Boy	4		
	"And Did Those Feet"	4		
1955 (August)	Old English Songs for Soprano		MS	
	Look, How the Floor of Heav'n (Shakespeare)	1		
	The Holly and the Ivy, a Carol of Nativity and Lent (anon., 1557)	2, 15		
	At the Spring (Jasper Fisher)	1		
(August)	Old English Songs for Baritone		MS	
	Consider, Lord (John Donne)	1		
	The Bell Doth Toll (Thomas Heywood)	1, 40		
	Remember Adam's Fall (anon., 15th cent.)	2, 30		
	John Peel (John Woodcock Graves)	3		

Year of Composition	Title	Duration	Publisher	Recording Companies
1956 (August)	Take, O Take Those Lips Away, from Measure for Measure, for any voice (Shakespeare)	0, 30	MS	
1957 (June)	Tell Me Where Is Fancy Bred, from The Merchant of Venice, for tenor (Shakespeare)	1	MS	
(June)	Was This Fair Face, from All's Well That Ends Well, for tenor (Shakespeare)	1	MS	
(July)	Sigh No More, Ladies, from Much Ado About Nothing, for tenor (Shakespeare) (2 versions)	1	MS	
(July)	Pardon, Goddess of the Night, from Much Ado About Nothing, for tenor (Shakespeare)	0, 30	MS	
1957 (Apr. 14 & 30 & Dec. 21)	Tres Estampas de Niñez, for soprano (Reyna Rivas)	6	MS	
(Apr. 15 & Dec. 21)	Todas las horas	2, 30		
	Son amigos de todos	0, 50		
(Apr. 15 & Dec. 31)	Nadie lo oye como ellos	2, 30		

WORKS FOR VOICE UNACCOMPANIED

Year of Composition	Title	Duration	Publisher	Recording Companies
1935 (December)	Go to Sleep, Alexander Smallens, Jr.	1	MS	
1937 (June)	Go to Sleep, Pare McTaggett Lorentz	1	MS	

WORKS FOR VOICE WITH VARIOUS ACCOMPANIMENTS

Year of Composition	Title	Duration	Publisher	Recording Companies
1926 (April & May)	Five Phrases from The Song of Solomon, for soprano and percussion (1 player)	6	AME	
	Thou That Dwellest in the Gardens	1		
	Return, O Shulamite	1		
	O, My Dove	1		
	I Am My Beloved's	1		
	By Night	2		
1927 (April)	Capital, Capitals, for four men's solo voices, TTBB, and piano (Gertrude Stein)	16	NM	COL
1931 (March)	Stabat Mater (in French), for soprano and string quartet, also for soprano and string orchestra (Max Jacob)	5	CC	COL
1951 (July)	Four Songs to Poems of Thomas Campion, for mezzo-soprano, clarinet, viola and harp (See listing under Chamber Music)	9		RIC

Year of Composition	Title	Duration	Publisher	Recording Companies
	WORKS FOR ORGAN			
1922 (January)	Fanfare	2	HWG	MGM & QR
(January)	Pastorale on a Christmas Plainsong	3	HWG	MGM & QR
(February)	Prelude	2	MS	
(June)	Passacaglia	8	MS	
December 1926– November 1927	Variations and Fugues on Sunday School Tunes	24	HWG	ESO
	Come, Ye Disconsolate	6		
	There's Not a Friend Like the Lowly Jesus	6		
	Will There Be Any Stars in My Crown?	6		
	Shall We Gather at the River?	6		
1940	Wedding Music	2	MS	
	1. To go in	1		
	2. To come out	1		
	CHORAL WORKS			
1920 (July)	De Profundis, for mixed voices, SATB (in English) (revised for publication 1951)	2, 30	WTB	
1921 (December)	Sanctus, for men's voices, TTBB (in English)	1, 30	MS	
1922 (August)	Tribulationes Civitatum, motet for mixed voices, SATB, also for TTBB (in Latin)	3	WTB	
1924	Agnus Dei, canon for 3 equal voices (in Latin)	2	MY	
1922–24	Three Antiphonal Psalms, for 2-part Chorus, SA or TB (in English)	5	LDS	
(January, 1922)	Psalm 123, Unto Thee Lift I Up Mine Eyes	1		OVE
(January, 1922)	Psalm 133, Behold How Good and Pleasant It Is, Brethren	1		OVE
(August, 1924)	Psalm 136, O, Give Thanks to the Lord, for He Is Gracious	3		
1924 (January)	Missa Brevis, for men's voices, TTBB (in Latin)	14	MS	
	Kyrie Eleison	1		
	Gloria in Excelsis	3, 30		
	Credo	5		
	Sanctus	1		
	Benedictus	1		
	Agnus Dei	2		

Year of Composition	Title	Duration	Publisher	Recording Companies
1924 (January)	Fête Polonaise from Le Roi malgré lui (Chabrier), for men's voices, TTBB, accompanied	7	MS	
1925 (March)	Agnus Dei, for men's voices, TTBB (in Latin)	1	MS	
1926 (August)	Sanctus, TTBB with children's voices, SS or SA (in Latin)	1, 30	MS	
1928 (August)	Saints' Procession (from 4 Saints in 3 Acts) for mixed voices, SATB; also for men's voices, TTBB; solos for mezzo-soprano and bass (Gertrude Stein)	4, 30	MY	
1934 (August)	Seven Choruses from the Medea of Euripides (trans. Countee Cullen), for women's voices, SSAA, and percussion (ad lib.)	9, 30	MY	
	O, Gentle Heart	1, 30		
	Love, Like a Leaf	1, 30		
	O, Happy Were Our Fathers	1, 45		
	Weep for the Little Lambs	1		
	Go Down, O Sun	0, 45		
	Behold, O Earth	1, 30		
	Immortal Zeus Controls the Fate of Man	1, 30		
(September)	Missa Brevis, for women's voices, SA, and percussion (ad lib.)	11	LDS	
	Kyrie Eleison	1, 15		
	Gloria in Excelsis	2		
	Credo	5		
	Sanctus	0, 30		
	Benedictus	0, 30		
	Agnus Dei	1, 30		
1937 (October)	My Shepherd Will Supply My Need (Isaac Watts's paraphrase of the 23rd Psalm) for mixed voices, SATB; also for men's voices, TTBB, and for women's voices, SSAA	3	HWG	
(November)	Scenes from the Holy Infancy, according to Saint Matthew; for mixed voices, SATB	9, 30	MY	
	1. Joseph and the Angel	3		
	2. The Wise Men (with tenor solo)	3, 30		
	3. The Flight Into Egypt	3		

Year of Composition	Title	Duration	Publisher	Recording Companies
1941 (September)	Welcome to the New Year, for mixed voices, SATB (Eleanor Farjeon)	1	MS	
(September)	Surrey Apple Howler's Song, a round (words traditional)	1	MS	
1949 (June)	Hymns from the Old South, for mixed voices, SATB	6, 50	HWG	
	1. The Morning Star (author unknown)	1, 20		
	2. Green Fields (John Newton)	2, 30		
	3. Death, 'tis a Melancholy Day (Isaac Watts)	3		
1953 (August)	Kyrie, for mixed voices, SATB (in Greek)	3	MS	
Arranged 1955	Four Songs to Poems of Thomas Campion, arr. by Virgil Thomson for mixed voices, SATB, acc.	9	RIC	
	Follow Your Saint	2		
	There Is a Garden in Her Face	2		
	Rose-Cheek'd Laura, Come	2		
	Follow Thy Fair Sun	3		
Arranged 1955	Tiger! Tiger! arr. by Virgil Thomson for mixed voices, SATB, acc., and for men's voices, TTBB, acc. (from 5 Songs from William Blake, for bar. and orch.)	4	RIC	
1955 (December)	Song for the Stable, hymn, SATB (Amanda Benjamin Hall)		CHU	
(December)	Never Another, hymn, SATB (Mark Van Doren)		CHU	
1958 (March)	Crossing Brooklyn Ferry, for mixed voices, SSATB, and piano (Walt Whitman)	7	MS	

CHAMBER MUSIC

Year of Composition	Title	Duration	Publisher	Recording Companies
1926 (February)	Sonata da Chiesa	15	NM	
	Cl. in E flat, tpt. in D, viola, hn., tbn.			
	Chorale	5		
	Tango	5		
	Fugue	5		
1928–1940	Portraits for Violin Alone			
(July 21, 1928)	Señorita Juanita de Medina Accompanied by Her Mother	1, 30	MS	
(August 31, 1928)	Madame Marthe-Marthine	1	MS	

Year of Composition 1928–1940	Title	Duration	Publisher	Recording Companies
(October, 1928)	Miss Gertrude Stein as a Young Girl	1, 30	MS	
(October, 1928)	Cliquet-Pleyel in F	2	MS	
(October, 1928)	Mrs. C. W. L.	1, 30	MS	
(October, 1928)	Georges Hugnet, Poet and Man of Letters	1	MS	
(November, 1928)	Sauguet, from life	1	MS	
(Sept. 15, 1940)	Ruth Smallens	2	MS	
1929	Five Portraits for 4 Clarinets 2 cl., basset horn, bass cl.	9	MS	
	Portrait of Ladies	3		
	Portrait of a Young Man in Good Health	2		
	Three Portraits of Christian Bérard			
	Christian Bérard, Prisonnier	2		
	Bébé Soldat	1		
	En Personne (chair et os)	1		
	Le Bains-Bar (waltz for vn. and pn.; also for 2 vns., 'cello, bass and pn.)	5	MS	
1930–1940	Portraits for violin and piano		MS	
(March, 1930)	Alice Toklas	3		
(April, 1930)	Anne Miracle	1		
(April, 1930)	Mary Reynolds	1		
(1940)	Yvonne de Casa Fuerte	2		
1930 (July)	Sonata for Violin and Piano, No. 1	14	ARR	
	Allegro	3		
	Andante Nobile	4		
	Tempo di Valzer	1, 15		
	Andante: Doppio Mov'to	5, 45		
1931	Stabat Mater (in French) for soprano and string quartet (Max Jacob)	5	CC	COL
(February)	String Quartet No. 1	19	ARR	
	Allegro Moderato	4		
	Adagio	4		
	Tempo di Valzer	5		
	Lento: Presto	6		
(November)	Serenade for Flute and Violin	5	SMP	
	1. March	2		
	2. Aria	1, 15		
	3. Fanfare	0, 15		
	4. Flourish	0, 20		
	5. Hymn	1		

Year of Composition	Title	Duration	Publisher	Recording Companies
1932	String Quartet No. 2	21	ARR	COL
	Allegro Moderato	6		
	Tempo di Valzer	3, 30		
	Adagio Sostenuto	4, 15		
	Allegretto	6, 40		
1942	Four Portraits for Violoncello and Piano, transc. by Luigi Silva	9, 15	MY	
	Fanfare for France (Max Kahn)	3		
	Tango Lullaby (Mlle. Alvarez de Toledo)	2, 25		
	In a Bird Cage (Lise Deharme)	1, 30		
	Bugles and Birds (Pablo Picasso)	2, 15		
1943 (September)	Sonata for Flute Alone	10	EV	
	Adagio: Allegro	3		
	Adagio	4, 30		
	Vivace	2, 30		
1947	Three Portraits, transc. for violin and piano by Samuel Dushkin	5, 30	MY	
	Barcarolle (Georges Hugnet)	1, 30		
	In a Bird Cage (Lise Deharme), unacc.	1, 30		
	Tango Lullaby (Mlle. Alvarez de Toledo)	2, 25		
1949 (January)	At the Beach, for trumpet and piano, also for tpt. and band	5	CF	
1950	Concerto for Violoncello and Orchestra, pub. for 'cello and pn. (See also listing under Works for Soloist with Orchestra)	21	RIC	
	Rider on the Plains	6, 30		
	Variations on a Southern Hymn	9		
	Children's Games	5, 30		
1951	Four Songs to Poems of Thomas Campion, for mezzo-sop., cl., viola and harp (also published for solo voice and piano; also arr. for mixed chorus)	9	RIC	
	Follow Your Saint	2		
	There Is a Garden in Her Face	2		
	Rose-Cheek'd Laura, Come	2		
	Follow Thy Fair Sun	3		
1954	Concerto for Flute, Strings, Harp and Percussion, pub. for fl. and pn. (See also listing under			

Year of Composition	Title	Duration	Publisher	Recording Companies
1954	Works for Soloist with Orchestra)	13	RIC	
	Rapsodico	2		
	Lento	4		
	Ritmico	7		

WORKS FOR ORCHESTRA OR BAND

Year of Composition	Title	Duration	Publisher	Recording Companies
1923	Two Sentimental Tangos			
	2-2-2-2, 4-2-3-1, 2 perc., hp., strings	5	MS	
	I	2		
	II	3		
1928	Symphony on a Hymn Tune	19	SMP	
	2-2-2-2, 4-2-3-1, tymp., 3 perc., strings			
	Introduction and Allegro			
	Andante Cantabile			
	Allegretto			
	Allegro			
	(to be played without pause)			
1931	Symphony No. 2	16	LDS	
	3-3-3-3, 4-2-3-1, tymp., 2 perc., strings			
	Allegro con brio			
	Andante			
	Allegro			
	(to be played without pause)			
1936 (February)	Suite from The Plow that Broke the Plains	15	MY	VIC & DEC
	1-1-3-1, 2-2-2, banjo-guitar (or piano), 2 perc. (incl. tymp.), strings			
	1. Prelude	1, 30		
	2. Pastoral (Grass)	1, 30		
	3. Cattle	3		
	4. Blues (Speculation)	3		
	5. Drought	1		
	6. Devastation	4, 30		
1937	Suite from The River	20	SMP	ARS
	1-2-2-1, 2-2-2, 2 perc. (incl. tymp.), strings			
	I The Old South	8		
	II Industrial Expansion in the Mississippi Valley	3		
	III Soil Erosion and Floods	6		
	IV Finale	3		

Year of Composition	Title	Duration	Publisher	Recording Companies
1937 (November)	Suite from Filling Station (See also listing under Ballets) 2-2-2-2, 4-2-3-1 (or 2-2-3), tymp., 2 or 3 perc., piano, strings	15	ARR	VOX
	1. Prelude	1		
	2. Mac's Dance	2, 30		
	3. Scene	1, 20		
	4. Acrobatics	3		
	5. Tango	4		
	6. Big Apple	1, 20		
	7. Finale	1, 30		
1937–1944	Portraits for Orchestra			
(1937)	The John Mosher Waltzes (No. 6, Family Life, in the ballet Filling Station) 2-2-2-2, 4-3-3-1 (or 2-2-3), pn., hp., tymp., 2 perc., strings	2, 10	ARR	
(1942)	The Mayor La Guardia Waltzes 2-2-2-2, 4-2-3, 4 perc., strings	7	MS	
(1942)	Canons for Dorothy Thompson 2-1-E.h.-2-2, 4-2-3, 3 perc., strings	3	MS	
(Arranged 1944)	Fanfare for France (Max Kahn), for brass and percussion 4 hns., 3 tpts., 3 tbns., side drum, field drum	3	B&H	
(Arranged 1944)	Cantabile for Strings (Nicolas de Chatelain)	4, 30	MY	COL
(Arranged 1944)	Barcarolle for Woodwinds (Georges Hugnet) Fl., ob., E.h., cl., bass cl., bn.	1, 30	MY	
(Arranged 1944)	Fugue (Alexander Smallens) 2-2-2-2, 4-2-3, 1 perc., strings	2, 30	MY	COL
(Arranged 1944)	Tango Lullaby (Flavie Alvarez de Toledo) Fl. (pic.), E.h., cl., bn., bells, strings	3, 30	MY	COL
(Arranged 1944)	Meditation (Jere Abbott) 2-2-2-2, 2-2-2, strings	1, 30	MS	
(Arranged 1944)	Percussion Piece (Jessie K. [Mrs. Chester Whitin] Lasell) 2-2-2-2, 4-2-3-1, 4 perc., strings	2, 30	MS	COL
(Arranged 1944)	Bugles and Birds (Pablo Picasso) 2-2-2-2, 4-2-3, no perc., strings	2, 15	MY	COL
(Arranged 1945)	Pastorale (Aaron Copland) 2-2-2-2, 4-2-3-1, strings	3, 15	MS	
1947 (December))	The Seine at Night 3-3-3-3, 4-3-3-1, 2 hps., 2 perc., strings	9	GS	COL

Year of Composition	Title	Duration	Publisher	Recording Companies
1948	Suite from Louisiana Story 2-2-2-2, 4-2-3-1, hp., 2 perc., strings	18	GS	COL
	I Pastoral (The Bayou and the Marsh-Buggy)	5		
	II Chorale (The Derrick Arrives)	2, 30		
	III Passacaglia (Robbing the Alligator's Nest)	6, 30		
	IV Fugue (Boy Fights Alligator)	4		
1948	Acadian Songs and Dances (from Louisiana Story) 2-2-2-2, 2-2-2, hp., accordion (or pn.), 2 perc., strings	14	GS	DEC
	I Sadness	2		
	II Papa's Tune	1		
	III A Narrative	2		
	IV The Alligator and the 'Coon	2, 15		
	V Super-sadness	1, 15		
	VI Walking Song	1, 30		
	VII The Squeeze-Box	3, 30		
	Wheat Field at Noon 3-3-3-3, 4-3-3, hp., xylo., 2 perc., strings	7	GS	COL
1949 (May)	A Solemn Music, for band 2 pic., 2 fl., 2 ob., 2bn., all clarinets, 4 sax., 3 ct., 2 tpt., 4 hns., 3 tbn., 2 bar., 2 tubas, tymp., 2 perc.	7	GS	MER
	Suite from The Mother of Us All 1-1-2-1, 2-2-1, hp., pn., 2 perc. (incl. tymp.), strings	18	MY	COL
	Prelude (Prelude to Act I, Sc. 1)	6, 30		
	Cold Weather (Prelude to Act I, Sc. 3)	3, 30		
	Wedding Hymn and Finale (transc. from Act I, Sc. 5 and Act II, Sc. 3)	5		
	A Political Meeting (Prelude to Act I, Sc. 2)	3		
1952 (October)	Sea Piece with Birds 3-3-3-3, 4-3-3, hp., 2 perc., strings	5	GS	COL
1956 (December)	Eleven Chorale-Preludes by Brahms, transc. by Virgil Thomson	25, 30	B & H	
	No. 1. My Jesus Calls Me Mein Jesu, der du mich	2, 30		

Year of Composition	Title	Duration	Publisher	Recording Companies
1956 (December)	No. 2. O, Blessed Jesus Herzliebster Jesu 2 orch. versions	3 each		
	No. 3. O World, I Now Must Leave Thee O Welt, ich muss dich lassen (first setting)	1, 30		
	No. 4. My Faithful Heart Rejoices Herzlich thut mich erfreuen	1, 30		
	No. 5. Deck Thyself, My Soul Schmücke dich, O liebe Seele	1, 15		
	No. 6. Blessed Are Ye, Faithful Souls O wie selig seid ihr doch, ihr Frommen	1		
	No. 7. O God, Thou Faithful God O Gott, du frommer Gott	3, 30		
	No. 8. Behold, a Rose is Blooming Es ist ein Ros' entsprungen	2, 15		
	No. 9. My Heart Is Filled with Longing Herzlich thut mich verlangen (first setting)	1, 45		
	No. 10. My Heart Is Filled with Longing Herzlich thut mich verlangen (second setting)	2, 30		
	No. 11. O World, I Now Must Leave Thee O Welt, ich muss dich lassen (second setting)	1, 45		
1957 (September 13)	The Lively Arts Fugue Ob., clar., hn., tpt., tbn., 1 perc., str.	1, 40	MS	

WORKS FOR SOLOIST WITH ORCHESTRA OR BAND

Year of Composition	Title	Duration	Publisher	Recording Companies
1931 (March)	Stabat Mater (in French) for sop. and string orch. (Max Jacob)	5	CC	
1949 (January)	At the Beach, for trumpet and band 2 pic., 2 fl., 2 ob., 2 bn., all clarinets, 4 sax., 3 ct., 2 tpt., 4 hn., 3 tbn., 2 bar., 2 tubas, tymp., 2 perc. (also pub. for tpt. and pn.)	5	CF	

Year of Composition	Title	Duration	Publisher	Recording Companies
1950	Concerto for Violoncello and Orchestra 2-2-2-3, 4-2, hp., cel., 3 perc., strings (pub. for 'cello and pn.)	21	RIC	COL
	Rider on the Plains	6, 30		
	Variations on a Southern Hymn	9		
	Children's Games	5, 30		
1951	Five Songs to Poems of William Blake, for baritone and orchestra 2-2-2-2, 4-2-3-1, hp., 2 perc., strings (pub. for bar. and pn.)	18	RIC	COL
	The Divine Image	3		
	Tiger! Tiger!	4		
	The Land of Dreams	3		
	The Little Black Boy	4		
	"And Did Those Feet"	4		
1954	Concerto for Flute, Strings, Harp and Percussion 1 or 2 hps., cel., 1 perc., strings (also pub. for fl. and pn.)	13	RIC	
	Rapsodico	2		
	Lento	4		
	Ritmico	7		

OPERAS

Year of Composition	Title	Duration	Publisher	Recording Companies
1928	Four Saints in Three Acts (Gertrude Stein) Soloists: sop., mezzo-sop., contr., tenor, bar., bass. Minor Soloists: 2 sop., 2 contr., 2 tenors, bar., bass. Chorus, ballet, four stage sets. Orch: 1-1-2-1, 2-1-1, accordion, harmonium, 2 perc., strings	90	MY	VIC
	Prelude and Act I	30		
	Act II	20		
	Acts III & IV	40		
1947	The Mother of Us All (Gertrude Stein) Two acts, 8 scenes, five stage sets. 25 singers, 6 silent actors. Principal soloists: 2 sop., contr., 2 tenors, bar., bass. Orch.: 1-1-2-1, 2-2-1, hp., cel., pn., 2 perc., strings	103	MY	
	Act I, with instrumental preludes	63		
	Prelude to Sc. 1 (with cut made)	4		
	Prelude to Sc. 2	3		

Year of Composition	Title	Duration	Publisher	Recording Companies
1947	Prelude to Sc. 3	3, 30		
	Prelude to Sc. 4	1, 30		
	Act II, with Prelude to Sc. 3	40		
	Prelude to Act II, Sc. 3	1		

BALLETS

1937	Filling Station (choreography by Lew Christensen)	24	ARR	VOX
	2-2-2-2, 4-3-3-1 (or 2-2-3), pn., hp., tymp., 2 perc., strings			
	1. Introduction	1		
	2. Mac's Dance (Pas seul)	2, 30		
	3. Scene (Mac and Motorist)	1, 20		
	4. Acrobatics (Mac and Truck-drivers)	3		
	5. Scene (State Trooper and Truck-drivers))	0, 45		
	6. Family Life (Motorist's Family and Truck-drivers)	2, 10		
	7. Tango (Rich Girl and Boy)	4		
	8. Valse à trois (Rich Girl and Boy with Mac)	2, 30		
	9. Big Apple (Ensemble)	1, 20		
	10. Hold Up (Ensemble)	0, 40		
	11. Chase (Ensemble)	1, 45		
	12. Finale (Ensemble)	1, 30		
Staged 1952	Bayou (choreography by Georges Balanchine, second version by Ruthanna Boris). Music: Acadian Songs and Dances from Louisiana Story.	14	GS	
	2-2-2-2, 2-2-2, hp., accordion (or pn.), 2 perc., strings			
Arranged 1954	The Harvest According (choreography by Agnes de Mille), arranged by Virgil Thomson from Symphony on a Hymn Tune, Concerto for Violoncello and Orchestra, and Suite from The Mother of Us All	40	MS	
	2-2-2-2, 4-2-3-1, hp., tymp., 2 perc., strings			

MUSIC FOR FILMS

1936	The Plow that Broke the Plains (Pare Lorentz)	27	MS	
	For Suite, see listing under Works for Orch.			
	1-1-3-1, 2-2-2, banjo-guitar, 2 perc., strings			

Year of Composition	Title	Duration	Publisher	Recording Companies
1937	The River (Pare Lorentz) 35 mm. For Suite, see listing under Works for Orch.	36	MS	
	1-2-2-1, 2-2-2, 2 perc., strings 16 mm. version	27		
	The Spanish Earth (Joris Ivens and Ernest Hemingway) in collaboration with Marc Blitzstein, a montage of recorded Spanish folk music	63		
1945	Tuesday in November (John Houseman) 1-1-2-1, 2-2-2, hp., 2 perc., strings	18	MS	
1948	Louisiana Story (Robert Flaherty) For Suites, see listings under Works for Orch. 2-2-2-2, 2-2-2, hp., accordion, 2 perc., strings	81	MS	
1957 (November)	The Goddess (Paddy Chayevsky) 2-2-2-2, 3 sax., 2-2-2, guit., pn., 2 perc., strings	100	MS	

INCIDENTAL MUSIC FOR PLAYS

Year of Composition	Title	Duration	Publisher	Recording Companies
1929	Le Droit de Varech (play by Georges Hugnet). Not produced. Accordion solo.		MS	
1934	A Bride for the Unicorn (play by Dennis Johnson) directed by Joseph Losey for the Harvard Dramatic Club. Male chorus, 3 perc. players		MS	
1936	Macbeth (for negro cast), directed by Orson Welles for the Federal Theater Fl., 3 clar., 3 tpt., 2 tbn., guitar, perc., strings, 4 African drums on stage		MS	
	Injunction Granted, a Living Newspaper, directed by Joseph Losey for the Federal Theater Pic., 3 tpt., 1 tbn., 16 perc. players		MS	
	Horse Eats Hat (Labiche, trans. Edwin Denby), directed by Orson Welles for Federal Theater, music by Paul Bowles, orch. by Virgil Thomson		MS	

Year of Composition	Title	Duration	Publisher	Recording Companies
1936	2-2-2-2, 4-2-3, 2 solo pns., 2 perc., strings; also cornet soloist, small jazz band, gypsy waltz orch., player piano, bass vocal soloist			
	Hamlet (for Leslie Howard) directed by John Houseman Recorder, hn., 2 tpt., 2 bagpipes, 3 perc.		MS	
1937	Antony and Cleopatra (for Tallulah Bankhead) directed by Reginald Bache Ob., 2 tpt., 2 perc.		MS	
1938	Androcles and the Lion (Shaw) for the Federal Theater (Not orchestrated by Virgil Thomson)		MS	
1940	The Trojan Women (Euripides, trans. Edith Hamilton) directed by John Houseman for CBS Workshop Fl., E.h., clar., tpt., hn., perc. and sound effects		MS	
1941	Sound Track of the Life of a Careful Man (CBS Workshop) 2 clar., 2 hns., org., 2 perc., strings, women's voices SA		MS	
	Oidipous Tyrannos (Sophocles) in Greek, produced at Fordham University Male chorus, fl., 2 hn., perc.		MS	
1952	King Lear (for Orson Welles), directed by Peter Brook for TV-Radio Workshop of the Ford Foundation 2 tpt., 2 hn., 2 vla., 2 'celli, 2 perc.		MS	
1953	The Grass Harp (play by Truman Capote), directed by Robert Lewis Fl., hp., cel., vn., vla., 'cello		MS	
1954	Ondine (for Audrey Hepburn and Mel Ferrer) (play by J. Giraudoux), directed by Alfred Lunt Fl., hp., str., qtet., cel., 1 perc.		RIC	VAL

Year of Composition	Title	Duration	Publisher	Recording Companies
1956 (June)	King John (Shakespeare) directed by John Houseman for the American Shakespeare Festival Theater, Stratford, Conn. 2 tpt., 2 hn., 2 perc.		MS	
(June)	Measure for Measure (Shakespeare) directed by John Houseman for the American Shakespeare Festival Theater, Stratford, Conn. 2 tpt., 2 hn., 2 perc., tack piano, boy sop. soloist		MS	
1957 (June)	Othello (for Alfred Drake) directed by John Houseman for the American Shakespeare Festival Theater, Stratford, Conn. 2 tpt., fl., vla., cello, bass, lute, 1 perc.		MS	
(June)	The Merchant of Venice (for Katherine Hepburn) directed by Jack Landau for the American Shakespeare Festival Theater, Stratford, Conn. 2 tpt., fl., vla., cello, bass, lute, 1 perc., tenor soloist		MS	
(July)	Much Ado About Nothing (for Katherine Hepburn and Alfred Drake) directed by John Houseman and Jack Landau for the American Shakespeare Festival Theater, Stratford, Conn. 2 tpt., fl.-picc., clar.-sax., 'cello, vla., bass, lute, tenor soloist		MS	

BOOKS BY VIRGIL THOMSON

1939   *The State of Music,* 250 pp., William Morrow and Co., New York
1945   *The Musical Scene,* 301 pp., Alfred A. Knopf, New York
1948   *The Art of Judging Music,* 318 pp., Alfred A. Knopf, New York
1951   *Music Right and Left,* 201 pp., Henry Holt and Co., New York

PUBLISHERS

AME   American Music Edition, 250 West 57th Street, New York 19, N. Y.
ARR   Arrow Music Press (now B & H)
B&H   Boosey and Hawkes, Inc., 30 West 57th Street, New York 19, N. Y.
CC   Cos Cob—Arrow Music Press (now B & H)
CHU   University of Chicago Press, 5750 Ellis Avenue, Chicago 37, Illinois
EV   Elkan-Vogel Co., Inc., 1714-1716 Sansom St., Philadelphia 3, Pa.
CF   Carl Fischer, 56-62 Cooper Square, New York 3, N. Y.
LDS   Leeds Music Corp., RKO Bldg., 1270 Avenue of the Americas, New York 20, N. Y.

MS	Manuscript
MY	Mercury Music Corp., 47 West 63rd Street, New York 23, N. Y.
NM	New Music Edition (now B & H)
PP	Privately Printed
RIC	G. Ricordi & Co., 16 West 61st Street, New York 23, N. Y.
GS	G. Schirmer, Inc., 3 East 43rd Street, New York 17, N. Y.
SMP	Southern Music Publishing Co., Inc., 1619 Broadway, New York 19, N. Y.
WTB	Weintraub Music Co., 853 Seventh Ave., New York 19, N. Y.

RECORDING COMPANIES

ARS	American Recording Society	NED	New Editions
COL	Columbia	OVE	OVERTONE Records
DEC	Decca	QR	Quality Records, Ltd., Canada
ESO	Esoteric	VAL	Valentino (R. F. T. Music Publishing Corp.)
MER	Mercury		
MGM	M. G. M.	VIC	RCA-Victor
		VOX	VOX

Index

Luxembourg, 109
Lynch, Father William, 191

McClendon, Rose, 84
McCormack, John, 19
MacDowell, 27
MacLeish, Archibald, 84, 85
"Madamoiselle from Armentières," 177
Madison Square Company, 18
Mainz, 39
Making of Americans, The, 82
Man of Aran, 103
Mandyczewski, Eusebius, 46
Mangan, Sherry, 61
Mannes, Leopold, 36
Mansfield, Richard, 18
Marlowe, Julia, 18, 19
Mark Twain Portrait, 193
Martinů, 95
Marxism, 51, 52
Massenet, 99
Masson, André, 60
Masters, Edgar Lee, 111
Matisse, 59, 60
Mattingly, Garrett, 9, 46
Meistersinger, 66
Mencken, H. L., 45
Mendelssohn, 172
Mercure, 133, 183
Mercury Theater, 87
Messiaen, Olivier, 230
Metropolitan Opera House, 31, 227
Milhaud, 39, 43, 129, 130, 175
Millerand, President, 38, 39
Miserere, 38
Mississippi, 180
Mitropoulos, 96
Moana of the South Seas, 103
Modern Music, 93, 250
Modigliani, 61
Modjeska, 18
Monteux, Pierre, 42
Moore, John, 37, 41
Morris, William, 111
Morrow, William, 87
Moses, Harry, 83, 107
Mozart, 41, 95, 97
Münsterberg, Hugo, 57
Murphy, Gerald, 85
Murray, Gilbert, 84
Murray, Robert Leigh, 16
Museum of Modern Art, 110
Music Critics Circle, 101, 110
Musical Club, Harvard, 45
Musical Quarterly, 251
Musique d'ameublement, 141
Musset, de Alfred, 66
"My Country, 'Tis of Thee," 157
Myers, Rollo H., 117

Nancy, 39
Nanook of the North, 103
National Institute of Arts and Letters, 112
"Negro *Parsifal,*" 82
Nelson, William Rockhill, 13, 20
Neo-romantics, 65
New England Conservatory, 36
New Opera Company, 100
New Republic, 52
New School for Social Research, 86, 214
New York City, 30 ff., 46, 73 ff., 80 ff., 84 ff., 90 ff., 141, 160, 172, 184, 214
New York Times, The, 105
Newman, Ernest, 93
Newton, John, 217
Nietzsche, 24, 34
Nijinsky, 18
North Easton Unitarian Church, 37
Norton, W. W., 87
Nottebohm, 46

Offenbach, Jacques, 100
O'Neill, James, 18
Opéra, Paris, 38
Orchestra, Boston Symphony, 36, 42
Orchestra, Kansas City Symphony, 20
Ormandy, Eugene, 251
Ornstein, Leo, 249
Oxford, Bishop of, 31

Paderewski, 18, 19
Paine, John Knowles, 35, 37
Palestrina, 38
Panic, 84
Pans, 22, 23, 25
Pansophists, 22, 23, 25, 27
Parade, 183
Parker, Henry Taylor, 42
Parsons, Geoffrey, 90
Perry, Ralph Barton, 34, 35
Pesaro, 40
Philadelphia Orchestra, 104, 251
Philharmonic-Symphony Society, 91, 94
Phoenix Theater, 84, 107
Picasso, 57, 58, 59, 60, 61, 62, 82, 89, 106, 249
Piston, Walter, 36, 74, 86
Polytechnic Institute and Junior College, Kansas City, 20 ff., 32
Pope Benedict XV, 40
Porgy and Bess, 83
Possibilities, 250
Post-Impressionism, 44
Poulenc, 39
Pound, Ezra, 53, 54, 59
Prix de Rome, 130
Prokofiev, 74
Protestant Church of St. Thomas, 39
Proust, 58